...tues of prayer. That day, hu...

..., as we watched a spoon bre...

...We watched a human being t...

...power of his... —the...

...Rabbi Zusya of Anipoli and...

...to flourish. Reb Zusya resp...

...Doctrine in the world. The st...

...s master's blasphemy. But Z...

...derstand," the master expl...

...in the street, you will turn...

...im. But what if there is no...

...unknown to us, He has cho...

...t He exists isn't worth a h...

...His place and practice justic...

...h AIDS patients who were...

ndred guests, discussing the

us dropped, including my own

and a seed grow in your hand,

material existence through th

spirit, given to us by God.

ndent once came to the great

why God had allowed atheism

theism was the single greates

his garments upon hearing h

ed his hands. "Don't you

time you see a hungry man

ng that God will look after

only you can feed him."

e is a God. But for reasons

n invisible. And the fact th

unless man chooses to act i

ess. Why did you work

The PSYCHIC AND The RABBI

The PSYCHIC
And
The RABBI
A Remarkable Correspondence

Uri Geller & Rabbi Shmuley Boteach
Foreword by Deepak Chopra

SOURCEBOOKS, INC.®
NAPERVILLE, ILLINOIS

Published simultaneously in the UK in 2001 by Robson Books,
London, UK H79HT

Published by Sourcebooks, Inc.
P.O. Box 4410, Naperville, Illinois 60567-4410
(630) 961-3900
FAX: (630) 961-2168

Library of Congress Cataloging-in-Publication Data

Geller, Uri, 1946–
    The psychic and the rabbi: a remarkable correspondence / by
Uri Geller and Shmuley Boteach.
        p. cm.
    Includes bibliographical references and index.
    ISBN 1-57071-786-9 (alk. paper)
    1. Spiritual life—Judaism. 2. Ethics, Jewish. 3. Geller, Uri, 1946–
4. Psychics—England—Correspondence. 5. Boteach, Shmuel. 6.
Rabbis—England—Correspondence. I. Boteach, Shmuel. II. Title.

BM723 .G45 2001
296.7—dc21
                                                    00-068769

Printed and bound in the United States of America

LB 10 9 8 7 6 5 4 3 2 1

To our wives, Hanna & Debbie
and to our children—
our light,
our joy,
our inspiration,
and to the Gracious God
responsible for these Beautiful Blessings

CONTENTS

FOREWORD BY DEEPAK CHOPRA

In May 1999, I was teaching a course in Oxford, England, entitled Seduction of Spirit. During the week, I happened to do an interview for a Dutch television show. At the end of the interview, the reporter handed me Uri Geller's card with a message saying he would like me to call him. The next day, as a result of my call, Uri and I met for dinner. I was overwhelmed by the elegance of his simplicity and felt I had met a long-lost brother.

That same evening, Uri got on the stage and in front of four hundred people touched a serving spoon that we had brought out from the kitchen. At his light touch, the spoon snapped in two and fell to the floor. The audience gasped. Then he proceeded to ask members of the audience to hold their keys in their hands, close their eyes, and mentally say "bend." Several keys bent out of shape.

At the end of the course, on a Sunday afternoon, I visited his home, which was full of beautiful mementos and great artwork. Uri gave me a piece of crystal as a present and casually asked, "Do you want me to charge it?" Before I could say "yes," he lightly touched it as it rested in my hand and the stone started glowing. The crystal became so hot that I had to drop it.

Later that afternoon, my wife and I drove to George Harrison's house to celebrate his son Dani's birthday. Uri performed remarkable feats at the house, including extraordinary mind-reading. I was wonder-struck—not just by his mind/body genius, but by his innocence, his kindness, his generosity, his alertness, his love, his present-moment awareness, and most of all, his humility.

Uri's unique talent lies in his ability to spontaneously integrate three domains of existence—the virtual, the quantum, and the material. Nature is the full expression of the integration of these three domains as one continuum of consciousness. The mind of the cosmos is constantly trans-forming itself from the world of pure potentiality into the world of information and energy, and then into the world of matter. This transformation is orchestrated by "intent," which must therefore be a force in nature. The principle of theology informs us that in nature, intended outcomes orchestrate their own fulfillment through the properties of infinite organiza-tion and infinite correlation. These qualities are inherent in nature's intelligence. The teaching of Vedanta informs us that this integration between the three levels is disrupted when our ego comes in the way of our spirit. Perhaps that is part of Uri's secret. More easily than the vast majority of us, he is able to get his personal self out of the way and "intend" from a deeper level of the submanifest order of being. This may be part of the mechanism. I am sure he also has a unique nerv-ous system that can tap into the deeper order of being. I was intrigued by Uri's abilities and became very interested to know more about his inner world.

The Psychic and the Rabbi is a fascinating collection of let-ters between Uri and Rabbi Boteach, author of *An Intelligent Person's Guide to Judaism, Dating Secrets of the Ten Command-ments, Moses of Oxford, Kosher Emotions,* and his international blockbuster, *Kosher Sex.* The two men are clearly close and inti-mate friends, and through their exchanges, we discover our own humanity. It is obvious that Rabbi Boteach is a wise man, bringing the richness of Judaic tradition to his thinking. Uri reveals himself with great honesty, and it is evident that at times he can be a challenged soul, seeking the deeper meaning and significance of his own existence. In his letters, we see him at times tormented, confused, vulnerable, yet full of wonder— and exposed, transforming but always spontaneous. This is the essence of spirituality.

I believe the time has come for Uri to use his extraordinary talents in the realm of quantum healing. There is a theoretical framework for that. I believe that by focusing his intention on transformation in the body, he will provide us with insight into abilities that all of us may have.

I hope to have many years of collaboration with Uri Geller. By understanding this extraordinary human being, we may all gain a deeper understanding of ourselves.

Deepak Chopra
The Chopra Center for Well Being
La Jolla, California

Introduction by Uri Geller

Shmuley Boteach is an impressive man. Broad-shouldered and dagger-eyed, with the wild beard of a prophet and the fast drawl of a comedian, he didn't introduce himself to me so much as detonate in my vicinity. The rabbi wanted me to lecture at the Oxford Union for his L'Chaim Society—and he got me, because what Shmuley desires he hunts down ruthlessly.

We should have had nothing in common. He was launching an international career, doing things no one had ever attempted before, like getting superpower leaders to address a Jewish students' charity, or writing books about having sensational sex after marriage. I was retreating from the adrenaline surge of TV chat shows and live appearances, focusing instead on my family and a series of novels about parascience. He was in the orthodox establishment—in it like a thorn, drawing blood at every step, but also committed. I have always been outside the establishment—all establishments: scientific, religious, artistic, entertainment, media. Now I'm in my fifties, and I seem to be regarded as a pillar of the anti-establishment.

We had talked for only a few minutes when I realized this man was going to become my brother. I was an only child, and I had always missed the guidance of a wiser, older brother. Here instead was a reckless, excitable rabbi, twenty years my junior, who gave advice so fast I could barely follow the ideas. Cynics say you can choose your friends but not your relatives—I have never been much of a cynic. Shmuley Boteach and I did not choose to be friends, but in the early weeks of our friendship we both seemed, independently, to take a conscious decision to forge a bond of brotherhood. Neither of us could have predicted the extraordinary discoveries that would follow.

We decided, when the correspondence was well underway, that we wanted to publish our letters. We were both concerned, however, that publishers would see our friendship as something exclusively Jewish, when it was nothing of the sort. My Jewishness has always been something private and personal—many members of the public seem to assume I am a Muslim or a Christian, and most UFOlogists are convinced I didn't come from this world at all. Shmuley is evidently Jewish, but that was irrelevant to our brotherhood—he might have been a Buddhist monk or a Baptist preacher for all that it mattered to me.

To test the breadth of appeal of our proposed book, I decided to seek an endorsement from a place that is very close to Jerusalem and completely unlike Israel—the Vatican. With a brief note explaining what Shmuley and I hoped to achieve in dissolving religious boundaries and awakening people to their own spirituality, I bundled up a few of our letters and sent them to the Pope. My admiration for Pope John Paul II is profound, and I appreciate the tireless efforts he has made to join Christian and Jewish hands in friendship. I hoped he might hear of our letters from an aide, and perhaps gain some pleasure and enjoyment from them—I did not expect a kind and loving reply, in the hand of his Vatican Assessor, Monsignor Pedro López Quintana, which concluded: "His Holiness invokes upon you and upon Rabbi Shmuley Boteach abundant divine blessings."

The Pope's blessing seemed to crystallize the central point of all my words with Shmuley—God loves not the divisions that human beings place between each other, but the people themselves.

Uri Geller

September 1999

Introduction by Shmuley Boteach

Like any reader of this book, I had heard of the amazing powers of Uri Geller ever since I was a small child. I understood that he could bend spoons simply by touching them, could make the magnetic needle of a compass move simply by looking at it, and could make seeds grow in his hand just by rubbing them. Up until my thirtieth year, my only contact with Uri came in the form of seeing him on the cover of books and magazines, always staring intently at the reader, always looking mysterious, indeed, hauntingly so. There was almost something spooky about him that made him at once fascinating and frightening. Uri was the kind of guy you'd love to show off at a dinner party, but wouldn't necessarily want to meet in a dark alley, even if you were twice as big as he was and it was you who had the gun.

When I moved to Britain to serve as rabbi to the students of Oxford University in 1988, I was told by friends that the enigmatic Geller lived just a few miles away in Reading. I had no reason to imagine that he would become something akin to family. Four years ago, *The Jewish Book Week* in London invited Uri and me to speak jointly at a symposium on the power of prayer. Uri spoke, and then I spoke. Uri bent a spoon, and then I spoke some more. Uri bent the keys of five members of the audience from a distance of at least twenty feet, and then I spoke some more. The pattern of the evening continued until, with the last of my speeches, the audience all drifted into a pleasant and deep sleep. It can be a real bummer when you're up against Uri on a one-to-one and your biggest trick is trying to keep your audience from slipping into an irreversible coma while he is out bending minivans in half just by looking at them. After the talk, both Uri and I sat at our respective tables to sell our books. The line to buy his books went twice around the auditorium. The line to buy mine consisted of a friend to whom I was giving a free copy.

Even my own wife was in the Uri line, waiting to get an autograph. So much for spousal loyalty.

In the eleven years that my wife and I lived with our six children in Britain, we were blessed with many close friends, but no relatives. Not even a distant cousin. It was therefore a blessing from heaven to have Uri Geller step into my life because he became an older brother to me. Ever since I met Uri four years ago, hardly a day has passed when he hasn't called two or three times to give me advice and guidance.

I can be a pretty hard-headed guy, sure of my own path, indifferent to people's advice, accepting criticism easily since I usually just shrug it off. Which only raises the question in my mind as to why I find it so easy to listen to Uri. But listen and follow I do, and Uri has become something of a mentor to me. Uri has always been a great human being and a proud Jew. But I hope that in return, I too have enriched his life by bringing him just a wee bit closer to his Jewish heritage and the faith of his ancestors.

Above all else, Uri has always tried to teach me how to maximize my human potential. If I wasn't giving enough time to my children, he scolded me. If I was wasting time on subjects that were of little value to others, he redirected me. And if I was allowing silly problems to needle and depress me, he uplifted me.

I am mostly a fire-fighter. Emergencies seem to erupt in my life all the time. And like a good fireman, Uri has been there to help me extinguish them. But he has then sat with me, in a comforting posture, and nursed me back to full health.

So here I am today, with a spiritual big brother. Looking forward to another day.

May God rain down His abundant blessings on us all,

September 1999
New York City

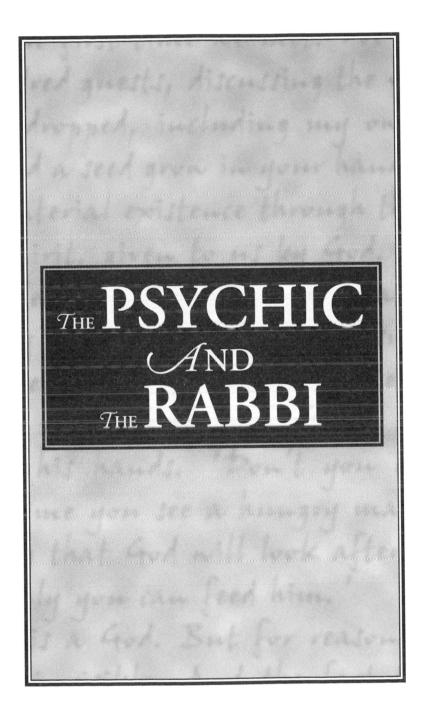

THE PSYCHIC AND THE RABBI

Dear Shmuley,

I love to get a reaction. I love it when people get excited, when they start to stare, when something about the universe is revealed to them that blows their minds. I must have bent a spoon for someone every day of my life since the sixties, and I've never tired of it. I love the reactions.

Some people nod and say: "Wow! I always wanted to see that. I always believed in it, but it's incredible to hold the spoon in my own hand and watch it bend." They're the believers.

Others shake their heads and swear. "I can't believe my eyes!" they say. Later on they reason, "It must have been a trick. I don't know how he did it, but it's got to be impossible." They're the skeptics. They won't let themselves believe, even though they have no real alternative.

And there are some people who refuse to look. "You'll trick me," they say, "and I won't be able to see how it's done." I really try with these people. One of them was a Nobel prize–winning physicist who asked to meet me but would not let me demonstrate my powers. I wondered how a scientist who could accept the incredible realities of quantum physics could refuse to watch someone else breaking the rules.

But at least he wasn't indifferent. It's those who don't give a damn that really upset me. Bending spoons is draining work. I'm low on power for an hour after bending just one spoon, so walls of indifference are hard to take. And when it's someone close to me, that's so much worse. When it's someone I really loved a long time ago, that does hurt me.

I won't tell you the girl's name. You've probably heard of her. She's a daughter of one of the West's most powerful families, and long before I married Hanna, I was in love with this girl. But she was a Christian, and her family didn't care for me and it didn't work out.

She never had children. When I was younger, I used to think, what if I'd married her, what would our kids have been like? How many would we have had? What would we have called them? But then my own two children came along, and all the might-have-beens ceased to matter.

A long time after we first met, she visited my home and stayed in the guest apartment. She had changed. Her vitality had gone, and she was sullen and distant, as if some essential piece of her mind had been cut out. On the third day of her stay, we went for a walk along the banks of the Thames behind my house, and I asked her to give me her copper hairslide so that I could bend it.

My energy is always greater beside running water. A good friend, the philosopher Colin Wilson, suggests this is caused by electromagnetic flow. And it's true, ghosts often walk beside rivers. In feng shui, running water carries chi, the lifeforce. Whatever, as soon as I began to stroke the slide, it bent. I handed it back, a twisted piece of metal. The pin dangled and dropped off.

"Sorry," I said.

"It doesn't signify," she said.

"But I blew your mind, huh?" I asked, more in hope than expectation. Her face still wore its blank gaze.

"It's pointless."

"I reveal the power of the human mind, and that's pointless to you?"

"You can bend metal. So look, I can bend it back." She turned it in her fingers.

"You can't mend the pin," I said, sulkily.

"That's a fact. It's useless." And she flicked the little shining crescent into the water.

"You're mad because I broke it."

"I couldn't care less. It means less than nothing."

That's the reaction I dread. The empty indifference, the hollow shrug.

"It does mean something."

"What," she said, "are you going to tell me there's a God, and a God who bends metal just for you?"

"You believe in God," I told her.

Her moist gray gaze was fixed ahead, and I saw what it was that had gone from her face. The little flame that danced in her irises. The life in her eyes.

"Do I? Do I believe in a God who lets babies in Africa starve, and who doesn't raise a finger to help when young men are wasting down to their bones because they're drug addicts and they might have shared a needle?"

I remembered her younger brother, who was a boy when I knew him. A boy of eleven back then. He died from AIDS at thirty-two.

"Do I believe in a God who is too busy to save one single solitary life from even one day's pain? Pain every, every, every day? But who takes time out from his busy schedule to materialize in this field and break my hairslide? Get real, Uri."

There is an answer to this argument. You told it to me once, Shmuley, and it made sense. But I can never remember what it is.

I said, "I didn't claim God was bending the metal."

"So what's the point?"

"So maybe it's a human ability."

"Pretty useless one, isn't it? The mystical power to break hairslides." She turned and began walking back to the house, and then broke into a run. I didn't try to follow her.

It was turning into evening, and the sky had got that washed-out color, like all the blue has drained into the earth and soon the blackness is going to spread in big smoky drops, like ink in water. The first star, which was really a planet, began glowing like a spotlight one million miles away.

I rested my back on a tree and stared out at it. Was there ever life on Venus? And if there ever had been and it was gone now, what would have been the point?

And if God was not helping me to bend that hairslide, why empower me to do it? Because I know the gift comes from somewhere outside me, the same way you know that visible objects are not fantasies generated inside your head but real matter, existing independently of your perceptions.

When you close your eyes, the sky is still there. And when I die, the power of human minds to bend metal will still exist.

Her brother had died. The sky was still there, but part of the boy's sister, my ex-lover, had drained away. I should have done more to help him. Maybe I could have lifted his pain for a day. Or just part of a day. I have worked with AIDS patients, people I never even knew. Why didn't I help with this one?

God watches as babies starve, and so did I. I saw the reports from Sudan. I shook my head and turned the page, and asked my wife, "What can I do? I am only one man."

What can I do?

But who knows what I might not do, if I tried?

Who would believe I had the ability to bend metal? No one, until they saw it with their own eyes. You can't take human limitation on trust.

That's the point. That was a point, and I saw it, burning brighter and more constantly, like the planet in the darkening sky. God lets me achieve something extraordinary to demonstrate how boundless is human potential.

There are no limits. Mankind can do anything. We can do for ourselves everything we wish God would do for us. We can prevent a child from starving. We can find a cure for AIDS. We can do every mind-blowing thing we ever dreamed of, if we all try together.

To believe in God, we must also believe in ourselves.

I went running back across the fields, to tell my friend, "There is a point. I know what the point is." But she had already driven away.

Yours with great love,

Dear Uri,

I was one of those skeptics who had heard of your powers, but always felt that a trick was behind them. But then my eyes witnessed what my mind refused to credit. I watched you bend a spoon. You will recall it was the first time we met. We were both on a platform in front of six hundred guests, discussing the virtues of prayer. That day, hundreds of jaws dropped, including my own, as we watched a spoon break in half, and a seed grow in your hand. We watched a human being transform material existence through the power of his will alone—the power of the spirit, given to us by God.

A student once came to the great Rabbi Zusya of Anipoli and asked him why God had allowed atheism to flourish. Reb Zusya responded that atheism was the single greatest doctrine in the world. The student rent his garments upon hearing his master's blasphemy. But Zusya grabbed his hands. "Don't you understand," the master explained, "every time you see a hungry man in the street, you will turn away thinking that God will look after him. But what if there is no God? Now, only you can feed him."

There is a God. But for reasons unknown to us, He has chosen to remain invisible. And the fact that He exists isn't worth a hill of beans, unless man chooses to act in His place and practice justice and kindness. Why did you work with AIDS patients who were total strangers? Because they weren't total strangers. They were your brothers and sisters, children of the one God, and you felt a congenital and unbreakable bond with them.

You are possessed of a most extraordinary and precious gift. But every human being is possessed of an ever greater gift. They can cause hearts of stone to melt into flesh. King Solomon said that love was like looking into a pool of water. Whatever you show is reflected right back.

I believe that we are all in a relationship with God, and a relationship is a two-way street. We don't have to bow our heads in submission when we witness emaciated children in the Sudan, or children riddled with cancer, and simply accept that this is the will of God. No. Our obligation in such circumstances is to reverse the suffering, and in situations where we cannot—such as in the face of incurable disease—then we are obliged to be defiant. The word "Israel" means "he who wrestles with God," and was a name given to Jacob after he had wrestled with the angel and prevailed.

That's why there does not exist, and never has existed, a proper rejoinder to the problem of suffering. Because the proper response is never to seek to understand it, but rather to obliterate it from the earth. Once when another Nobel Laureate, Elie Wiesel, delivered a lecture to our students in Oxford, a young woman arose from the audience and with tears in her eyes asked why there had been a Holocaust. Wiesel responded, "That is an immoral question. Because if I answer it, I fear that you might sleep easier tonight." An answer is an attempt to reconcile tension. We shouldn't want to know why young children starve or why so many people go to bed lonely. We should only want it to cease and work and pray our hardest until suffering vanishes from the earth.

I believe that evil and suffering are not a necessary part of our universe, and that the forces of good will eventually triumph. As a Jew, I am not part of a tradition that believes that there is any inherent good within suffering. I reject utterly the balderdash that tells us that suffering ennobles our character and teaches us to value the truly important things in life. There is no good which suffering helps us to achieve that could not have been attained through a painless means. All suffering is difficult to bear, but it is especially difficult when patronizing and insensitive arguments are offered by clerics as to the redeeming qualities of suffering, implying that it is somehow good that we are in so much pain. As Jews, we might excoriate God for the Holocaust. But we must also offer humble thanks for the longevity of the Jewish nation. A relationship is indeed a two-way road, and we cannot simply holler when things go wrong. We must allow our hearts to swell in the face of all that is beautiful.

Sometimes in the modern world it is possible to lose sight of the beauty of life. And this is what makes your extraordinary gift so powerful. For we are a generation that worships the senses. We love sex because it feels so good, and we reject love as an illusion caused by an evolutionary need to propagate the species. But your immense talent in bending hard metal with the soft gray matter of the mind teaches us that the most precious things in life are actually those that cannot be seen, touched, heard, tasted, or smelled. Like love itself, the world's most powerful forces are those that are so infinite they cannot be limited or constrained by the flesh.

Ultimately, the power that cannot be seen is God Himself, the source of all hope. Your friend who walked away in disgust because no divine power had saved her brother from AIDS still believes deep down that AIDS will one day be cured. But why? Maybe there will always be diseases that will overcome the best efforts of mankind. And yet, we still burn the midnight oil in the certainty that our efforts to better our planet and rid the world of war will indeed bear fruit. This is because deep down we all believe in hope, in a brighter future, and have faith that history has a direction. That we are all headed toward a better and brighter tomorrow. Against all the historical evidence of war, famine, and incurable disease, the flame of hope still burns brightly and irrationally within the breast of man.

Hope was a difficult thing for Jews to imagine after the Holocaust. And yet, they built a nation that continues to endure after seven wars in five decades. The reason for their enduring faith in their history was that their return had been foretold, it had been promised. Yet we humans often make the mistake of believing that history is causal, that the events of today are caused by what happened yesterday. In reality, however, the events of today are controlled by the promises of tomorrow. Because we will something to happen in the future, we can make it happen today.

You have the brilliant power to remind us of the greatest lesson of all. That every human possessed of a spark of the divine can cause reality to bend to his or her will.

Two thousand years ago, a poor and illiterate shepherd boy named Akiva was challenged by Rachel, daughter of the richest man in the Holy Land, to become a scholar and win her hand in marriage. He despaired of reorienting his life. Filled with melancholy, he walked into the woods and witnessed a huge rock that had a hole piercing it through and through. What was strong enough to penetrate the rock? He looked up and saw a small stream that deposited a tiny drop every few seconds onto the rock. With persistence, the water had bored a hole through that which seemed impenetrable. Akiva took the lesson to heart. He went back and began to study. Twelve years later, he was the greatest Jewish sage alive.

We might not be able to feed every starving child in the world today, immediately. But with the determination never to give up, we can alleviate their hunger, one by one, drop by drop, until we have made a gaping hole in the world's indifference.

Reciprocating all of your immense love,

Dear Shmuley,

It was great that you were able to visit my home last week. I felt a terrific flow of energy between us, which was still hanging like static in the room hours after you left. You were almost horizontal at one point in our conversation, staring up at the ceiling with one hand reached across the top of your head, flipping your skullcap up and down. (Did you realize you had that mannerism? Does your wife tell you, "Stop fidgeting with the *kippah*, Shmuley"?) You were lying back, but there was so much force concentrated in you, I was prepared to see you blast out of my sofa like a rocket.

And my mother—she loved the fact that I had a rabbi in the place. It doesn't happen often. We get a lot of sports stars, journalists, business types, and occasionally a passing head of state or member of the royal family, but rabbis are fewer and further between. My mother has an apartment in the west wing of the house, and when she wants to inspect my guests, she pops into my kitchen and looks through the window at the driveway. She was impressed I had a rabbi over—and she's not someone who's easily impressed.

I'm saying this lightheartedly, because it's easier to admit a difficult truth this way. I feel more comfortable with secular society than I do with conventional religion. I don't go to synagogue regularly, I don't rest on the *Shabbat*, and I don't usually find it easy to talk to rabbis. Even though my Jewishness is an essential part of my personality, I tend to avoid its formal elements in everyday life. And that's a difficult thing to admit.

Jewishness is at the root of my soul. After all, I was brought up in Israel, and I shed blood for my country. The festivals and the fasts do not pass me unobserved—not always, anyway. But that's because they are part of my culture, and culture doesn't have to be a religious thing. Any lapsed Christian who spends a fortune on celebrating Christmas will tell you that.

But while my material life is much influenced by Judaism, my spiritual life is not. That's the core of it. And I know it's a contradiction. It makes a note of guilt sound deep within my body, a note that tolls so low I feel it as a vibration rather than hear it as a sound. A tremor of guilt. I appreciate that Judaism is a religion, not a set of social laws, and yet I do not live my life accordingly. I know that the *Torah* was not written as a book of etiquette, so I feel a kind of hypocrisy when my habits draw me back to Jewish customs while my mind recoils from the Jewish faith.

And this feeling of guilt has to confront another thread buried deep in the tangle of my soul. This one is thick and wiry, and if ever I suffered enough pressure to pull my spirit apart, this red thread would be the last of all to snap. Red is for rebellion, the rebellion in my mind and in my spirit. I've woven a career from this red thread, brittle though it is. Rebellion against science, rebellion against preconception, rebellion against the norm, rebellion against the possible. Every time I see a theory or a proposition that's designed to fit me into someone else's pattern, I get a thrill from ripping it apart.

So, this conjurer thinks my metal-melting powers are some kind of magic trick: how come his car keys just bent in his pocket? This scientist claims my body merely discharges a greater electromagnetic flow than is usual: watch his face when I will a radish seed to sprout in my hand. This guru desires me to renounce all worldly possessions and spearhead a movement of new international holiness: sure, I'll meet him—but I'll turn up for the talks in a $5 million Sikorsky helicopter.

And sometimes I think that the red in my head goes right back to my Jewishness. For organized religion was in many ways my first experience of other people's patterns. Judaism went much deeper than the social strictures of school and family. It attempted to mold my soul, reshape my essence to fit its compartments—and there was no place in those compartments for my paranormal powers. According to the rabbis, only prophets worked miracles, and anyone else was just making a nuisance of themselves. So by the time I was twenty, I thought religion was a steaming pile of platitudes.

There are plenty of reasons why a twenty-year-old man cannot express himself honestly through his actions. First of all, there are too many people ordering him around for him to choose his own actions freely—I'm talking about army officers and parents and employers and girlfriends and, yes, rabbis. And then, a twenty-year-old can easily mistake the urgings of his loins for the demands of his soul—many times I thought I was doing exactly what I wanted when it was nothing but what my dick wanted. And then, a twenty-year-old soul is still in its infancy.

In the intervening thirty years, I have located gold and oil all over the planet by dowsing, become a multimillionaire, tried to starve myself to death, fathered two beautiful children, written several books, and bent enough cutlery to fill an aircraft carrier. And it has gradually, very, very gradually, dawned on me that Judaism was not acting on a grudge when it tried to fit me into the pattern. It was nothing personal. The ancient authors of the Torah and the Mishnah did not give Uri Geller ingeniously subtle punishments—though when I was a child it definitely felt that way.

I have more confidence now. I can tell the difference between rebellion against ill-conceived patterns and the indiscriminate fear of all patterns. I'm still the world's least likely candidate for an evening of bridge at the club—I've never joined a club; in fact, after the army, I never joined anything—but at least I can see why people might want to play a few rubbers.

And I can see why you love being an Orthodox Jew. You're a rebel, Shmuley—that thick red thread is always whipping your soul into a frenzy. People find it tough being in the same club as you. But you want to belong, and so you fit your rebellion and your Jewishness together until they fit perfectly.

I know that I don't want to belong, but sometimes I wish I could want to. I know that sounds querulous and spoilt, but there's a real ache at the root of the pain. Other people, people like Shmuley Boteach, can keep a foothold on organized religion without sacrificing their rebellious souls. So why do I feel it's impossible for me?

Without a foothold, I suppose there's no rock—there's nothing but water. It's like being at sea. Often, I relish that freedom, but when darkness gathers overhead, I am overwhelmed by the terrifying knowledge that below me is nothing but fathomless water. I know that darkness gathers over you too. But beneath your feet there is an immovable expanse of rock.

Shmuley, for the first time in my life I have met a man of orthodox religion whose thoughts I can truly understand. We are on the same wavelength. For someone who practices telepathy seriously, this is not a vague metaphor. Because I feel that when we speak, I understand the ideas behind your words. That is rare. It offers me an opportunity, one I don't want to let slip.

I know you are busy—I know how busy! But for the sake of our new friendship, I am asking a favor: when I ask a question, try and listen to the questions hidden inside.

I cannot think I will ever want to stand beside you on the rock, day and night, for eternity. I love the open water. But it would be good to know that there's a place on your rock where sometimes I can rest my feet.

With much love,

Dear Uri,

Your letter read almost like a confessional. Of all your remarkable gifts, it's your honesty that I find most refreshing. Considering that your authenticity has been so repeatedly challenged, I am always taken aback at how forthcoming you are about yourself. Perhaps it's the same for me. People expect perfection from their rabbis, and like the rest of us, I am not perfect. But, like you, I always try to be honest and open, because I don't wish to compromise my humanity by pretending to be an angel. And besides, honesty can disarm. Perhaps mine is at heart an attempt to preempt people's judgmentalism by offering my soul before it is scrutinized. Perhaps yours is a self-defense mechanism too, almost daring your adversaries to come clean with their real intentions.

I do not believe in coincidences, Uri, and my meeting with you was certainly no accident. After we first met, I was amazed to discover that your biographer is Jonathan Margolis, a very close and dear friend. The nicest bit of flattery that has ever been channeled in my direction came from Jonathan. He called me up one day and asked if I minded being included in his will. I was delighted and asked him how much I would be inheriting. He told me that it wasn't money, but he had put into his will that the only rabbi that could eulogize him upon his death would be me. Did I mind? he asked. *Did I mind?* I wept. There could not have been a more beautiful statement of love. Death is what keeps us honest. It's the one thing that can't be manipulated. Paradoxically, the last moment in life is the first moment of truth.

Religion turns you off, you tell me. You're a rebel and you refuse to conform. You can't be straightjacketed, and religion has therefore become to you nothing more than a collection of platitudes. I sympathize with your feelings. Religion, once seen by man as a fountain of life, has become a barren desert, incapable of imparting the inspiration, guidance, or passion that it once embodied. But for me, Uri, religion actually confirms my individuality and allows me to maximize my own spiritual and material potential as an individual. The highest purpose of religion is to help people discover what it is about them that makes them special. Without religion, none of us would have developed the moral knowledge to swim against the social tide of complacency and indifference. We would all have conformed. Abraham and Moses—they were not social lackeys. They were revolutionaries.

You'll tell me that I too am merely offering even more platitudes, and I therefore must explain. Religion is the answer to our three greatest and most deep-seated needs: 1) to cure loneliness, 2) to overcome boredom, and 3) to surmount the challenge of meaninglessness.

Every human being goes through three levels of loneliness. The first is simply aloneness, a feeling of solitary isolation, which can be remedied just by being around other people. The second is what we may call pure loneliness, a feeling of lacking in appreciation. The greatest human need is to be needed. We need to be needed and want to be wanted. We want to feel that we are special, that there is a unique contribution to the world that only we can make. Real loneliness results not from having no one who loves us, but from having no one who *needs* our love. This loneliness is remedied by entering into a loving relationship with a man or woman who tells us they need us, that the sun wouldn't shine for them tomorrow if we were not around. Whether we are aware of it or not, we all seek to share our lives with such a person. We want to be the center of someone else's universe.

The third level of loneliness is contained deep within our hearts. The deepest loneliness is the fear that we never will be understood, that there is no one out there who can truly fathom our depths or fully grasp our pain. True loneliness is having an ache that no one can heal, an aspect of ourselves that no one can comprehend. And here is the greatest paradox of human existence. What makes me special is the fact that there is no one else like me. But this crucial fact also ensures my isolation and loneliness. Here lies the reason that so many choose to become conformists. All they are looking for is companionship, and they sense that in order to really bond with somebody else, they must first relinquish their uniqueness. Every relationship, then, involves a fundamental compromise of one's personality and character so that two people can find common ground. And while this compromise may serve a higher purpose, it is a compromise nonetheless.

In this recognition lies the ultimate reason for religion. People cry out to God as the only being in the universe that can truly understand them without this compromise. Since God is the architect of man and provider of his soul, He can comfort us in our loneliness without us conceding or altering our individuality. Herein also lies the highest reason for prayer. It is the belief in God and communion with Him in prayer which assures lonely human beings that they don't need to change in order to be special. God will always be there to understand them. So religion is the ultimate liberating force. This is something that mere spiritualism or spirituality can never impart. They can make you feel good and uplifted, but never understood.

You call yourself a rebel, Uri. But this is *because* you are a Jew, and not in spite of that fact. Before the Jews, all lived by the principle of might makes right. The strong suppressed the weak. Many centuries later, Darwin only reasserted what all the world had once believed: that the world operates by the law of the jungle in which only the fittest survive. In this world, fate was supreme. Nothing could be made better. The concept of progress was empty.

Into this world came the Jews with their radical ideas of monotheism and ethics. They taught that righteousness was greater than brute strength, that the weak had a protector in the personal God of history. They asserted that there was no fate and that man can permanently alter both himself and the earth. One caste of people was not superior to any other. The Jews became a nation of do-gooders in a world ruled by anarchy and tribal chieftains, and this is the origin of anti-Semitism. The Jews have always been the world's revolutionaries, undermining the hegemony of the oppressors. And the oppressors don't like it.

In a world in which a man could not be a ruler unless he were a conqueror, where an emperor of Rome could only hold onto his throne if he expanded the borders of empire, Isaiah and Jeremiah thundered in marketplaces that peace was greater than war and that a time would come when great men would beat their swords into ploughshares. Uri, these were no conformists. All the prophets were firebrands, radicals, and agitators, and it was the passion and conviction of their religious faith that gave them the courage to defy the social norms of their times and swim against the current of complacency and inequity.

What you are rebelling against is the endless and meaningless role of arcane ritual to which religion has been reduced.

This is something that I can empathize with very easily. But your rebelling against religion without having had the opportunity to study it properly and gain an appreciation of its true depth and beauty is a great pity. It is comparable to the man who watches a husband and wife going about all the menial responsibilities of their married life together. He watches them change the diapers and take out the rubbish, and concludes that marriage itself is rubbish. But this man has never been a part of such a relationship, and so cannot see its beauty and the invisible love that motivates these actions.

Like many people today, you feel that religion represses your freedom. This constitutes the main reason that people dismiss religion. It doesn't give them wings. People want to see miracles and experience the divine. They want fireworks, and religion doesn't seem to offer them. Certainly, no rabbi or priest in the world can reproduce your amazing feats of paranormal genius.

But this is a juvenile approach to life. Only romantics who haven't learnt what love is seek endless poetry in a relationship rather than prose.

Religion is a proclamation, a manifesto on the part of the deity, that this is My intrinsic will, that if you want to draw close to Me, this is what you must do. The book of Psalms declares that "From my flesh I shall perceive God." By understanding ourselves, we come to understand, in a vague and imperfect way, the perfect mind of God. Just as we have needs, so does God. And all religion is a communiqué of what those needs are. But, by accommodating those needs and living in accordance with the divine will, we bring God into our lives so that we never feel forsaken or lost.

I personally hate loneliness. And that's why I am religious. I hate the feeling of being abandoned, in a cold impersonal universe, alone against the elements. Some would say, therefore, that religion for me is a crutch. To that I plead guilty as charged. For some, money is a crutch; for others, success and the adoration of their peers are the props they lean on throughout life. Given that all of us need something to sustain and support us, I choose to support myself against the Rock of Israel.

To turn to the issues of boredom and meaninglessness: these are difficult for someone like you, with your enormous success. You can do things that no one else on the planet can replicate. God has seen fit to deliver unto you powers that cause mouths to drop and eyes to pop. But what should you do with your powers and success? How can you realize their potential?

That's more of a problem than many would believe, for it is precisely due to the fact that we are the most successful and financially prosperous generation of all time that we are also the most bored. We have so much extra time. Not knowing what to do with it, and valuing space and possessions over and above time and special moments, it is all too easy simply to squander our lives in endless acquisition and pleasure. The Talmud says that when you have nothing to do, you do what you ought not to do. How many wars have started simply to alleviate human boredom and unease? The philosopher Robert Nesbitt says that most wars came about as a result of too much energy and not enough engagement. How many people take drugs and commit vandalism and crime simply because they weren't preoccupied with something higher?

The purpose of religion was to give people something glorious to do with their lives, something extraordinary to which they could devote their time. God commanded the Jews in the wilderness of Sinai to use their gold to erect a holy Tabernacle. This is important because so many today use their gold to buy drugs or see another movie. While the rest of the world were wasting their lives bowing to stones and worshipping the sun, Abraham, our grandfather, was out under the unbearable heat of the desert looking for wayfarers to whom he could offer hospitality. He was educating his children to love wisdom, to cherish books, and to devote their lives to contemplation and the pursuit of knowledge. And today, while many people worship

Eminem or Destiny's Child, we offer a wholesome alternative—the pursuit of Godliness and goodness.

I remember, and still so deeply regret, how I wasted my childhood on television. My parents were divorced, my mother had two jobs to support us, and I had little supervision or guidance. I watched TV day and night and became a terrible student. By the time I started rabbinical training school at age fourteen, I had read only one, perhaps two, full-length books. It was religion that taught to me to love learning, to love God, and, most important of all, to love goodness. To try and find people who were humble and kind. In you and in your friendship, I feel that I have found this, and much more. Hoping that we will meet one day in the tent of Abraham.

With much love,

Dear Shmuley,

I have been kneeling among my photographs. In one of my cabinets, I keep boxes of pictures from my childhood, from my early career, from my modeling days. I almost never look at those. But one packet I take out, every two or three months, when my family is not around. It is something I do, like a recurring dream that happens when I am awake. (There is a recurring nightmare too, a real one, which also dates from this time.)

I spread the pictures on the checkered marble floor of my hall, and I examine each one in turn. They are the images from my army days, and I will never be able to banish them from my mind, neither the memories nor the photographs which I cannot help but return to.

Many of my friends died in the Six Day War, that blitz from nowhere, a do-or-die conflict for Israel. I was a sergeant on leave, recuperating from pneumonia, when the Klaxons went off all over the country. I understood without being told that my army and my homeland were risking their existence on one throw of the dice, and that it would be nothing if the coming battle were to cost me my life—it could also cost the lives of every Israeli I had ever known and loved. I was proud to be fighting alongside my comrades and my father. He had not been part of my life for a long time, but this was war. War made it different.

I remember my frantic scooter ride across Tel Aviv, fist hammering the little hooter, as I scrambled to rejoin my unit. I was at the head of eight men, driving a command car. If I'd been fully fit, I would have been detailed to an armored car, like my dearest friend, Avram Stedler. I caught sight of Avram refueling at a roadside stop, and as I ran to greet him, I knew we were saying good-bye. I made him shake my hand, though he didn't want to. Before the week ended, I had hauled him from the wreckage of his vehicle. His driver and captain had died when a Jordanian tank shell hit them. Avram was the gunner, and the blast had torn away his left leg.

Avram died, but not at once. He lay in the shelter of a ruined building for several hours, in convulsions of hope and agony, waiting for the medical helicopters that I swore I had summoned. But the only radio handset I could find was perforated with two neat bullet holes. There was in fact no way of calling for help. So I lied.

And then I lied again. Avram was staring in disbelief at the mangled mess that had been his body, and he begged me to tell him his genitals were still there. "For God's sake," he asked over and over, "Uri, look and tell me. Tell me honestly, is everything all right?" I told him, "Avram, you've still got the hairiest balls in the army."

But his organs had been torn away, right to the base of his spine. I was already nursing a bullet-wound in my hand, and what remained of my unit had to be got away from there. I wish I could tell you my best friend died in my arms. He didn't. In the end, we all die alone.

I remember that when I look at the smiling faces in these old photographs. Many of them did not live. If they had wives, those girls were soon widowed. If they had children, those children grew up orphaned. I hope they are always comforted by the truth that their fathers were some of the bravest, most unselfish men who have ever lived. I look at my photographs and I am glad I knew them. Those were exceptional days, and extraordinary men lived in them.

It is not a maudlin urge that drives me to take out my pictures again and again, and to study them when I am alone. I think I am reminding myself of someone I was. Though the army never took to me, and I was as much an outsider then as I have ever been, still I was one of those soldiers. I was an Israeli paratrooper in the Six Day War. If I had never done anything else—if I had died instead of Avram—then that would have been enough, and much more than enough.

For a short time, I suffered nightmares about the fighting. I was wounded twice, the second time so badly that I thought I was dead. I still don't know what hit me—shrapnel from an exploding enemy tank, I think, but it could have been bullets. There was impact in my left arm and then, after a split second that lasted several eternities, a massive blow to my forehead. Then a black tide, and as it washed over me, I thought: "I'm dead, then. Not so bad." I didn't feel regret, or disappointment, or disbelief. I was dead. It happens. Only, as it happened, I wasn't.

I think about my friends as they lived, not as they were in their last moments. When I close my eyes and think of Avram, he has both legs. And both balls, probably. Though I can recall them vividly, the slaughterhouse images don't haunt me, perhaps because my school in Cyprus during the Troubles overlooked a mortuary, and we would press against the fence and squint through the slats to see the corpses of Greeks and Turks on the slab, with their blood oozing into the drainage grooves. They were the bodies of strangers, and I was in the thick, callous armor of youth. So when I looked at bodies of friends, what I saw were the friends, not the bodies.

When those comrades died in front of me, I felt myself protected by a sense of the unreality of these images. I remember seeing corpses lying at the roadside during the first hours of the land battle, and asking my driver, "Why are they sleeping in the day?" He looked at me like I was a self-obsessed idiot. That look still stings me now. But that's how war was for many men, something so unreal, it was easier to believe the corpses were sleeping.

I keep going back to my photographs. It's something which I will always do, just as my left arm will always fail to extend properly. That's a trivial reminder which jogs my memory with death. Much more disturbing is my recurring nightmare.

Shmuley, I killed a man. He was a Jordanian soldier, and my unit was advancing into rocky hillside that his unit was abandoning. He took two shots at me from a badly sheltered vantage. I guess he wasn't much good as a soldier. He was out of position, and he panicked. I turned with my gun halfway to my shoulder and looked into his face. We were both bad soldiers. I should have been hitting the ground, my gun should have been permanently ready to fire, and I shouldn't have given a damn what was in his face.

He had a moustache. Even as I pulled the trigger, I was thinking: "That moustache makes you different from me. You're an Arab."

If I had hesitated any longer, he would have fired again. But he didn't. I killed him.

The nightmare began weeks later, when the sense of unreality that had sustained me began to slip. Now it returns two or three times a month, and I wake up feeling disturbed. Not screaming or sweating, but depressed for the duration of the day.

In my dream, we're somewhere like the battlefield, but there's no sound of gunfire. It's barren and burnt, and there are bodies around us. Maybe it's hell. We don't have our weapons. The Jordanian soldier steps forward and grabs my uniform, and he's crying. His face is nothing like the blank and terrified mask that I saw when I killed him. It's full of pain and disbelief. He is shouting at me in Arabic, but I understand him—"Why did you kill me? Why did you kill me?"

I want to give him all the answers. They are simple and they stand out in everything I've told you. I have no doubts about them. If I hadn't killed this man, I wouldn't be alive now. I would have died instead of him, and maybe now I would be invading his dreams and grabbing his uniform and screaming at him in a Hebrew that he could understand. And if his country had not threatened my country, and if his tank crews had not blown my friends to pieces, and if our governments had talked instead of compelling young men to be inept, unwilling soldiers...

Why did I kill you? Why do you have to ask?

He has been asking since 1967. I truly do not know if this is his soul, returning again and again to beg the answer, or if my own soul, at a deep, hidden level, cannot understand the horror that overtook it. I hope it's my soul that bears the burden; I want to think his soul is at peace.

I'm not telling you this because I want reassurance, Shmuley. I don't need to hear my justifications repeated by my friends. I have been tutored in them for many years by my wife and my mother, and now I believe in them myself. I make some atonement for a killing that was beyond my control, by refusing to handle weapons—I admit I collected guns in the seventies, and I still own seven or eight, but I cannot abide to touch them now. They are locked in a safety deposit box in New York, and I pay the rental because I could not open it to sell them or even think of asking anyone to do that. It is cleaner to keep the box locked.

If that recurring dream is the bewildered cry of a dead soul—and part of me thinks that it must be, that in some way this is not a dream but a confrontation—then the Jordanian soldier cannot understand what I've done and why I did it. I know what I did, and my conscious mind has explanations for it. Maybe my unconscious mind doesn't.

But what does God think? I know you believe in a God who sees and judges. A God who gave a simple law to Moses— "Do not kill." A God whose commandments were clear, without room for justifications and validations and explanations and life-or-death decisions. "Do not kill."

The part of my mind that has no explanations knows exactly what God thinks. I killed. So I must live with it.

With very much love,

Dear Uri,

Your latest letter confirms to me that you are one of the least understood men on the planet. On the face of it, you are a man possessed of an extraordinary ability to control matter with the power of your mind alone. What is overlooked, however, is that concealed beneath your amazing gifts is one of the most introspective and thoughtful hearts that I have witnessed.

Unlike you, I have never had to witness the horrors of war. But when I was just ten years old, I witnessed two innocent police officers killed right before my very eyes. We lived in a decrepit part of Miami Beach where there was much drug dealing and violence. A group of us were playing hide-and-seek at a derelict hotel when we suddenly heard shots going off. A young man came flying out with a gaping wide hole in his chest. Within seconds, his body was bathed in blood. His dark green suit reddened. A tall, unshaven man quickly emerged from the same corridor just moments later. He carried a large shotgun that was still smoking. Barely ten fen feet from me, he stopped to reload. Seized with fear, I stood immobile, looking right at him. He returned the stare for just a moment which to me seemed like an eternity. Then he turned and fired on another man, killing him instantly. That day I felt a terror that I have never since experienced.

I mention this to you because we should distinguish between the story described above and your own personal experience of the Six Day War. In the horrible sequence of events to which I bore witness, an evil man took two innocent lives. In your painful story, you took the life of an assailant who first sought to murder you. You write of the excruciating pain that you still endure in the knowledge that you have shed human blood, that you have taken a human life. But what if that life had already been forfeited before you ever took it? What if there was no life to take?

In the Ten Commandments, God never tells us not to kill. Rather, He commands us not to *murder*. There is a critical difference. Murder involves taking an innocent life. Killing involves saving oneself from harm. Murder is where someone preys on an unsuspecting and undeserving victim. Killing is where a human being takes a life in order to save another— perhaps when that person's own life is at threat.

All human beings are endowed with the gift of life. What is more important, they are entitled to the life with which they are endowed. But this life is both a responsibility and a privilege. The latter can be forfeited when the former is ignored. One who comes into the world and determines to use his life to destroy that of another has waived his privilege to this blessing. Man was called forth by God from nothingness in order to practice love and promote justice. Those who serve as an obstacle to God's plan have no purpose in the cosmos.

So when you kill someone who is trying to kill you, Uri, you are actually doing something moral, strange as it may seem. You are bringing goodness into the world by purging the world of evil. Is there anyone that would deny that the fight to stop Hitler and kill off his SS was a courageous act of great morality?

Such a bold and highly controversial statement requires elucidation. How do we know what is good and what is bad? Indeed, how do we know that killing is bad at all? I am a religious man, Uri, and as such I look at God as the ultimate arbiter of right and wrong. Something is good because God says it is good, and something is evil when God declares it thus. Without God, there can be no absolute good or evil. We are left aching in a world of moral relativism where no man ever has the authority to declare someone else's actions immoral or unlawful.

Such relativism is the basis of modern-day political correctness which says that no faith has the right to superimpose its values on the rest of the world. But such an easy and blithe dismissal of dearly held beliefs is difficult for the heart to accept. Everyone has an innate belief in absolute ethics that are binding on all humanity, notwithstanding their protestations to the contrary. Whenever liberal Oxford academics tell me that there is no such thing as absolute morality, I always ask them whether a man is ever justified in beating his wife. Understandably, they always answer to the contrary. So I continue to play devil's advocate. "Let's say he catches her in bed with another man. Can he beat her then?" "No," they say, "let him throw her out or divorce her. She does not belong to him and he is therefore never permitted to strike her. She is not his chattel or his possession. He can terminate the relationship, but he can never hit her." They say this with great conviction, not catching on to the hole that they're digging for themselves.

Saying that a man is never ever justified in beating his wife is a tacit acceptance of the belief in absolute morality. Saying that something is always wrong is an acceptance that some things are not relative, but absolute.

Most people today believe that the highest goal in life is to be happy. Because happiness is their God, they basically interpret anything that makes them happy as good, and anything that makes them unhappy as bad. But such superficial and relativistic definitions of good and evil present many problems.

For instance, if a heroin addiction makes someone happy, is that good? And what about an extramarital affair? Is that good, so long as it provides pleasure and brings happiness?

In solving these dilemmas, most people would go along with the argument that says something is good if it makes a lot of people happy, not just oneself. This is called utilitarianism, where goodness is defined as the maximization of happiness for the largest group of people. But utilitarianism also presents problems. Suppose your best friend is severely depressed and asks you to kill him. He hates every moment of life and he asks you, as his most trusted colleague, to give him a fatal injection of morphine. Because this will make him happy, should it be done? And suppose he is a burden to his family and friends, although he is still in his twenties? Does it become moral to murder him just because so many will be satisfied with the results?

These are questions that are never easy to answer. In your tragic story, you describe the excruciating death of your friend Avram, and how you lied to him by telling him that his body was OK and that help was on the way. Is lying under such circumstances allowed? Is killing in war allowed? How can we say what is good and what is bad?

God is ultimately the source of all law, and it is He who determines the morality of every human action. Without God, there can be no good or evil because there is no absolute standard by which these are defined. Uri, if Hitler had won the war and succeeded in imposing Nazism on a conquered Europe, then it would have been considered good for Jews to be killed. This is something that all humanity living in the wake of the Holocaust must contemplate. This insight serves to underscore how important it is to base morality on divinely communicated ethics. Mankind has been a very poor guardian of good and evil throughout time. Goodness must be anchored in a divine definition unassailable by humans, rather than being rationally articulated.

There are many parents out there who couldn't care less for their children, who have not only failed to look after them, but actually abandoned them or scarred them in very deep and unalterable ways. Do these children have an obligation to honor their parents? Or can they simply tell them to get stuffed? If morality is based only on logic and reciprocity, then irresponsible parents have earned whatever contempt their children show them. But for Jews who abide by the Ten Commandments, it is different. God commanded us, "Honor your father and your mother." However our parents may have treated us, we are under an obligation to show them honor, even when we don't feel any love. Without this commandment, there would be anarchy in the world because the younger generation would not always esteem the older generation, and tradition, ethics, and wisdom could not be handed down. In a relativistic world shorn of the absolute, chaos results.

Indeed, since science today has abandoned God as the ultimate arbiter of good and evil, this chasm opens before us. Evolutionary "ethics" is all about the strong devouring the weak, thereby making the species better by weeding out those who are genetically infirm. Take for example the view offered by Nobel Laureate Francis Crick, one of England's greatest scientists and the man who deciphered the double-helix code of DNA, who suggested that it may be necessary to redefine the concepts of "birth" and "death." He recommended that the time of birth be redefined as two days after parturition so that there would be time to examine the child for genetic defects. If its defects were sufficiently deleterious, the infant could presumably be eliminated with impunity because it had not yet become alive. Similarly, Crick offered a new definition of death, proposing that it occurred when a predetermined age, such as eighty or eighty-five, was achieved. At that time, a person would automatically be declared dead and all of his property would pass on to his heirs. Crick is not a monster. Rather, he is a scientific reductionist. His definition of life and death demonstrates the limits of human reason. Why should the state, with its limited resources, have to look after a child whose mental age will never be greater than that of a five-year-old? There is no logical answer to this question. There is only a religious one: God created every human being in His image. As such, all life, regardless of health or capacity, is sacred and infinitely valuable.

Adolf Hitler remains the most written-about, perhaps the most fascinating man of the twentieth century. Half a century later, why does his memory still haunt us? I maintain it is because deep down we are troubled by what we see as the logic of what he did. Indeed, why should we not euthanize the severely mentally handicapped? There is no answer, once we have done away with religious belief. If there is no God, then life is not holy. And if life is not holy, then we may terminate those lives which only consume and never produce.

To go back to your torment over having killed a man in combat, I believe it is a mistake to regard the taking of life in any form as a bad thing. The same God who outlawed murder also said that it is imperative to defend one's own life. And all our ethical absolutes derive from this God. You did not murder, Uri. You killed someone who was trying to take your life. Had you not killed him, you would have sinned against God by demonstrating in what low esteem you hold your own life. A man who watches a thief break into his house and does nothing, does not value his possessions. You valued your life, and you took the necessary steps to safeguard it. Hence, ever since you killed the Jordanian soldier, you have had terrible nightmares about the event. But the time has come for you to get over it because neither you nor I are the arbiters of morality. The same God who taught us about the sacredness of life and the sanctity of the soul also commanded us to do our utmost to preserve our lives at all costs. Far from doing anything wrong, you obeyed His commandment by defending the soul given to you.

Uri, you did what you had to do. In general, there are three areas of activity in life. The good things, the bad things, and the necessary things. Into the first category fall actions like giving charity and being nice to every person one meets. Into the second category falls conduct like deceit, murder, theft, and arrogance. And into the third category fall things like killing and divorce. Killing is never a good thing, but it is sometimes a necessary thing.

During the Six Day War in which you served, the tiny and highly vulnerable Jewish state was attacked by five Arab states led by Gammal Abdul Nasser of Egypt, who helped to seduce the entire Arab world into a war against Israel with his promise of the total and final annihilation of the Jewish state. Indeed, there was little good reason for Jordan to be in the war, and they only came in after the war had begun, with the cynical motive of making further territorial gains.

You joined a nation that was fighting for survival, that had nowhere else to go save into the sea. Your adversary lifted his rifle to ensure that you returned home to your mother in a bodybag. The Talmud declares, "He who comes to murder you, rise to kill him first." You are a hero, not because you took life, but because your actions saved life. There is nothing more noble than that. A nation that barely twenty years earlier had lost half of its number in the death camp crematoria could not have endured another catastrophic defeat.

It is time for you to let go of your demons, to let go of your nightmares, and accept that you did the right thing. To love life is not only to share iced tea with your neighbor, but also to be prepared to stop your neighbor when he becomes an aggressor. The Jews can no longer afford to be the world's perennial victims, because the world shouldn't have any victims at all. None. Never.

Judaism has always been part of a tradition that takes dreams seriously. The ancient Rabbis said that there are two key elements that identify a dream as containing prophetic import: first, the dream is so vivid that it causes the dreamer to awaken, and second, the dream follows a mostly logical and sequential pattern that could actually happen in waking life. Your dream seems to possess both key elements. And it means that you should take it seriously. But rather than focusing on the Jordanian soldier who pleads with you in your dream, the next time he interrupts your sleep, grab him by the shirt collar and ask him why he chose the path that forced you to stop him. Ask him why the nations of the world have a problem with the life of the Jewish people. Tell him that the nation of Israel is an eternal nation, whose heart, like yours, will beat until the end of time.

But still we hope, we pray, and we clamor for that end of time in which all nations will live together as brothers and all will affirm the infinite value of every human life.

Pledging myself as your brother in peace rather than comrade in arms,

With all my love,

Dear Shmuley,

My God, your letter made me think. I put it to one side when it arrived, because I wanted to devote my mind to it, but for several weeks my mind has been exclusively devoted to murder. Deliberate murder, callous murder, murder with no redeeming feature—except that it is done for entertainment. In a book.

I've been writing a crime mystery. It's the first time that I've tried it, and if you ever want to give your morals a holiday, you should try it too. My killer uses a blowtorch—very messy. Very destructive. Very therapeutic.

So last night I typed the last page, and then the title page— I called it *Dead Cold*—and e-mailed the whole lot to my publisher. An hour later I picked up your letter.

You told me a story, shocking and vivid, about a murder you saw in Miami when you were ten, and it kicked me out of my fantasy world. Because murder in real life isn't entertainment. Thrills and drama in a novel are fine, because you can close the book and switch off the illusion. It's not just the writer whose morals take a holiday. The reader comes too.

What you saw in real and vicious life was very close to something I witnessed in Cyprus. This was during the civil war, when I was sixteen. I don't want to fall into the trap of making entertainment from it, so I shall describe what happened only briefly. A British soldier was walking in the street with his wife. He was holding her hand, and on his shoulders he was carrying their two-year-old daughter. A Greek terrorist sidled up behind him and shot him in the back. I will never forget how the woman screamed.

We share a common experience, one that has probably affected both of us as we grew up and came to terms with violence and our own mortality. And one that still affects us now. I don't believe it's possible for a young boy to witness a horrific incident so swift and total and remain unscarred. The killings in Miami must have recurred in your nightmares, just as the killing in Cyprus loomed again and again in mine. Death comes suddenly, death can be random, death happens as we do our jobs or laugh with our families. Death can visit anywhere, and nowhere is beyond its reach. These are not easy ideas for the young, but you and I were confronted with them early in our lives.

What puzzles me is how our experiences remain invisible to all but our closest friends. When we sat at your dinner table the other week, our common experience was not laid out on the table with the wine glasses and the soup plates. Yet the first time that we met, both of us sensed we were kindred spirits, and that suggests coincidences in our lives. But not necessarily this particular coincidence. It would be easy for two friends to go through life without ever guessing that some of their closest bonds even existed. And if friends do not know these things, enemies will certainly never guess.

I told you in a previous letter how I had shot dead a Jordanian soldier during the Six Day War. I shall never know anything of him. Only that he had a moustache. All the rest— where he lived, who his family was, who he loved—is just my imagination, and I force these thoughts out of my mind whenever they appear. But even if I had known anything about him, I would still have had to kill him, because he was trying to kill me. Even if we had known each other all through our childhoods. Even if he was the boy who sat next to me in school. Even if he was my brother.

As an American, you know that the wounds of the Civil War are still raw, more than a century later. That war almost destroyed the nation, because brothers really were compelled to kill brothers. All those wise words about love and family—a war like that reveals them to be baseless. "Blood is thicker than water," says the English proverb. But it is thinner than bullets.

Forget all the carefully reasoned arguments about when it might be permissible to kill, the let-out clauses that apply in the Sixth Commandment. Men will kill even when they are destroying their own country, even when they are killing their own flesh and blood. When a man kills, he knows at that moment that the Commandments don't apply to him. Or, if they do, they don't matter. Afterwards, he might try to find a way to justify his action within the context of the Law. But when the Commandment might have counted, when the Law could have prevented a crime—at that moment the basic rule You Shall Not Kill was simply ignored. The other rule applied: Kill If You Want.

In civil law, where morals aren't an issue, I think most people would accept anything as OK so long as it can be proven legal. You can break a fingernail in McDonald's and sue them for $10 million—if the courts uphold your claim, that astronomical compensation is acceptable. Most people would cheerfully paint their fingernails red, white, and blue for $10 million, but that isn't the issue: what matters is whether a judge rules one fingernail is worth that much money. Morals don't come into it.

Morals do matter in religion. They're one of the chief reasons people follow a faith—for moral guidance. And a lot of essentially God-loving people are repelled by organized religion because they see professional clerics acting like lawyers, trying to prove what's legal, trying to screw the maximum in heavenly compensation out of God.

I know Catholics who won't go to confession, because they expect to be told to say a succession of prayers in penitence for a big sin—a sin so serious that they can't forgive themselves. One male, married friend had sex with a young man in a hotel after a business meeting, and he has not been to church since. He used to confess at least once a month. But we had a long telephone conversation about six weeks after the event, and he told me that he feels revolted that this side of his sexuality got out of control. He can't forgive himself.

He has told his wife, incidentally. They've got a good marriage, and they're dealing with it. But he cannot tell his priest, because his priest will tell him God is forgiving (in exchange for those prayers), and my friend believes that's a lie. He has broken a Commandment. God shouldn't forgive so easily, and the priest shouldn't say it's all washed clean.

To make his peace with God, my friend has had to step outside his church. When he begins to forgive himself, I think he will permit God to start forgiving him.

It is the same acceptance of my own guilt that makes me reject your explanations about the Jordanian soldier. What does it matter whether one edition of the Torah reads Thou Shalt Not Commit Murder, and another says You Must Not Kill. I know what God meant. I knew when I was a soldier, too. And I knew I had put myself into a position where I might have to react instantly against God's Laws in order to save my own skin. That is what happened. I became a soldier because I loved my country and was willing to fight and kill to protect it. I began breaking that commandment the minute I put on the uniform. And because I love my country, I would do it again…even though I risk killing another innocent, fumbling, incompetent soldier—another soldier who joins up because he loves his country.

How can I expect God to forgive my flagrant, reckless disobedience? If I am to make my peace with him and allow him to forgive me, I will have to speak for myself in the court of judgment. If I ask a lawyer to speak for me, I might save my soul, but I'll abandon my morals. And according to what I understand of God in my heart, that doesn't make sense.

Hi again Uri,

You say in your last letter that when we met we felt ourselves to be kindred spirits. Indeed, it was so almost instantly. When first I met you, I expressed my gratitude to God because I felt intuitively that you would grow to be a soul-friend, someone who fathomed my depths and understood me without my having to even confide or verbalize my pain. With most friendships, you enjoy the benefits of the friendship only when you are in the company of your friend. With a soul-friend, however, the joy comes from merely knowing that they exist, even in a far-off land. Just knowing that you exist and that you care for me brings me comfort and joy.

But I cannot attribute a friendship so precious to our sharing mutual coincidences, as you write in your letter. Our friendship is based on something much more profound. Every human being has a gift given to him by the Creator to share with the world. What we share in common is that our particular gift for reaching people has been profoundly and sometimes maliciously misunderstood. In your case, this is due to the fact that people expected the world's greatest psychic to be utterly detached from the world and to assume a false posture of spiritual piety. In my case, it is due to the fact that I am a rabbi and the world expects all clerics to be aloof and all too serious. Those who tell jokes on television, or ever adopt a flippant demeanor, or, heaven forbid, write a book about sex, must by definition be self-serving and interested only in their own popularity.

We have both been dismissed as only capable of doing a few tricks, real or imagined. And this mutual experience is the reason that we appreciate each other, rather than adopt the attitude of a cynic. Both you and I desire and need to be loved. We live in a cold world that would rather dismiss than embrace, condemn than honor, attack than defend, subdue than uphold. What you and I share, Uri, is that at times we have both been robbed of our very humanity. In your case, you have a gift that points people to truth—but most prefer to live with their own lies.

One of the penitential prayers that we recite on Yom Kippur reads, "Forgive us, Oh Lord, for the sin of having proud eyes." It is a prayer asking for atonement for our arrogance. But the Hebrew verse, translated literally, reads, "Forgive us, Oh Lord, for the sin of *lifting* our eyes." Perhaps you remember the famous lyrics to the Bob Dylan song "Blowing in the Wind": "And how many times does a man close his eyes and pretend that he just doesn't see?" This is the sin that we most need atonement for. God gives us signs, but we lift our eyes and pretend we don't see. We overlook our truest mission in life. To look at someone and pretend you don't see their pain or their humanity is a sin: to look at a man of great spiritual gifts and pretend that he does them with trickery and electrical transmitters; to listen to a rabbi and, instead of focusing on his message, pretend to see only whether or not he enjoys appearing on television.

I am glad you raised the subject of the American Civil War. It is one of my favorite subjects, and I am a bottomless pit for good books on the subject. But the greatest story of the Civil War is not that of a nation torn asunder by politics and ethical issues. Rather, it is the story of an individual, Abraham Lincoln. Lincoln demonstrated to all, to the end of time, the power of one person to dictate the course of history. There isn't a shadow of doubt in my mind that had it not been for Abraham Lincoln there would be no United States today. When all seemed lost for the North—repeated military disasters due to the incompetence of mediocre military commanders—and unspeakable opposition and hatred tried to break the back of this untested leader, he never succumbed. Instead, he showed superhuman vision and strength to keep his nation together and, ultimately, free the slaves. Lincoln had been elected leader of the United States and, by God, united they would remain. It was because of his determination that the terrible injustice of slavery was abolished. Without him, there would not have been the political will to undermine this unjust institution. In survey after survey, taken from every personal and political angle, Lincoln is referred to by experts and laymen alike as America's greatest president.

And yet, Uri, he did many things during the war of which, from the content of your last letter, you would have strongly disapproved. You speak of God's commandments as strictures without exception or excuse. People all have inalienable rights. And yet Lincoln suspended the writ of habeas corpus for almost the duration of the war. Tens of thousands of suspected traitors were arrested and held without trial on flimsy evidence. He was accused of being a tyrant by both Southerners and many Northerners, Democrats and his own party of Republicans. He sent hundreds of thousands of young men to their deaths in war, all in the cause of this abstract notion of united nationhood.

And still he never flinched. War is war. Even just and moral men must sometimes compromise their most cherished principles in order to safeguard justice. But this is no compromise. Harsh measures can constitute the very essence of goodness. Your own uncompromising stance on this issue, not allowing countries to fight for their rights, denies good men a just cause to live for, and sometimes to die for. Human life, while sacred, is not everything. Nor is it the highest of values. Don't we give our lives over to our families and to God and to service to humanity? Aren't these cherished goals more important than human life, indeed superseding it at all times? It is a heresy that today young men and women are taught that the most noble thing they can live for is their own happiness.

Lincoln repeatedly attributed his endurance during the hellish years of 1861 to 1865 to the inspiration he derived from the Bible. In the darkest moments, when it seemed time and again that all was lost, he would retreat into the privacy of his study and read about Moses and how, walking with God through the arid plains of Egypt, he brought a mighty and tyrannical empire to its knees and freed its slaves. He would read about the prophet Elijah and how he never bent to the will of the unjust king, Ahab. He read of Job and how he wouldn't permit his spirit to be crushed amid crippling inhuman suffering. From these figures, Lincoln derived strength. He knew that he too could walk with God—even through the valley of the shadow of death—so long as the cause was just. Yes, Uri, life is a blessing. But what makes it a blessing is that it can be devoted to glorious and noble causes. Selflessness, compassion, goodness, charity, prayer, forgiveness—these things make life worth living. To paraphrase a famous saying on the subject, life is only worth living because there are things worth dying for.

What disturbs me about your letter is that it equates oppressor with oppressed, persecuted with persecutor, murdered with murderer. Do you not accept that killing a truly evil man, like Hitler—a murderer—is good? I do not believe you when you tell me that you put on your uniform only because you loved your country. Jews have never been good at fighting and have no glorious military memories. There are no Jewish Napoleons, Hannibals, Julius Caesars, or Montgomerys. Jews would rather be praying, laughing, or making love than doing stupid things like fighting wars. Those young Israeli soldiers, including yourself, donned their uniforms because over the centuries so many of their prayers went unanswered, so many of their dreams remained unfulfilled. Israeli soldiers don their uniforms reluctantly, but they do so simply because they want to live. I am a man of faith and prefer the Bible to the sword. But, Uri, until the messiah comes and makes the world perfect, there are still times when we must lift the sword.

I consider pacifism evil. Even as a Jew, I have always had great admiration for and felt inspired by many of the truly beautiful ethical teachings contained in the New Testament. But "turning the other cheek" is not one of them. To turn the other cheek is to invite aggression. To turn the other cheek, to lower your guard and allow yourself to be stepped on, is to desecrate the divine spark contained within the breast of every human being. Just as we are commanded to uphold goodness, we are also commanded to resist evil. Those who stood by and watched passively as Hitler trampled on everything good and decent in Europe were themselves evil. The real enemy of goodness, Uri, is not the evil one himself, but the silent one. The evil one might one day be turned to good, but the silent one is condemned by his own passivity. We cannot get so easily off the hook by claiming that we are not our brothers' keepers. God's cry to Cain in the book of Genesis rings down through the ages, "The blood of your brother calls out to Me from the earth."

During the Holocaust, God too was a Silent One, seemingly standing by passively as one million innocent children were converted to dust and ashes. Yes, Uri, the Lord Himself has much explaining to do as to why He did not kill, why He did not send a plague to destroy the evil Nazis. Didn't Moses himself, the same man who brought down the Ten Commandments, kill an Egyptian who was beating an Israelite slave to death?

You tell me that your married friend who engaged in homosexual relations with a younger man cannot now forgive himself. He no longer attends church because he is afraid that his priest will forgive him. Yet, he somehow summoned the courage to tell his wife. Good on him. But why does he fear confessing to God? Would he prefer a God that struck him down the moment he pulled his trousers down? Why can he not conceive of God as a father, as a parent? As a being in which to confide, rather than one before which to keep silent? A God whom we can love rather than only fear. A parent also delivers to a child the rules by which he must live. When the child is unwell, it is the parent's responsibility to search out the correct antidotes against that which has poisoned him. Hence, our need to confess. Breaking our marital vows—with members of the same or the opposite sex—is poison. And we run to God not for forgiveness, but for healing. He who gave us life is He who can renew our lives as well and restore our innocence. We must talk with Him. Isn't that why your friend told his wife? Because he felt that he had harmed something precious and he wished to renew his commitment to his wife so that the marriage would not only survive, but flourish? He sought forgiveness, and what kind of good human being doesn't forgive? And why does your friend deny God the opportunity to practice goodness and forgiveness also?

It is time your friend awoke from his nightmare of torment and despair. Let him be washed in God's love and in his wife's embrace, forgive himself, and move on. Let him speak, and be heard.

Passionately yours,

Dear Shmuley,

I was standing outside an Italian restaurant in Bristol one night last week. The rain was hitting the street in gusts, and I had the collar of my coat turned up to protect my face. There's a pleasure in that kind of weather, when you know you're going to step into a warm restaurant and order bowls of steaming pasta. The sting of rain on your head stimulates the appetite and the intellect, so I was happy to stand and wait for my friend, a journalist who had run back to her car to pick up some notes.

A man in a pink blanket came up to me. I was watching his reflection, the back of him, in the dark windows of the shops across the street, and the fact he was a human being didn't register properly at first. I was conscious only of a pink triangular shape that was flapping against the mirror images of oily rainbow puddles on the road, lit by yellow sulphur lamps. And there was no head on the triangle. That was the weird part, I remember now. It was a moving shape without a head.

I looked down the street at the shape, and seeing it from the front I realized there was a head, but it was bowed down against the rain—because the pink blanket didn't have a thick collar to be turned up.

The man didn't raise his head even when he'd shuffled close enough to speak to me. I knew what he wanted, and I was already reaching in my pocket for some change. On a night like this, he wasn't an autograph hunter. He didn't know or care if he knew me, he hadn't even tried to look in my face. I was just someone who chanced to be standing on the street in the rain, and that was enough of a chance for the man in the pink blanket.

The blanket was sodden across his shoulders, and they were not thin shoulders. This beggar was well built. I didn't catch what he said, but the hand he held out was broad with long fingers. When I didn't pour money straight into his fist, I got a glimpse behind the matted hair of a strong face, broken-nosed and sharp-eyed. He might have been a drug addict, but he wasn't wasted. If he was a drinker, he wasn't drunk. There was life and fight in him.

For a few moments, I kept my hand in my pocket with my fingers closed over my money. This headless shape in pink was probably stronger than me. If he wanted to try and rip the wallet out of my coat, he might succeed. Or if he wanted to kick himself out of the gutter, claw his way out of the freezing rain and into a place in the sun—he might succeed at that too. This wasn't a helpless bundle of rags. It was a man. What was going to do him more good—a few coins or a few good words of advice? And then I remembered something. So I gave him the money.

My friend, the journalist, came round the corner as the shape in the blanket backed away from me, muttering something—maybe thanks. And he saw her, and he probably thought he ought to beg from her too, in case his luck was on a roll. She swore at him.

She said to me as I hung up my dripping coat and we pulled out our chairs, "You didn't give him anything, did you?"

"Who? The head waiter?"

"Don't try and lie to me, Geller. I can see right through you when you do that. That ciderhead outside, you gave him something."

"It's cold, he was wet."

"So? He chose to be out there. We have unemployment benefit in this country, there's about two million people who manage to live on that without standing in the pouring rain."

"He must have been desperate or he wouldn't have asked."

"Desperate for booze. Or smack. Or desperate to make a hundred pounds a night by walking about in a blanket."

"You think that's how much he makes?"

"I bet he's got a nice little house, rent paid by the council, and something like an army invalid's pension that probably lets him run a car, and his food and heating on the DHSS. All he has to do is dress up as a beggar one night a week, and he's got all the free beer in the world. Beats working."

"Maybe I'm an easy touch."

"Easy? You're a free gift."

"When I was young," I told her, "we didn't have any money. We lived in a one-room apartment in Tel Aviv and my mother had to wait in coffee shops and mend dresses to earn a few shekels for our food. Sometimes she went without eating. Sometimes we both did."

"Did you go out begging?"

"Of course not."

"So why give away your money now?"

"Because I've been lucky. Because I'm sitting down to eat hot food in dry clothes, and because I don't have to beg anything from anyone. Because that was luck money, OK? I give away my money so I keep my luck."

But that wasn't what made me give the man in the pink blanket my change. And my friend knew I was lying, because, like she said, she could always see it in my face.

Shmuley, I've got a question for you, and it won't sound like it has much to do with bowls of pasta and pink blankets. I want to ask you, even though I know you're an Orthodox rabbi, and Orthodox rabbis are supposed to answer this question in only one way.

I want to know, am I right to be waiting for a savior to turn up? A messiah? The savior of the Jews? When I'm standing in the rain and the whole city is indoors, except for the beggars and the taxi drivers, is it possible that somewhere in the world a little boy is growing up whose life has been prophesied for thousands of years?

I've always believed it. That's one of the first things any Jewish child learns—the savior will come. It's a promise. All the prophets said so. A belief like that, that begins when you're almost too young to speak, it stays with you, like believing your father is better than any other father, and that God loves you above all. Your mother tells you these things, and both of you so badly want them to be totally true, so the belief goes very deep.

Later, as you're growing up and you're wriggling away from the simple beliefs, parts of them still cling to you. And then, when you're completely grown up, those simple beliefs are the ones you want back. Only, of course, nothing is simple anymore.

That meal I had a week ago. Two or three days later, my journalist friend sent me a copy of the evening newspaper, and there on the front page was the man in the pink blanket. Unmistakable. The headline was something about terror on the streets, blackmail, intimidation—aggressive begging. The man in the pink blanket was pictured holding out his hand to a young mother, and she did look scared. In another picture, he was begging from a child. And in a third picture, he was scoring some small change off an elderly man who was pushing his wife's wheelchair. Down the side of the page, my friend had scrawled, "Nice guy!"

I looked at the face of the man who gave the money, the pensioner whose wife was disabled. I wanted to know, "How come he's thinking the same thing as me?" Because this elderly man wasn't handing out luck money. He was giving away something he perhaps could not easily afford to lose.

This man could have been Jewish, though he was probably Christian. He was waiting for a savior who hadn't shown up. The Second Coming, if he's a Christian. Small difference, frankly—he was just waiting for the messiah.

The reason I gave money to the man in the blanket, the same reason I always want to give money to beggars, is the idea that one of them might be the savior.

What if the savior has come to earth? If the story I've believed since I was a child is true, he's here, he's come to save me and all of us. But all of us have rejected him.

Because, let's face it, we are not open to saviors. Politicians who pledge to save us, yes. Pop stars and journalists and filmmakers and TV actors—we're open to them. And advertisers, especially. If our souls are to be saved, Shmuley, it won't be the rabbis who'll do it—it'll be the advertisers. They'll wash us all whiter than white and transport us to a biologically improved Heaven with airbags as standard and a smoother, richer taste, and 20 percent extra in every pack. Messiahs can't do this. Only advertisers can.

So when the savior comes—and I truly believe, like a child, that if he isn't here already, he is coming—he'll soon be destroyed. The messiah will be obliterated in a political mine-field, with a bad TV image and no Hollywood agent, with a lack of perceived hipness in the seven to thirteen age group, and, critically, no ad agency prepared to touch him.

I'd like to ask you all the questions that bothered me as a teenager. Will the savior bring world peace and will he be for Jews only? And if so, what will happen to our non-Jewish friends, and how could the prophets be so sure anyway? But all that seems so naïve now. As if those schoolboy questions will ever get the chance to matter.

I just think that when the savior comes, we'll reject him and humiliate him and make him hate us. Until he's reduced to standing on freezing streets in a waterlogged pink blanket, begging. Begging with aggression. I'll give him a couple of pounds, if he thinks it will help. But somehow, I think he came for more than that.

Yours with love,

[signature]

Dear Uri,

I was just a boy of thirteen. Already, because of my parents' divorce, I had become a cynic. I found myself at the bottom of my school class. While others did their homework, I consumed copious quantities of television. My parents—partners in the archetypal relationship that had been responsible for my existence—had separated before my very eyes. I slowly sunk into the cynicism of believing that every star that illuminated the dark night would one day cease to shine. And that any two people who fell in love would one day end up as bitter adversaries.

The one ray of light in my life was Lubavitch, the worldwide Jewish education network that had a branch in Miami. Although I was very young, I already had a moped. On most nights, I would ride the three miles from my home on Miami Beach down to South Beach where the Lubavitch Rabbinical College was situated. There I would sit and *kibitz* with the young rabbinical students, most of whom were about five years older than me.

I became exceedingly close to one of them, Shnooki (Shneur Zalman) Fellig. Shnooki told me that for my Bar Mitzvah present he would take me to New York and arrange a private audience with the world's most famous rabbi, the great leader of Lubavitch, Rabbi Menachem Schneerson, known simply and affectionately as "the Rebbe." I waited for hours in a line to see the world's foremost Jewish spiritual leader. Finally, I was ushered in to see him. He sat, I stood. I handed him a letter that detailed the ongoing pain I felt from my parents' divorce. I told him that other kids in my school from broken homes had seemed to adjust to the circumstances far better than I had. I told him that I felt broken to my very core.

He looked up from reading my letter and stared at me intently with his rich blue eyes. As he gazed upon me, I saw in his eyes not the look of authority, but a deep sea of infinite kindness. He asked me when my Bar Mitzvah had taken place, and I answered. Then, in a soft and gentle voice, he told me the words that I shall never forget, for they pierced my heart and have become ingrained on my soul. "You have no room to be a cynic. I say this not only because you are quite a young man, but especially because I see now that you will grow to be a great light, first to your family and your school, then to the

Jewish people, and finally to the whole world." I could not believe that a colossus of such stature could have uttered words of such great portent to one of such insignificance. "And I bless you today," he continued, "that these words which I utter shall materialize and be fulfilled. Now go and fulfill your destiny."

I emerged from his room radiating hope and energy. In those brief and simple words, a man had taught me to believe in myself. I would never forget that blessing, nor the one who had delivered it. The very next day, I returned to Miami and told my mother that I would be leaving my Jewish day school and enrolling in a proper *Yeshiva* where I would train to be a rabbi. My mother thought that I had taken leave of my senses. She also feared losing me to what she considered to be a life of ascetic fanaticism. Nevertheless, a year later I was at Lubavitch Rabbinical College in Los Angeles. I had run to the shining streaks of light that the Rebbe had illuminated for me. And I have never looked back. The test of true greatness is the ability to inspire greatness in others—the Rebbe was a great man. With his help, I had found my calling in life, to immerse myself in the faith of my ancestors and try, to whatever limited degree, to impart healing to the world.

Twenty years later, I am still on this path through life that I chose with the Rebbe. Being a rabbi has become my life's work, the labor which every morning inspires me to get out of bed and begin. It is something for which I still feel great passion and enthusiasm, in spite of many hurdles. Yet today, Uri, the question of what gets us out of bed in the morning is more difficult to answer than ever before. In his book of psalms, King David beseeched God that he be granted the privilege of being one of those people who greet the dawn, who actually get up at the crack of dawn because they look forward to a brand new day—but where can we find that kind of enthusiasm?

Surely this can only come from the belief that tomorrow is going to be better than today. This is the essence of Jewish messianism and the reason why it is perhaps the most important gift which Judaism gave the world. We human beings are all innately messianists. We all have an irrational hope, at the core of our being, that our cumulative efforts actually make a difference.

Yet many historical movements have carved themselves out in opposition to this idea of people being able to make a difference. The tragic nature of fate and its disregard for humanity was the essence of the theater of the Athenians. If Oedipus is fated to kill his own father and sleep with his mother, then however much he tries to change that destiny, there is simply nothing he can do. Hindu beliefs incorporate similar principles to this very day. And the modern scientific world also believes in fate, although of course far more sophisticated words are used: behaviorism, determinism, and genetics. In part, the study of genetics is a study of how people are fated to behave in a certain fashion because of their cellular construction. Many scientists today believe that man is an intelligent animal, ruled by whim and instinct, with no real freedom of choice.

This is why Judaism, with its message that man was utterly unscripted, was so radical in ancient times. This idea makes man not only dignified, but also accountable for his actions. We believe in our power to change things both through action and the spoken word. Simply stated, Judaism taught that history is like a line. The beginning of that line is creation, and the end of that line of history is what we call the messianic future. The day will come, in the not-too-distant future, when the world indeed will be perfected. Nation will never again lift sword against nation, and no man will again teach his son the art of war. Messianism is about historical progression. History is linear rather than cyclical. We are not doomed to forever repeat the mistakes of our ancestors. We can break free of historical determinism and chart a new direction into the light.

Two and a half thousand years ago, frail, white-bearded Jews, with names like Isaiah, Jeremiah, and Zechariah, stood in the dusty marketplaces of the holy land and foretold of a time when the wolf would dwell with the lamb, and the earth would be rid of poverty and disease. The great men would be those who beat their swords into ploughshares, and no man would again teach his son the art of war. And do you see what has happened, Uri? We have attempted to build our world according to their predictions! We have sought to create a world embodying their vision. In other words, rather than allow war and conflict to continue to rule history, we are all racing to make the messianic predictions of Isaiah a reality. The promises of tomorrow are governing the events of today.

Billions upon billions of dollars have been poured into the fight against cancer and AIDS. Now how do we know that this isn't just wasted money? After all, no cure has yet been found. Maybe there isn't one. It could very well be that all this money is simply wasted, that in the final analysis man will forever remain at the mercy of cruel and indifferent elements. Maybe we've come up against a killer disease that can't be cured. And yet, there are no large groups of protesters hanging about outside the U.S. Congress or the British Parliament protesting at the squandering of public funds on the fight against incurable, lethal diseases. There is a reason: all of humanity has been infected by the optimism of the prophets. Without even knowing it, all of us are messianists, believing in the ability of man to conquer death and disease.

Uri, from the outset the history of humanity has been a history of wars—family feuds, tribal wars, national wars, world wars. It seems that from the very beginning we have been killing each other and haven't stopped until this very day. Even the great German philosopher Hegel predicted the inevitability of war, since men were always striving to distinguish themselves at each other's expense. Yet, after the most appalling war in the history of the world, the Second World War, the United Nations was set up, and since then, conflict on such a global scale has been averted. The founders deserve credit for their bold initiative and, even more important, for giving credit to the man who inspired the entire idea, the prophet Isaiah. Across the street from the United Nations Plaza in New York is the Isaiah Wall which reads, "They shall beat their swords into ploughshares, and their spears into pruning hooks; nation shall not lift up sword against nation, neither shall they learn war any more" (Isaiah 2:4). Those men came together because of an ancient promise that has influenced history and has dictated man's deepest longings ever since it was uttered. The result today is that generals are no longer heroes. They have been replaced by the winners of the Nobel Peace Prize. Hence, Uri, messianism, far from being just another tenet of Judaism, is actually the engine by which all civilization advances and develops. But in order for this engine to work, we must all play our part. We all have to believe that we have a role to play in bringing redemption to the world.

You ask me about who the messiah will be and suggest that it will be someone we despise. I have news for you, it ain't me. But there will of course be one great messiah who will appear at the end of days. Judaism does not accept that messianism is only a process of social and historical evolution. Essential to the messianic age is the messiah himself, a human leader who will spur humanity to finish off the job. An orchestra without a conductor will not make music but noise. This is the much-hoped-for, much-prayed-for messiah who will lead the world to the promised land. He will be a very wise man who, through his charisma, holiness, integrity, and force of personality, will persuade mankind to let go of their false idols of money and power and instead join God as junior partners in the perfection of the world and the end of all human strife. But until that time comes, each one of us is the messiah. God has given each of us a part of the world that only we can redeem, that only we can uplift. And for that corner of the world, we are indeed the messiah.

For my six young children who await my arrival at home to read them a bedtime story, I am the messiah who brings them redemption. The same is true for you and your children, Uri. I remember how I once asked your son Daniel what it was like to be your son. I told him that it must be incredibly difficult to be the son of a great celebrity, and how, with all your media appearances, you probably didn't have a lot of time for him. "No, no," he responded. "That is absolutely not the case. My dad has all the time in the world for me." And then there is your mother, whom you care for and who lives with you in your home. Once when you were a helpless child, she was your personal messiah who fed and nurtured you. Now that you are grown, you look after her. All of us have our corner of the world which we have to look after. The man who will ultimately be the messiah is not someone who will claim to have all the answers. Nor will he disenfranchise those who claim to have other solutions. Instead, he will harness every unique aspect of every contributor so that the world becomes more complete than ever before—to the point where the critical mass of goodness is reached, and the hidden light of Creation is finally manifest for all to see.

Hence, you were absolutely right to give the beggar money on that cold night in the rain. You did the right thing not because he may be the messiah; rather, because you are the messiah, and you have an obligation to redeem every portion of the world that comes into your reach. Every time a man sticks out his hand in your direction, for that moment, he becomes your responsibility. You are afforded an opportunity to undertake a redemptive act.

My fears are not the same as yours, Uri. I do not fundamentally fear that the messiah will come and we will reject and despise him. On the contrary, I think the world is crying out for leadership, and when a righteous, holy man comes along and preaches a message of peace, we will all go out and embrace him. What I fear is that when the good side of our nature reveals itself, we will despise it for its weakness. That when our messianic capacity for hope and forgiveness tries to shine through the darker side of our personality, we will squash it for fear of becoming too soft. When we open our hearts, we will fear being taken advantage of and will therefore rush to shut it down. That after a friend has insulted us or hurt us, when we find ourselves longing to see that friend again, we will step on that feeling and tell ourselves that he is not worthy of our friendship, for fear that he may hurt us again.

All of us have a little messiah within us, Uri. It is the still small voice that whispers in the ear of the man on the golf course that, although a little harmless pleasure never hurt anyone, still he was created for higher things. It is the thunder of conscience that pierces a man's heart when he goes for yet another shopping spree after turning away the hungry man with just a few coins. The messiah within us is the soothing rain that quenches the fire of our passion as we are drawn into an illicit relationship that will compromise our integrity and marital vows. It's that voice within us that we dare not forsake and we dare not despise.

But if the collective efforts of humanity all add up to the perfection of the world and the redemption of mankind, then why do we need a messiah at all? There is a simple answer to this question. There is a deep paradox at the heart of humanity. Even when we do good things, our ego is mixed into it in an inextricable blend. Most acts of charity involve the need to be recognized, which is why you will see donors' names on hospitals and universities. The man who will find the cure for AIDS will also be trying very hard to win a Nobel prize, and the man who cures cancer will be doing it for the history books just as much as for the victims. There is always so much of our own ego mixed into all our efforts. So although we can do so much to perfect the world, the final touches will have to be done by God. The crowning achievement of all humanity's efforts will have to be placed by a non-human hand that is untainted by human ego, uncorrupted by the human desire to be recognized.

In the final analysis, the real messiah will be someone who will teach us common sense. Common sense says that we all have to inhabit this planet together, so let's not fight or kill each other. Common sense says that if I'm in trouble, I would look to you for help. So why not help all those who are in need so that one day someone will be there for you as well?

Hoping you will always be there for me on a rainy day,

Dear Shmuley,

Tonight there was a parents' evening at my son's school. You know Daniel, you know what an extraordinary mind he has, and you know how I love to hear him praised. So I had to wear a suit and a tie, and submit to being teased by the rest of my family who pretended I looked like a door-to-door insurance salesman—but it was worth it. I would wear anything to listen to educated men and women describe my child as "brilliant," even nothing but a *tefillin* and an embroidered skullcap—and Shmuley, I would let you sell the Polaroids to the *National Enquirer*.

Mixed with the joy, you understand, there is a futile longing. I am fifty-two years old and I have an eighteen-year-old son who is now legally a man. Legally, intellectually, emotionally, physically. I am a man whose boy is a man. And I am not an old man, I do not think, neither in mind nor body, and certainly not in my emotions. Not an especially wise man, and not at all a cautious one, and probably not a man who has learned as much tolerance as he would like to imagine he has. All the same, a man of fifty-two.

I am sitting at my PC, thinking about how far it is from eighteen to fifty-two, and an hour has passed since I began to write this letter. Outside it is black and 3 A.M., and the lights of my study shine back at me from the window. The security lamps in the grounds are glowing as distantly as stars. The windowpanes appear like frozen membranes of skin, the way glass does on the coldest of nights, and my reflection looks very solid on the other side. It is an image of me staring back from the outside of my house.

My house is my greatest possession. All my other possessions are inside it. My family is inside it, my life in every way is inside it. But this wraith of me is outside the house. And it is too real an image to be a wraith. If my spirit was to flash across the gap into the me outside, that reflection would become Uri Geller. I would be out in the cold, outside my life, staring in through the window at a reflection that looked real and safe inside all the trappings of its existence. A man's life is more than just his body—my life inhabits my body the way that my body inhabits this house. The house holds everything I need and love, but in the end, it is only a house. Only a body.

The more-than-a-wraith outside in the freezing night could be a clone of me. Uri Geller in every way, except that it is not Uri Geller.

If a true flesh-and-blood clone of me exists, something grown in a test-tube by aliens or the Mossad, I don't want to meet it. It would be outside my life, on the other side of the glass. If I let it in, it might try to take my identity. How would anyone know which was the real Uri? Would I know? Would we both believe we knew? I know what you're thinking—you're thinking, "Go to bed, Uri, these are cheap sci-fi ramblings; you'll hit the delete button in the morning." But I have read up on this, more than once. This story of identical selves goes way back before cloning. Every culture has this myth of doubles, doppelgängers, fetches, *vard-gers*, subtle bodies. In ancient Egypt, the soul's double was the *ka*, which remained with a corpse when the spirit ascended to paradise. Part of every tomb was sacred to the *ka*, and a priest was appointed to serve it and feed it.

So many people have written of seeing a friend's double—and, more terrifyingly, their own—that I cannot believe that these stories are all exaggerations or inventions. Goethe met his own self on a lane near Drusenheim. He looked a little older, and more richly dressed. Eight years later, when the poet was a wealthy and successful man, he was walking near Drusenheim when he met his younger, poorer self. Which one was Goethe, which was the reflection? Which was inside his life and which outside? Goethe also described in detail how he met the double of a friend, while that man was dreaming of meeting Goethe. Shelley and Maupassant both wrote of meeting their doubles. Both were dead, months later. The Irish believe that to meet your "fetch," or your own self, is an omen of long life in the morning and a portent of death in the evening.

I am an encyclopedia on the subject. I did not acquire this knowledge by accident. In 1973, when I was living in New York State and my relationship with Andrija Puharich had reached explosion point, I acquired a double. Or a clone—call it what you will. Andrija, as you know, was a scientist who met me in Israel and brought me to America for tests funded by the Pentagon. Along the way, I became famous, which was my agenda, and I became the focus of some prophecies from outer space, which was Andrija's agenda. The agendas didn't match. I came to feel Andrija was manipulating me, and Andrija felt I was betraying him. We could agree on nothing—the weirdness around me became so intense that, far from simply bending spoons, it was warping everything in our lives. There were days when I was at the eye of a poltergeist storm. I believed the phenomena were erupting from my frustration and unhappiness; Andrija believed they were warnings and manifestations from the other worldly prophets. Different agendas.

One night I was with a group of friends at Andrija's house in Ossining. The confrontations were exhausting me, and I slept early in the evening. Everyone in the house says they saw me asleep, and that I didn't get up or leave the house. At the same time, 2,500 miles away in Germany, I was seen by a couple I have never met before or since. They were making love in their bedroom, in a hotel I had never visited. They heard a knock, and more knocks, insistent and repeated, at the thin door to the passageway. At last, they stopped what they were doing and the man pulled on his trousers and opened the door, half angry, half fearful that the manager had come to ask them to keep the noise down. And when he opened the door, my double was standing there. It held out its hand and proferred a piece of stone, which the man took. The double did not speak. The man stared and asked, "Are you Uri Geller?" and my double still did not speak. "What the hell...?" said the man, and my double turned and walked away.

It was obviously a case of mistaken identity. This German must have seen someone else, maybe someone pretending to be me—the real Uri Geller was asleep in Ossining. I don't even remember having any dreams, and it is not possible that I could have flitted to Germany—it is not possible even to think of a reason why I would have wanted to.

But the stone the man was given came from Andrija's house. The couple were so bewildered and scared by what had happened that they found my phone number and told me their story. When I didn't believe them, the man flew to New York. He showed the stone to me, and later to Andrija. It was certainly the same piece of amethyst, cased in coarse rock, that had lain on a bedside table at Ossining. Beside the bed I had slept in. And the stone was no longer on the table.

Who was it in Germany? Who took the stone from America to Europe? Was that me? Was it actually me, Uri? Two Uris? And am I still out there? Where did I go? If that is me, who am I here now? Is that me, the Germany me, out in the icy garden? And have I been locked out of my life, on the other side of frozen glass, for twenty-six years? Did I make myself, did I split away from myself? Or did Andrija's alien prophets manufacture me? Do we share the same philosophy, myself and I? The same morality? And if not, which of us is right? Of all the things that happened to me in 1973, that is the one I understand least and fear most.

Cloning is not paranormal, not the way that sheep and monkeys are cloned in laboratories. Dolly the sheep is not Doppelgänger the sheep. I understand that. I understand the biological concept of replacing the nucleus of an egg with DNA material from another animal. I know it is a procedure with a very high failure rate; I know that Ian Wilmut's team at the Roslin Institute did not set out to create clones, but were simply investigating how farm animals could be genetically improved; I know that some skeptics claim Dolly is an ordinary sheep and not a clone, because cloning is impossible. You see, I am an encyclopedia on all aspects of the myth of doubles.

I believe, though I don't know for certain, that human cloning will occur within ten years. And when it does, I may be ready to overcome my terror of doubles. I shall want to purchase a clone of myself.

Maybe I'll be sixty-two when the technology becomes robust and affordable enough to be worthwhile. I'll pay to have a donor egg cleaned out and filled with my genetic material: my blueprint for a new human being. The lab will employ a willing womb, a professional mother, and when the baby is born, I shall hold in my arms a perfect Uri, a Uri that I cannot remember having been. Hanna and I will raise my child—my child, not ours, for this creature will be something quite different from the wonderful boy and girl Hanna and I created, the children who cannot imagine yet how much they are loved. The little Uri-child will be something else: a repeat of me, like a digital replay. When a CD player's laser returns to the start of a track, it transmits exactly the same signal as it did before, digitally identical. That is how my clone will repeat me. And if I live to be eighty, the Uri-child will be as old as Daniel is now, just eighteen, just a man.

There are companies that will do this. Already on the Web, firms are offering to take genetic matter and store it until it can be reproduced by cloning. Valient Venture Ltd., based in the Bahamas, offers to manufacture babies at $200,000 a time for infertile and homosexual couples. Their scientific director, Brigitte Boisselier, says that when the technology is perfected, the company will set up a lab in a developing nation where there is little danger that human cloning will be outlawed. I don't know what Valient Venture's overhead could possibly be, but I know I would be willing to pay substantially more than $200,000, which is, after all, the price of a luxury car. For a yacht, the wealthy pay at least ten times more—I think a baby must be worth more than a yacht.

The Uri-child will live a different life from mine. My father was not a young man when I was a child, but he was not in his sixties. He was not around much either, and I love to be with my children whenever I can. I was brought up in Tel Aviv, and my mother had to work sixteen hours a day as a seamstress and a waitress just to put food on the table. I lived on a kibbutz, I went to a Catholic school in Cyprus, and these are not experiences I intend to inflict on the Uri-child. What would be the point? I could send the boy to Cyprus, perhaps even to my old school, but he would not have my teachers. The civil war was raging in my boyhood—even if there is another war, it will be nothing like the one I saw in the early sixties. I can reproduce my genes, but I cannot begin to reproduce my experiences.

The Uri-child will have my looks. He will share precisely the mix of my mother and father embodied in me. He might even be said to have eight aborted brothers and sisters, as I have—because though I shall be raising him as my son or my grandson, he will truly belong to my generation: he will be my clone; he will be me. Will he have any of my character? Perhaps everything that is in my nature is a product of my upbringing. The Uri-child could be like me in every twist of every cell, and possess a personality utterly unlike mine. After all, he will have a different soul, for sure, and perhaps it is the soul that makes the man.

What I will wait to know most desperately is this—will the Uri-child be psychic? Is that in my genes? Will it be in his? Will I be able to train him in MindPower, teach him to read minds and break metal with a brush of his fingertip, help him to see with his psychic eye events that happened scores of years ago and thousands of miles away?

Or is that a gift which was given to an ordinary child named Uri Geller in Tel Aviv some time during his childhood? I have always felt that my psi abilities had some connection to an outer force, as though I was not wielding them myself. Perhaps that force chose me randomly, and would not dream of inflicting the same double-edged talent upon the Uri-child.

Imagine a Uri Geller, living long after I am dead, with no power to receive telepathic images or bend spoons. Maybe a Uri Geller with a steady job and a normal social life. Maybe a Uri Geller with a simple faith in God.

Imagine that.

Yours with the deepest affection,

Dear Uri,

The world barely knows what to make of the first Uri Geller, and here you are telling us that we will have to contend with another! Perhaps even a whole tribe of Geller spoonbenders, circumnavigating the globe, destroying the earth's eating utensils.

OK, OK, Uri, I know what you're thinking. It's unfair of me to superimpose my own visions of world domination and make you an unwitting partner. But it is true that since Debbie and I love having you, Hanna, Shipi, and the kids over for the weekly Sabbath dinner, we have no spoons left at all, and our own children are now forced to eat soup with straws.

I did find your latest ruminations about cloning absolutely fascinating, and I want to deal with them seriously.

Let's begin with a debate I had last Tuesday with a group of young people. I dismissed the modern notion that you must first love yourself before you can enter into a relationship. I have never understood the meaning of such balderdash. Which should come first, love of self or love of the other? Have you ever met a person loved by no one who finds comfort in the fact that they love themselves? Is there a woman on earth who has discovered that her husband has cheated on her, and yet feels no pain because she is in love with herself?

But these people would have none of it. They insisted that you could not give your love to others if you did not love and appreciate yourself, but I steadfastly maintained that loving oneself was a form of arrogance. Loving oneself pulls us into ourselves, leaves us feeling content, like we don't need anyone else. Often a woman will tell her girlfriend, "Forget your relationship with Steve. He's not ready for a relationship. He's too in love with himself." Self-love breeds conceit and lessens our dependency on others. It renders us incapable of truly learning from others since our love of ourselves turns us into know-it-alls.

Although I stood firm, Uri, I did concede that every individual has to believe that he has something unique to contribute to others. This is not love of self, but rather a profound belief in our ability to contribute. In other words, we have a fundamental need to *esteem*, rather than love, ourselves. We are all born with the capacity to enrich our environment. In that sense, we can love our uniqueness, and this should be translated into a positive contribution to the lives of others. Rather than pulling us more into ourselves, it causes us to gravitate to those who surround us. But, seen in this light, love of self, or self-appreciation, can only be truly realized through contributing to others. Through the reflection of other people, we come to find our own uniqueness.

If Martin Luther King Jr. had loved himself more than his people, he would have stayed at home while they suffered the daily humiliation of racism. But his love for the poor and the helpless, coupled with his belief in his power to make a difference to their lives, made him into a formidable leader. The contrast between this sort of self-esteem and that of a man who is in love with himself could not be more acute. Egomaniacs will believe that they are the path of righteousness, and everyone must conform to their cue. This was the kind of megalomania demonstrated by Hitler and Pol Pot.

The opposite of feeling love is loneliness. I remember once, as a child of about ten, two years after my parents' divorce, I sat home one night watching television and could sense that my mother was depressed. I asked her questions, and she gave me only monosyllabic responses. To me, she seemed lonely. I went over and hugged her and said, "Mom, you don't have to feel alone. I am here and I love you." She put her arms around me and told me that she loved me too. But I could sense that I had not alleviated her pain, and she drifted back into her own thoughts. It was then that I understood that her loneliness came from the fact that there was no one to need her in her totality, as a woman, as a full human being. I just needed her for her mothering instincts; there was no one in the home who was her equal—in age and maturity and with similar needs—no one who relied and depended on her.

Human loneliness is only assuaged when we find someone to receive that unique gift that only we can contribute to them. But the person who needs this love has got to be our equal. A subordinate relationship does not have the power to make us feel special. You can already see, Uri, where I am headed with this. The greatest need of every human being is to be loved. We all need our uniqueness as individuals to be appreciated, substantiated, and reciprocated.

To feel loved, there are two essential prerequisites. The first is that the person who loves you cannot be a relative. They have to choose you, and relatives—no matter how much they love and appreciate you—can never choose you. Hanna makes you feel special because she chose to marry you. (And that is why the *Cabbalists* always said that the husband/wife relationship is the loftiest of all.) But no matter how much Natalie loves you, she can never make you feel unique. She can make you feel love and nurse you in your old age. But she cannot *choose* you.

Secondly, the person who loves you must acknowledge the fact that you are irreplaceable. In fact, I would say that this is the definition of love. To love is to acknowledge that the object of affection has no double. Tell a parent who has lost a child, God forbid, that the loss is no big deal since you can go and adopt a new child, and they will dismiss you as mad. The child has no double and is totally irreplaceable. This is why so many people today are afraid to love, because they are afraid that if they put all their eggs in one basket, the person they love may reject them and they will be destroyed.

My favorite verse in the Bible, and by far the most moving, is that which declares that man was created in the image of God. But what does this strange metaphor mean? Some have interpreted it only in a legal sense. They say it means that like shadow puppets, we must always obey the will of God. Others have interpreted the verse to mean that, like God and unlike the animals or even the angels, we have freedom of choice. Unrestricted by fate, we are the arbiters of our own destiny.

But the real meaning of this verse, Uri, is that each and every one of us is the one and only. It is telling us that in the same way that God is utterly unique, every human being has no equal, has no double, has no doppelgänger. There is only one God, and since you are made in His image, there is only one of you, too. You are never extraneous, you have no replacement, and you can never be made redundant.

There are three uniquely human privileges that follow from this lofty biblical description. As the Jewish scholar Rabbi Yitz Greenberg says, every human being is endowed with the three gifts of 1) infinite value, 2) equality, and 3) uniqueness. These are independent of any factor such as heritage, status, wealth, or background. The ancient rabbis of the Talmud said that saving one life is equivalent to saving the entire world, because that one life is equal to the value of the entire world. Since God is the source of all human importance, and we are all made in His image, no human being can ever be more valuable than another.

And that is how I know that we do not have a doppelgänger, that we have no double, that we actually have no equal. In the same way that none of us are identical on the outside, none of us are identical on the inside. I once heard from a great rabbi that God's infinite power is manifest in the fact that no two snowflakes are alike. But an even greater demonstration of that power, Uri, is that no two individuals are alike—which is precisely why they are individuals.

Tyrants have long understood that if you wish to control a man, all it takes is the destruction of his feeling of uniqueness. Hence, amidst the various degradations that the Nazis inflicted on the Jews of the concentration camps, the most important was replacing their name with a number. Primo Levi discusses how after numbers had been branded on the arms of the inmates, what resulted was an "anonymous mass, continuously renewed and always identical, of non-men, already too empty really to suffer. One hesitates to call them living. One hesitates to call their death 'death'." Levi describes how the Nazis created the *muselmann*—camp slang for a skin-and-bone walking corpse, or living dead. As another author points out, the *muselmann* may be called the most truly original contribution of the Third Reich to civilization. Once you destroy a man's sense of uniqueness, then you have blotted out the image of God that resides within.

The denial of our uniqueness is ultimately the source of all human misery and unhappiness. You speak of your amazing mother and how she worked impossible hours as a seamstress to support you. Unfortunately, this is something we share in common. My mother worked two jobs to support her five children after her divorce. Once, she came home on a Friday afternoon just before the Sabbath, with tears in her eyes. I asked her what had happened. "They fired me," she told me. She worked as a bank teller and had made an error that cost the bank $1,000. She had apologized and begged for the money to be deducted from her wages. They refused. "But I have young children to support," she pleaded. "Well, you'll have to find work somewhere else." "But I know the systems and the customers better than anyone else. How will you manage without me?" "We'll get someone else who knows them just as well." And this is what ultimately caused her so much pain. Being told that she wasn't special, that she was easily replaced. She cried the whole Sabbath long.

I maintain that this is the main reason we humans so fear death. We hate having to face the possibility that the world will somehow manage without us. Life tells us that we are unique and irreplaceable, while death tells us that no one is irreplaceable. Hence, Judaism has always seen life as holy and death as an abyss. Death is where the darkness and the lies that tell us we don't really matter finally overtake us.

I recently participated in a television debate in which a thirty-something feminist told me that marriage is dead in this age of female financial independence. Why should any woman want to forfeit her independence just to be attached to a man? I told her that she was not in touch with her deepest human desire, which was not independence, but the corroboration of her uniqueness. And that corroboration comes, oddly enough, from someone else forfeiting everything to be with you. That's why marriage is so much more special than living together. A relationship of commitment and sacrifice is all about the corroboration of the individual's uniqueness. It is about being told that we have no double. And this is also why marriage has always been associated with holiness. Because when you make one person the center of your universe, love them, worship them, and make them feel like God, you corroborate the holiness of that person and prove for all to see that indeed they are created in God's image.

Uri, this is why I feel saddened at how many people refuse to acknowledge their dependency on others. A young woman at Oxford, who had sworn to remain single ("I refuse to put all my eggs in one bastard," she told me), once took umbrage at my statement that she needed a man. "I don't need a man. What a sexist statement you are making. A typical male." I countered, "Do you need a telephone?" She acknowledged that she did. "Do you need a house?" She acknowledged that she could not live in the street. "So you are prepared to admit that you need pieces of plastic and bricks and mortar in order to live, but not another warm human being to nurture and cherish you always?"

There are many sins in a relationship, Uri. A husband can be neglectful of his wife. A woman can aim biting, cynical comments at her husband. But the worst sins of a relationship involve making a person feel they are not unique, that they are easily replaced. It's when a woman tries to talk to her husband, but he is instead immersed in the television that she feels most offended. She is so ordinary that she doesn't even merit a response. Similarly, when a man cheats on his wife, he is telling her that there is someone who can take her place. But the worst sin is where you so completely overtake your partner's identity that there is nothing left in them to feel. They have become you and have lost all their individuality.

I remember as I grew up as a small boy in Los Angeles that my parents had these friends who would occasionally come over to our home on Friday night for the Sabbath dinner. Isaac was a stern man who would silence his wife in our presence for virtually every opinion she offered and raise his voice at her for every gesture that was not to his liking. I remember witnessing the slow deterioration of his wife's personality until she had been completely pummeled into obedience. Finally, at a

Passover seder at our home, which they attended with their children, she was passing around the saltwater when she accidentally spilled some on the table. All of us were aghast as he yelled at her that she was stupid and clumsy. We were all appalled, but she was not. She simply cleaned up the spill and sat down. She had long since ceased to feel embarrassment. She was a non-person. She had lost all feeling. He could no longer hurt or humiliate her. He had destroyed the soul within.

Yes, Uri, the greatest sin in the world is to rob someone of their dignity, their uniqueness, and make them into your double, your appendage. And the greatest *mitzvah* is to help a person find themselves. The Torah obligates us to return a lost possession to its original owner. Is there any more prized possession than our individuality? Thus, an unhealthy relationship is one in which we lose ourselves to the other person. And a healthy one is where the love of the other helps us to discover who we really are. Hence, Uri, maybe you're right. Perhaps there is a double of me out there. But I hope I never find him. And I hope he never finds me.

There is a final consideration. When I was younger, Uri, I used to hate the Sabbath, with its endless laws prohibiting television and music. I saw it as the ultimate burden and would treat its approach with dread. It was only when I got older that I began to appreciate and anxiously await its beauty. This was not due to the peace and tranquillity the Sabbath brought from the harried and busy life I led. To be sure, I now love the stillness and silence of the Sabbath, and the opportunity it affords me to focus exclusively on my wife and children, friends and guests. But I mean something more than that. When I started working and building the L'Chaim Society, I found myself feeling like an inventor, a creator. After staging events with world-renowned celebrities drawing thousands of people, I felt that perhaps I was more unique than other people. Perhaps I was the most unique. Arrogance and conceit filled my head. But then, every week with unbroken regularity, the Sabbath came along to dispel my illusions. For one day a week, I was reminded that I was not the creator. Indeed, like everything else around me, I was created. Part of the created world. In losing myself to become one with the universe I was actually able to find my truest self. Whereas, on the other days of the week, I had to celebrate in my work and productive capacity, on the Sabbath, I had to revel in my passivity—in being rather than doing, in existence rather than productivity. I learned on the Sabbath that it is as important to know when to stop creating as it is to know when to create.

Uri, our world is incredibly creative. Technology breaks all bounds. With such manifestly impressive achievements behind us, we can easily forget that we also are created. We have to know when to stop creating. The Sabbath is a weekly reminder that the knowledge of when to stop creating is as important as creation itself. And the first great shot across the bow of human creative genius is human cloning. Amazingly, *Time* magazine reported that 98 percent of Americans were against human cloning. It is as if, for the first time, humanity has said collectively that we have created just a bit too much. We are now overstepping the bounds. Science has gone from Albert Einstein to Dr. Frankenstein, and we are all protesting the transgression of sacred human boundaries. Every human being is born with certain inalienable rights that include not only life, liberty, and the pursuit of happiness, but especially the right to be a unique individual. Nothing can take that away from us.

And here I close the circle that I began at the beginning of this letter. That's why, Uri, the human desire to be immortal—your willingness to spend $200,000 to be immortal—is misguided and misplaced. You have to achieve immortality specifically through the gift which you give humanity, the gift which transcends your spatio-temporal reality. The love you give to those around you is your everlasting legacy and the guarantor of your immortality. The ancient rabbis proclaimed long ago that whereas man dies, the good deeds he does in this lifetime are eternal. The son you refer to, the love you bestow upon him, the man you have helped to create—that is what is eternal. He is everything you are, but much, much more. All parents know and feel this. They all know that their children are their betters, and that is why our greatest desire as parents is "to have our children have all those things that we never had." To reach all those things that we never attained. Your son will be a giant standing on the shoulders of a giant. And nothing will stand in his way. He will see from afar. He will see distant horizons and vistas. And, ultimately, nothing will be outside his grasp.

Rather than wasting our time (and money) on creating our doubles, we have to ensure that our children never become our doubles. We have to teach them to be unique, to be special, and to treat all other people as if they are special too. We have to give them the strength of character to swim against the tide of conformity. As the ancient rabbis said, "In a place where there are no men, stand up and be a man."

I have learned this lesson from you. Because while you are a famous and highly successful celebrity, with unique powers that truly have no double, you treat all those you encounter as if they were as famous and power-laden as you. And that is a great gift indeed.

Wishing you love from the singularity of my being,

Dear Shmuley,

When I was nine, my parents divorced and I was sent to a *kibbutz*. Something happened to me before I left my home and my school in Tel Aviv, and I should explain it to you, so you can understand how I was feeling and what my life was like when I had to leave my mother. But even after forty years, I feel guilty and ashamed about this thing. I'll tell you about it some other time.

I was nine years old, and I had to leave my home because there wasn't a home anymore—just my mother with her ancient Singer sewing machine in a one-room apartment and my father with his army barracks and his army brothels. And I had to leave my dog, Tzuki. But I was also leaving all the fights, the screaming, slapping, spitting bouts, and the long days of glowering anger and the long evenings of hissed insults that had been the script of my parents' break-up. So a country home and a new family and the chance to ride a tractor seemed like a good thing to a small boy. Plus, I was leaving behind the situation that had made me so ashamed.

But I was homesick. I hated being a city boy among the kibbutz kids. I was teased and mocked from the minute I woke up till the minute I fell asleep, sobbing silently under my blanket. I hated picking oranges, I hated digging potatoes, I hated eating oranges and potatoes. I was scared my mother would visit me, because the kibbutz kids jeered viciously at me about her lipstick and her city clothes. I was scared my father wouldn't come to visit, because this was 1956 and he had been sent to fight in the Suez War.

Worst of all, I missed my dog. You told me once that the love of a dog was not enough to make a man feel special. You are completely wrong. There is no love on earth like a dog's love, and if you allow yourself to return even a piece of its devotion in the same way, without judgments or reservations, you will learn a great truth about your own capacity to love. A dog forgives everything, a dog lives and loves for the instant, a dog is faithful. If I had always loved the people in my life the way my dogs loved me, my life would have been much happier. When I feel angry now with my children, because they will not be exactly who I want them to be, or angry with my wife, because she is too much the woman she has always been, it is so good to remember a dog's love and to reach for that in my own heart. It is so good to love my family for being with me at that instant, and for being mine. A dog's heart is limitless, and I only wish mine was.

And if I know this now and can say it, think how much more intensely I felt it when I was nine years old and utterly alone. I would stand in the fields on the north face of the hill, with the red roofs and white walls of the kibbutz at my back, staring across the thirty miles to Tel Aviv, where some other child was looking after my dog Tzuki. With every spark of my energy, I would try to remember how his rough coat felt beneath my fingers and how his nose was cold and his mouth was hot when he licked the palm of my hand and the side of my face, and how his whole body twitched in my hands when I lifted him because he was wagging his tail so hard. I tried to recreate Tzuki in my mind. I tried to make him real enough to hold. And one day, I managed it.

I know that it was an afternoon, because I was a long way from the other children. I had been working my way apart from them all day, to avoid their jeers, as we dug potatoes. By the time I had enough space to stand and dream about my dog, the others were a hundred yards off. So it must have been during the afternoon. I was standing with my eyes closed, willing myself to remember every scent and sensation about Tzuki, and I felt him in my arms. His front paws were scrabbling at my tee-shirt, and he was trying to lick my face, but I was hugging him so tightly he couldn't wriggle free. His coat was as wiry as a brush and the wag of his tail was running right through him.

For a few moments, I did not open my eyes, just thrilling to feel my dog with me again. Then I looked at him, and he was not there. I shut my eyes in surprise, and I could still feel him. I was holding a dog, my dog. All my senses told me so. Except my sight—and when I opened my eyes again, there was no Tzuki. The touch of fur and paws melted in my arms. I was standing alone on a kibbutz hillside once more, and I never did see Tzuki again. The family who were caring for him moved from Tel Aviv before I returned.

I have thought about this many times. All through my life there have been so many phenomena, countless events where my senses have seemed to lie. So much of what I have seen, I cannot possibly have seen, because it defied physics. So much of what I touched and heard and smelled cannot possibly have been, unless all of reason is wrong. But if I cannot trust my senses, I am nothing but a mad man. And only a very weak man would believe in the theories of physics and the philosophies of reason when his senses were proving them totally false.

The dog in my arms was too intensely real to be imagination. It existed. It was warm and it was breathing. But it was not such an ordinary dog that I could see it. I conjured it from my soul, or Tzuki's own vital energy traveled to me because I needed him so desperately, or...or what? The answers I have given myself during the past forty years are all so vague. I have an instinctive understanding of what may have been happening, but I cannot define it. That would be like trying to describe a scrap of mist.

I read of a girl—a patient of Dr. Oliver Sacks, the neurologist at Albert Einstein College of Medicine in New York—whose name was Bhagawhandi. She was nineteen years old, dying of a brain tumor, and in her mind she was in India. She saw visions of the villages and gardens she knew as a child, and as the disease deepened, she saw the people she had loved and lived with. Dr. Sacks wrote: "We would see her rapt, as if in a trance, her eyes sometimes closed, sometimes open but unseeing, and always a faint, mysterious smile on her face." The doctor diagnosed epileptic convulsions of the temporal lobes, provoked by the tumor. The steroids she was taking may have contributed, and it was even possible she had some schizoid illness unconnected to the tumor. He also hinted that there may have been a paranormal basis—that Bhagawhandi's spirit was somehow returning to India.

I thought of Tzuki and of Bhagawhandi when I learned that brain researchers at the University of California in San Diego had proven a connection between temporal lobe epilepsy and ecstatic visions. The neurologists were calling a point behind the forehead, between the eyes, the God Spot. Brain scans were performed on epileptics prone to visions and on non-epileptics who were deeply religious. In both groups, brain activity in the God Spot soared when emotive trigger words were used— phrases from prayers, passages from the Bible. In some cases, the words triggered real states of holy ecstasy. Similar scans were done on a group of agnostics with no religious inclina tions, and their God Spots barely seemed to respond to the key words. This study certainly fits observations of some saints and mystics, such as the Franciscan monk St. Joseph of Copertino, who could be plunged into trance by a line from a psalm or the mention of an angel.

There are many explanations for the San Diego findings. For thousands of years, mystics have associated the region called the God Spot with the "third eye," or brow *chakra*, the source of much spiritual sensation and understanding. It is here, for instance, that I sense my energy building when I perform psychokinesis, in particular when I deflect a compass needle without touching it. Perhaps the neurologists have inadver tently found proof in our brain synapses not of God but of the reality of *chakras*. Maybe Western science is about to catch up with the yogis of four thousand years ago.

Perhaps anything that thrills us is registered in the tempo-ral lobes. The ecstatics and the epileptics were thrilled by bib-lical phrases, because they were religious people. The agnostics were not—maybe their foreheads would have lit up when the baseball scores were read.

But perhaps they are right at San Diego and Albert Einstein College. Visions of a childhood home might be evoked by a tumor pressing on the temporal lobe. Perhaps a rush of some chemical secretion in the brain can conjure the smell and warmth and touch of a beloved dog. Perhaps God, the vastness that I feel as a love and a power pervading the universe, is only a synaptic frenzy between my eyes. I know they believe they are right at San Diego. And I don't know how to prove them wrong.

With my greatest love (like a dog's),

Dear Uri,

Your letter asks me to prove the existence of those things that exist outside the realm of the senses, but which we nevertheless all experience to be true. These are the moving moments in our lives when we are lifted to a higher plane of experience and life begins to make sense. Metaphorically, we go to the mountaintop and achieve a higher sense of clarity.

Even now, such experiences seem extraordinary to us. Imagine, then, what it must have been like for the Jewish people when they emerged from the cauldron of Egypt. Until then, they had been pagans because they could only have faith in those things that were true to their senses—they denied the existence of everything else. Like their Egyptian overlords, they worshiped the material things that sustained them. Hence, they worshiped the sun, the moon, and the stars, rather than the invisible Creator. But along came an imperceptible God in the wilderness who demanded that the Jews repose a belief in an invisible Protector that they could not see, hear, touch, or smell. The Jews were challenged to accept that it was specifically those things that escape the senses that are the most real of all. They were being schooled in the belief that it was their sensory perception rather than their imagination that was playing tricks on them.

And so it has remained unto this very day. We, as their descendants, continue to respect and cherish those things that we cannot see. No one has ever seen love. For that matter, no one has ever seen electricity. But we know they exist because of their effects, the sparking to life of TVs and stereos all around the world. And the same is true of love: it can be experienced, and its effects can be seen, but it remains permanently invisible to the senses. When we encounter a man and a woman who refuse to be separated, we know that love has captured them in its paws.

You know, Uri, that for eleven years I have served as a rabbi to students, and I have learned that one of the principal distinguishing characteristics between the more mature and less mature students is the degree to which they imbibe this message. The less mature students want sex. But the more mature students understand that the external desire for sex is the product of an internal desire for intimacy. They are the students who want love. But even those students who try to ignore this message are susceptible to its appearing unannounced in their hearts and minds.

I remember one good-looking twenty-five-year-old male student, who slept with at least two women per week, coming to me one morning, looking like his world had fallen apart. "Shmuley, I took another stranger home last night. I thought we had a great night of sex. But in the morning, I woke up and looked in the mirror and hated what I saw. I have become something that I despise." His heart had been torn asunder by these casual sexual experiences. His indulgence in the immediate gratification of his senses was rendering him incapable of seeing the eternal within the ephemeral, and the hidden within the obvious. In short he was becoming blind.

Often, Uri, it seems to me that the wisest among us are those who reject what they see and embrace the feelings that cannot be grasped. When I was a young rabbinical student studying in Jerusalem, every day I passed by the home of an elderly woman who had been widowed twenty years earlier. After a while, I befriended her, and she used to invite me into her apartment and make me tea. Once, when I was extremely tired, I plonked myself down in a chair at the head of her dining room table. This gentle woman immediately became upset and asked me to switch chairs. Not knowing what I had done to upset her, I sprang to my feet. Then she explained, "That is the seat that my husband sits in, and it is disrespectful for anyone else to sit there." "Sat in," I corrected her. "That is the seat that your husband sat in, and I am so sorry that I have disrespected his memory. Please forgive me." But she would not be corrected. "That is the chair that he *sits* in. He has never abandoned me. He is still with me, perhaps even more than when he was alive. When he was alive, his love for me and the time he spent with me could only be finite. He could only love me with his body. But now he has no limitations and he is with me always. I feel him wherever I go."

I, of course, thought the woman was madly sentimental at best, and downright batty at worst. But there was a strange and haunting sincerity that rang through her words. "My husband's love is like a shield protecting me at all times. Even now I feel him."

Many years later, I saw another example of the power of a departed human spirit to be present even when it is absent. I was invited to deliver a lecture at a synagogue in New York for a charity named after a boy who had been killed in a car crash. His father introduced me to the audience and I spoke for about an hour. After the event was over, we chatted over coffee. He asked me to provide counseling to him and his wife. "We have been fighting a lot lately. Over our son, you see. I go to see him every day in the cemetery, and my wife is very unhappy." Knowing that his son had died, and that he had no other, I said, "Yes, I can imagine that after the tragic loss of a child there can be much recrimination and mutual guilt and blaming of each other." "No," he told me, "that's not why we're fighting. We're fighting over our *living* son, not our dead son. Every day, I go to the cemetery to talk to him. He loved football and the New York Jets, so I tell him about how they're doing and bring him newspaper clippings. I tell him the latest gossip in the family. And then I cry and tell him how much I miss playing with him. I tell him that I cry at night thinking about all the time that I spent at the office and on business trips when I could have been at home playing with him and singing him lullabies. But my wife says that our son died, and that I have to let go. She wants to put his life behind us, and live with the reality of his loss. She says that to do it any other way will drive her crazy. But I can't do that. He is my son. I can't leave him all alone in that cold, stone cemetery. I may not be able to hold him and hug him. But I can still love him."

That night, another man drove me home. I suppose that the emotion of the night caused him to open up. He told me that he had two children. Well, actually, he said, he and his wife have three children. Their third child, a son, had been born severely mentally handicapped. He had been denied oxygen to the brain for seven minutes during the delivery, after the umbilical chord had wrapped around his neck. "My wife," he told me, "refused to hold the baby or even see him. The nurses fed and changed him. When I began making plans to bring the baby home, my wife told me that if we did, she would kill herself. Her depression and the blame she put on herself for the baby's condition were such that her doctor told me that he feared she would carry out her threat. With the heaviest heart I have ever felt, I sought out an adoption agency. There was a family in Montana that already had two handicapped children, and they adopted him. My wife made me cut off all contact with the family, but I secretly kept in touch. But when my wife found a drawing that was sent to me by a little boy in the mail, she moved out of our house for a full month. We have two older daughters of marriageable age, and my wife thought that if anyone found out that they had a retarded brother, no one would want them anymore, thinking that they had defective genes or something. That was ten years ago, when our son would have been eight, and I have had no contact since. I think about him all the time. But that's all he is. A distant memory that brings me nothing but sadness. I think the time has come for me to let go as well."

Now I ask, Uri, which child is the more real? The dead son, killed in a car crash, who is visited every day in the cemetery by his father, who still talks to him as if he were alive, or the living child, somewhere thousands of miles away, whose parents, even for the best of reasons, have abandoned him? I would contend that the dead child is far more alive. He continues to affect the life of his parents, while the little boy in Montana is alive to his parents in nothing but name.

And as this man who had given up his child for adoption spoke, Uri, I was immediately plagued by terrible pangs of conscience. I thought to myself, "Do I hug my children enough? Will I one day live with the same regrets, God forbid, once they're older and out of my care? Am I a dream father, or a real father? Do I exist in nothing but name?"

I have never told you, Uri, that the book of Proverbs is one of my favorite books of the Bible. In it, King Solomon declares that a child is like a bow shot from an arrow. Even after he leaves your care and jurisdiction, if you guide him, if you impart to him a feeling of inspiration, he will continue to pursue the path you have shown him. Is that not life, Uri? Can we not say that to inspire someone, even from beyond the grave, is to be far more alive than ceasing to make any impression on them even if you are standing just inches from their nose. In other words, what good is sensory perception if it leaves absolutely no trace?

The mystery of those things that are hidden being more real than those that are overtly present goes all the way back to the Creation itself. The Jewish esoteric discipline of the *Cabbala* considers how God creates the world. The dilemma is straightforward: if He were to reveal His infinite presence undisguised, He would overwhelm the earth's inhabitants. And if He were to remove Himself completely, the world would be an empty void. God overcomes this through a process of creating a void within Himself. This is not a void per se, but rather an absence, a concealing of His countenance. In other words, creation comes about by the paradox of God being simultaneously present and absent. God is present enough for us to experience Him, but hidden enough for us to deny Him and thereby assert our own identities. In the Cabbala, this is known as *tzimtzum*, the great mystery of contraction and condensation.

The same paradox is prevalent in parenting. The objective in effective parenting is to be both present and absent simultaneously. In the metaphor I quoted earlier from Proverbs, the arrow, once released, is endowed with an invisible force. Good parenting is that very same force, an invisible voice of conscience that accompanies a child on his journey through life.

You have often served for me as a voice of conscience, Uri. Although I still have my doubts about telepathy, I cannot deny that on countless occasions, far more than statistics could explain or predict, as soon as I have thought of you, you called me on the phone just moments later. It is almost like you are present and absent with me all the time. Perhaps this is the highest form of friendship. When we don't actually have to be present in order for us to feel close to each other.

But alas, we live in a visual world where sensory perception and immediate gratification are everything. Men want women who are beautiful. They are like sexual drug addicts. They need that immediate buzz as soon as they look at the woman. They crave the instant "high" that visible beauty can bestow. Discovering her hidden essence is far less exciting by comparison. But it is they who miss out, since they end up making love to a body rather than a person.

Parents, likewise, are often far too visible in their children's lives. Many of them seek to be proactive teachers rather than hidden guardians, and continue to hammer and chisel away at their children as if they were pieces of marble, not realizing that they are destroying their individuality, creativity, and sense of security. By emphasizing the active side of parenting, parents show their children that they will be judged by how they behave and act, rather than by who they are. Look at many of today's high achievers, the kids who excel at university and to whom I serve as rabbi at Oxford. The more they propel themselves to achieve, the more likely they are to experience free fall into a state of insecurity.

Like the invisible force imparted to the arrow, the parents must become the invisible voice of conscience that stays with the child, guiding his or her actions at all times.

The Talmud explains how Joseph prevented himself from sinning with the wife of Potiphera. A vision of his father Jacob flashes before his eyes just before Joseph succumbs to the temptations of another man's wife. Here he is, seventeen years old, hormonally driven and responding to his adolescent stimuli. A beautiful woman throws herself at him, and yet he resists because his father is with him in the room. Jacob cannot be seen, indeed he is hundreds of miles away. But Joseph visualizes him—he becomes the invisible voice of conscience. This is not radically different, Uri, to your having felt the presence of your beloved pet who made you feel warm and loved.

The role of parents in the life of a child is still crucial, but it is in its hidden qualities that its essence emerges. In the case of your father, Uri, you will please forgive me for saying so (and who am I to judge?), but he seems to have left little trace. He chose not to be a father, and, consequently, his effect on you was minimal to nonexistent. But then your dog, a creature which showered you with love in your loneliest moments, showed you constant love and companionship. Of course, that is something that I can appreciate. Yet the Torah tells you to honor your father, and not your dog, because your father gave you something that your dog never could: life itself. In this respect, whatever choices our parents make in regard to our upbringing, for good or for bad, they will always remain the most important people to us.

But to return to our point for a moment. You asked me how we could know whether or not experiences that seem illusory are real? To answer that question we must first define the meaning of real. The Talmud says that a river that dries up even once in seven years is called "waters that lie," meaning they're not real. Real does not mean that something stares you right in the face. Nor does it connote something that you can see, smell, hear, touch, or taste. Rather, something is real when it moves you—especially on the inside. Anything that has the effect of shaping and changing its environment is real, even if it cannot be sensed. This is what makes our emotions real, even though we can't taste, touch, or see them. Existence is defined as the ability to make an impact. But if something just dries up then, like the river above, it is not real but merely an illusion.

We all have dreams, and the question really is: are our dreams real? They certainly seem real, especially while they're happening. A Chinese poet once wrote: "Last night I dreamt that I was a butterfly. This morning I have awoken and I cannot remember if I am a man who dreamt that he was a butterfly, or if I am a butterfly who now dreams that he is a man."

So, what is the answer? Are our dreams real? Or mere fantasy? The answer depends on the extent to which we translate them into reality. One man will have a dream about finding a cure for AIDS, but will wake up in the morning and dismiss the dream as the silly stuff of fantasy. But another man will have a dream of building a homeland for the fellow members of his wandering people. He will wake up in the morning and proclaim, "If you will it, it is no dream." And he will be remembered in history as a great man, by the name of Theodor Herzl.

About thirty-five years ago, a black man who had spent time in prison in pursuit of racial equality, spoke to 250,000 in front of the Lincoln Memorial in Washington. His message, "I have a dream...that one day my children will be judged for the content of their character rather than by the color of their skin." As you know, Uri, I travel frequently between Oxford and

London, seeing as L'Chaim has branches in both cities, and I often listen to tapes of great speeches of the twentieth century. But there is no speech as good as the one Martin Luther King Jr. delivered that day. And although he did not live to see the fulfillment of his own dream, it did happen in his children's lifetime. He made his dream real.

And just as a dream is translated into reality through a tangible program of action, the same is true of human life. A man lives on, Uri, through the good deeds he has done, and through the inspiration he bequeaths to subsequent generations. Hence, the Talmud says that the righteous, even after death, are still alive, since so many living people hang on to their memory and continue to be inspired by their wisdom and example. Even though they can't be touched, they can still be felt. Whereas the wicked, the Talmud adds, even while alive, are really dead. If they were hit by a garbage truck tomorrow, nobody would care and nobody would miss them. No void would be created by their disappearance. Hence, even as they breathe and walk the earth, they are dead and as dust. Their lives are a passing wind, a fleeting memory, that leaves no trace.

I have told you, Uri, of how the Lubavitcher Rebbe, Rabbi Menachem Schneerson, was the formative influence of my life. While being the most celebrated and influential Jewish spiritual personality of the twentieth century, he also had time to take a personal interest in people and guide their lives. I was one of those souls who found solace and comfort in his guidance. I described to you how I went to him at age thirteen and told him of the devastating effects of my parents' divorce upon me. Rather than allow me to succumb to cynicism, he lifted me and inspired me to become a rabbi. He told me that by embracing a profession that was about mending hearts and healing wounds, I would ultimately find healing myself.

But then, after ninety-four years, he died. I heard the news from my father over the phone, one Sunday morning in Oxford. It was the first great loss that I had experienced on a personal level. It was odd hearing my father tell me how my father figure had died. Debbie immediately broke into tears, but I remained focused on reining in my emotions and getting to the airport so that I could make the funeral in New York that was to take place that afternoon.

Ten hours later—I was just able to make the beginning of the funeral, which took place in a steady New York drizzle—I witnessed the most confusing sight of my life. On the one hand, as soon as they brought out the coffin, thirty thousand women, pressed together behind police barricades, let forth the strongest wailing sound that I had ever heard. It was like an avalanche of grief cascading down upon all of us that nearly knocked me over. On the other hand, downstairs in the Rebbe's enormous synagogue, more than ten thousand men sang and danced while their leader was being laid to rest. Many said it was a travesty. How could they be joyous upon the occasion of this great man's demise? I myself was outraged and deeply hurt. I wanted to cry unhindered. I wanted to feel the pain and experience the loss. But there they were, dancing undeterred. And they defended themselves, "He is not dead. We feel him with us at this very moment. His love and guidance remain with us. He is more alive than ever." I remember being torn with emotion. Who was right?

Did you feel your dog's warm breath and cold nose against you that day? Or were you just dreaming? Perhaps you were tired and lost your senses? Or perhaps you tapped into a higher reality.

And in the final analysis, Uri, the conflict of whether or not you were just dreaming that day will always be with you. But only now will you be able to decide if it was real or not. If your dog's love continues to influence you—if its memory makes you more forgiving of other people's flaws, if it causes you to give more charity, if it teaches you to be more polite, even to those who do not deserve it—if his memory teaches you to show unconditional love even to those who unfairly criticize you, then it was real. And if it doesn't, then it was false. You were only dreaming.

An old Jewish joke comments on how fortunate it was that Sigmund Freud and Theodor Herzl, although both Viennese Jews who lived at the same time, never actually met. Because if they had, Herzl would have said, "Sigmund, I have a dream." And Freud would have said, "Really Theodor. How long have you been having these dreams?" And the State of Israel might have remained nothing but a passing fancy in Herzl's head. Perhaps it would have emerged as a novel or a play. But certainly there would have been no geographical space to absorb millions of refugees from the Holocaust, the former Soviet Union, and Ethiopia.

As for me, Uri, I offer to you sincere thanks from the bottom of my heart for having strengthened my absolute belief that it is the invisible things in life that are the most precious and powerful. You did this partially by demonstrating the amazing powers of your mind. But especially by demonstrating how the love you show your friends travels with them wherever they go. Hoping that God will be with you in all your physical and mental journeys.

I remain your real and never illusory friend,

Dear Shmuley,

You speak the word "father" with deep love and affection. To you, a father is a teacher, a protector, a noble ideal, and a fervent principle. Your fierce desire to be a worthy father to your children is so powerful that anyone can see it, even if they have known you for only a few minutes.

To me, "father" means the man who forced my mother to have an abortion in the back of a Tel Aviv taxi. My mother had eight abortions. I was the ninth child. How I survived the first weeks in the womb I have no idea. Did I have the protection of all those unborn souls, my brothers and sisters? After eight backstreet abortions, it was a miracle my mother could even conceive. All her desperate hopes for a child that would live were focused so intensely on me, and perhaps all the snuffed-out energies were channeled into my own energy, so that I was born with special mindpowers—nine lives in one life. She told me of this private holocaust only recently. My father died twenty years ago, and I cannot ask for his side of the story, but all the details are so like him: the bullying rages when my mother confessed she was pregnant again, the blame flung at her, the cheap solutions, the solitary visits to vicious, seedy doctors, the brutal contempt which answered for his sympathy. And the nadir of all this, the abortion by a doctor who did not even have a room to perform his work in, so that my father's taxi was used—the vehicle she had bought him with her savings, to give him a chance of earning money after the war.

My father was not an evil man. He was brave, and I loved him. My mother loved him too, or she could not have endured so much horror. They had been married eight years when I was born—they met in Hungary, were married in Budapest's most lavish synagogue, and fled separately to Palestine as the Nazi storm broke. My father's ship was strafed by British machine-guns three times as it made for safety. Twenty refugees were killed. Later, he fought for the British, in the Jewish Brigade of the Eighth Army under Montgomery, and then fought against them in the *Haganah*. My parents were apart very much, and this did not change after I was born. My photographs show him as a proud father, his arms bearing baby Uri proudly, his face beaming a father's embarrassed, delighted smile. He was a roguishly handsome man. My mother says he could woo any woman with a smile, and he smiled often. But I rely on my photographs for my memories. He was not in my life very often, until I was years older.

Once he gave me a dog. I adored him for that and I always will. He loved dogs. Once, he hauled me out of bed like a sergeant rousing his ragbag of conscripts, screamed me to attention, and made me stand with my feet perfectly together and my fists at the seams of my shorts. I was four years old. Once he beat me, tied me by the wrists with his belt to the toilet cistern, and left me dangling in the tiny dark room for hours. But I had done a very awful thing, and I deserved this.

Last time I wrote, I wanted to tell you about this, but I held back. It is not that I have never confessed what I did. I told my classmates and my teacher, then my mother and father, I told the scientist who wrote my first biography, and then I told the world when I wrote *My Story*. That was twenty-five years ago— half my life away. The shame has not grown any less in those years. I still cannot understand what I did.

I stole a Torah scroll and ripped it up. All my class had been told to bring a scroll to school, and my family did not possess one. My mother did not come from an observant family, and we had no money but for what my mother could scrape from her seamstressing and waitressing, for the money that my father was paid he did not spend on us. So I had no scroll. And I was envious. I was red-faced and furious with envy when I saw what beautiful scrolls the other children had, because this meant they came from homes with more money and more ceremony and ritual, and more family. I felt like I didn't have a family, because I didn't have a scroll. So I crept back into class when the others were at prayer, and I took a dazzling white scroll from a desk and slipped it into my bag, and took it home. I don't know whether I was seen, or if I said something that betrayed me, or if the glowing envy in my face whenever I had looked at the scrolls had warned the teacher what was in my mind—perhaps it was some kind of telepathy, but I had not been home an hour, with the uselessly stolen Torah hidden under my mattress, when I saw the teacher striding up the street to our apartment building.

In my panic, I tore up the angelically white paper and flushed it down the toilet. And so it was there that my father chose to punish me, slashing at me with his belt and finally roping me to the cistern pipes with it so that my bleeding hands were puffy and white, and my feet barely touched the tiled floor. That was just the beginning of the punishment. My classmates would not speak to me—the girl I had fallen in love with, desperately, ignored me—the teachers treated me like a criminal, and my mother nodded when my father yelled at me. Only my dog forgave me, and that was simply because dogs do not understand.

My father forgot about it. He never bore a grudge. For him, life was for living, and living was done in the present. When I was at the *kibbutz*, and the Suez crisis was at its worst and my father had been fighting the British again, he took a day's leave to visit me. I did not know he was coming, but I saw the speck of dust rising out of the plains and stood and watched for almost half an hour, knowing it was him, until the speck became a ball of dust that rolled in through the gates, and my father leapt out of his jeep and took me on a ride through the heat haze that was more wonderful than any boy dared hope for. Even now, I would call it the happiest day of my life.

My father was a powerful man. He never rose above the rank of sergeant-major, but he could silence a busy street with one look. I remember walking into a noisy coffee bar behind him. The room was silenced—people held their cups at their lips and held back their words and gazed at him as he walked to the bar. A film star would have that effect, but a film star who was not yet famous, because there was no jolt of recognition—just a roomful of people saying, "Who is that?" That was my father—always a film star who was not yet famous.

His looks got him girls, and he had a lot of them. They were not especially good-looking—and I should know because I met enough of them—but they were, I suppose, willing. My mother blamed herself, because after eight abortions and a live baby, she had become dumpy. My father wanted slim women. It was a normal desire for a married soldier of his type—nothing to hide, not even from his wife and son. The girls used to come and whistle in the street for him if he was late. We would be eating, and a coarse note would blast up from the gutter, and my father would writhe in his seat and say, "I have to be off, I have to be going. I have someone to see." Once, when I was seven or eight and we were walking in the city, he dragged me into a phone booth and made me wait while he spoke to his girlfriend. Suddenly the phone was thrust in my face—"Say hello to Trudi," my father ordered.

From my father, I learned to be alone and to trust myself. Other people come and go, loving you sometimes and vanishing when you have just become used to their way of loving. In the end, nothing can stop them from leaving. I learned to be alone, because that's sometimes the way we all have to be.

For years before he died, I had a nightmare. I was letting myself into my father's apartment in Tel Aviv, the one he shared with his second wife. They married in the sixties, when he was starting to settle down, and though they didn't have children, their marriage seemed pretty happy. There wasn't much cash, and one time on the phone my father got angry with me and then burst into tears. I owned an apartment in Tel Aviv that I rented out, I had lots of money, why wouldn't I let him stay there? He wasn't asking me to support him, he was just asking me to give him something I owned and didn't need. I tried to tell him the apartment couldn't ever be his, because my mother had paid for it, with the money she earned after he walked out on us for the final time. He didn't listen. He was too ashamed, I think, at his tears.

In the nightmare, I went into the tiny rooms where he lodged, and a body under the window rolled over and stared at me. With my face. There was a dead man and it was me. After years of this dream, when Hanna and I were staying in Rome, I had a call saying that my father was very ill and I must go to him immediately. My stepmother's voice said "very ill" in that way people have when they don't want to tell you over the phone of a death. He had died in the apartment, from an angina attack, under the window of my nightmare. After that, the dream stopped.

I love my father, but I cannot revere him. He was a man, with as many brutal faults as any man I know. And as much kindness. He chanced to be my father. Does that demand reverence? I know you will say it does, because the commandments order us to honor our fathers and mothers. But you know by now that I do not trust God and his commandments. Why should I? God is a father, and not to be trusted.

With much love,

Dear Uri

Ah, Uri, the tortured relationship we all have with our fathers!

As you know, my parents divorced when I was eight years old, which meant that we moved with my mother from Los Angeles to Miami, where my grandparents lived. This meant that, like you, I could not be close to my father, neither geographically nor emotionally. We were separated by 3,500 miles, a lot of history, and even more emotional baggage. For years, I judged my father for having been absent, even while my mother was still married to him. He was an immigrant to the United States from Israel and Iran and worked incredibly hard to build up his business. I felt angry and bitter that everything seemed to be more important to him than his family. I remember the resentment that swelled in me as a child when we were told that we could not be at dinner certain nights since important business contacts would be my father's guests. I also remember how my father would go back to Israel every year, armed with suitcases of presents for our poorer cousins, when often our own birthdays were forgotten or neglected. I had anger in my heart.

Every Sunday night, we would call my father on the phone, mostly because we were forced to by my mother. I was really under the impression, however mistaken, that my father didn't care to hear from us anyway, so why should I inflict myself upon him like some unwanted virus?

Much of my childhood in Miami was spent searching for a lost father figure, which resulted directly in my becoming a rabbi. There was a local rabbinical College in Miami, run by Lubavitch, and they offered a summer camp, which I attended. I latched onto my older counselors and tried to emulate them. I loved being around them and continued visiting them after the summer had ended. With money I had saved up, at the age of twelve, I even bought a moped—something which was totally illegal at my age—in order to travel to see them at the Rabbinical College three miles from my home.

You have seen me many times, Uri, and know me to be vertically challenged, the politically correct way of saying that I am very short (I always tell people that, in my case, I am vertically at war). Well, at age twelve, I was about two feet tall (a "slight" exaggeration, if you'll pardon the pun). I would drive around Miami on my moped, barely able to reach and hold on to the handle bars. I was so tiny that it looked to most people as if the moped was being ridden by itself without a driver. Often, I was chased by the police who found it curious that a moped was being ridden by a headless horseman. On one occasion, I had to hide for two hours behind a bush while the police searched for me at night with spotlights and trained dogs. One of the dogs eventually found me, but mistook me for a garden gnome and let me go.

I went to a religious school in Miami. Most of the kids came from two-parent homes. I always felt like the odd man out when the teacher told us to go home and practice our daily portion of Talmud with our fathers. I felt closer to the Captain from *Gilligan's Island*—which I watched religiously every day—than I did to my own father. I was a terrible student, angry and cynical by the time I was thirteen. Amidst the great Jewish affluence of Miami Beach, we lived, all six of us, in a one-bedroom apartment, and my mother held two jobs to support us. The result was that my two brothers, my two sisters, and I had an incredible devotion to my mother and felt quite distant from my father. Indeed, when my sisters got married, both at age nineteen, they told their fiancés that they had to live within walking distance of my mother or the marriages could not go ahead.

Uri, it has taken a long time, but over the past decade, especially since my marriage, I have begun to make peace with my father and have, thank God, become much closer to him and now feel very loving and intimate with him. Several factors have contributed to this rapprochement, but none as important as this simple fact: I have ceased judging him. In fact, I arrived at the conclusion many years ago that it is neither my right nor my prerogative to judge any fellow human being (although I continue to reserve the right to judge their actions, as I shall discuss). I also discovered that my father was a much, much better man and a much more devoted and loving father than I ever knew.

All the while that I grew up in Miami Beach, I falsely convinced myself that my father did not really love or care for me and my siblings. Indeed, his infrequent visits to Miami seemed to confirm that view. The way I saw it, he would come for a weekend and we would all exchange perfunctory conversation. He would pretend to be interested in us, and we would pretend to be interested in him. I remember the cold peck on the cheek I would give him while he waited for a taxi to take him back to the airport. Inside, I was praying that the taxi would arrive quickly so that the awkward moment of his good-bye would speedily pass. He always had a problem showing affection, and I didn't see the point in us going through the play-acting of pretending to like or miss each other.

I had no way of knowing what pain and torment he was in from being separated from us until years later. When I was fourteen years old, I went to a Yeshiva boarding school back in Los Angeles. One day, a rabbi came to visit the Yeshiva, and on hearing there was a student named Boteach, he came over to introduce himself. "I know your father," he told me. I wasn't really interested in talking to him and didn't respond. "Don't you want to know how I know your father?" I just kept looking ahead, pretending that I didn't hear him. "Well, I will tell you," he continued. "After your mother took all of you and moved to Miami, your father was a complete wreck. I was the rabbi at his new synagogue. My wife and I would invite him over to our home for *Shabbat* dinner, and he would sit there crying in front of us all, inconsolable, because he had lost his children. At times, it was so bad that we thought of not inviting him back because his sobs ruined the *Shabbat* atmosphere for our own children. For two years, he walked around Los Angeles haggard and unkempt. Like a walking corpse, his life had been taken away from him." I was in shock. My father? Crying? And over his children? Why, he never even showed that anything could hurt him like that. I didn't even know he had a heart that could be broken!

Little by little, I became exposed to this unknown side of my father, the part of him to which I had been oblivious and which I had before never made an effort to discover or understand. What I discovered surprised and humbled me. The more I learned about my father, the more I understood how spoiled and insensitive I had been for judging him in the first place. I began to respect him as a heroic figure who had overcome much adversity and pain in life to try and provide for his family. I began to respect him as a heroic figure who had overcome much adversity and pain in life to try and provide for his family. I had made out as though I was the only one who had any pain and my father had none, when in truth he had suffered much in life, but still preserved his integrity and resolve.

When I was nineteen, I went to study in New York at a rabbinical boarding school. My father's younger brother Eliyahu came to visit me from Israel, and I was showing him around the city. I went to a hat store and bought myself a beautiful new black hat, the kind that young rabbis wear, made from beaver skin. It cost me $150, and I paid for it from the cash my father gave me as my monthly allowance. Immediately afterwards, I took my uncle to the top of the Empire State Building. A gust of wind then whisked my new hat right from my head and up toward Central Park. I am sure that some pious and saintly Hassidic Jew was pleasantly surprised to see a beautiful new hat rain down on him from heaven, and convinced to this day that it was in recompense for a life lived in holiness. And perhaps it was.

I was of course upset that this had happened. But I turned to my uncle and said, "That's a shame. We're going to have to go straight back to the hat store and buy another one." And that's what we did. When I had paid for the hat and we got on a bus, my uncle started to cry. His eyes swelled up and tears ran down his cheeks. I asked him what was the matter. And he told me. "When I saw you callously pay another $150 for your hat, without so much as batting an eyelid, flashes of memory came before my eyes. I remembered our childhood in Isfahan, in Iran. We were a family of thirteen children living in abject poverty. I remembered your father, and how, when he was a tender boy of ten, he would put upwards of one hundred pounds of carpets onto his back and go to the marketplace early in the morning to help feed the family. We wouldn't see him until late at night. When he returned, he was so hungry that he couldn't even wait for the food to be served by our mother. He ate it straight out of the pot. And there wasn't even that much left.

At six o'clock the next morning, he would start off again, with his torn shoes and unwashed clothes, so that his younger siblings could eat and be clothed."

Suddenly, I began to understand that, whereas I had always focused on my own suffering, my father had internalized so much suffering by comparison. My father was a hero, and I didn't even know it. He grew up in an absolutely impoverished Jewish family in Iran, the second child of thirteen. His father was never well and found it impossible to support the family on his own. My father therefore had to go out and work from the age of eight. The entire family lived in a tent and barely subsisted on the meager food that they had. To this day, my brother has a picture on his wall of my father's class at school in Iran, before he had to drop out and go to work. All the kids have patches on their dusty and ugly clothes. Their sallow faces show not a single smile.

Another uncle told me a story of how, when my father was already older and the family had emigrated to Israel, my father would drive from Be'er Sheva to Tel Aviv at the crack of dawn every morning to sell goods in the Israeli market and bring bread to the family table. After several months, he was so tired that he could not keep his eyes open as he traveled. He would then take the scissors that he used to cut the fabrics for customers and stick them into his legs to keep himself awake. When I asked my father about this story, he would not go into the details. But he lifted his eyes, looked at me, and said, "Who cares about my legs? The important thing is, I didn't miss the market. Not once. I never missed that market. I never let my family down even once."

As a rabbi to university students, Uri, I constantly have to listen to students complain about their parents. They are many and varied. But almost never do the students make an effort to understand their parents' own circumstances. Kids today believe that they all have a right to complain. And they do. But they do not think that their parents too might have complaints—against God and against life itself. Sure, we believe that our parents scar us with their neglect and indifference. But never do we think to ourselves that someone might have scarred them in the very same way. Maybe our parents would also like to raise a fist toward the heavens and rail against the injustice. But perhaps they cannot afford that luxury since they have too many responsibilities.

We have every right, Uri, to judge people's actions. The world is not a free-for-all, and anarchy cannot prevail. But while we can judge people's actions, we cannot judge *them*. One of the most beautiful of the rabbinical teachings proclaims, "Never judge a man until you are in his place." Unless you step into his shoes you cannot know why he does the things he does. Similarly, King David writes in Psalms, "May all sin vanish from the earth," and the Talmud points out, "Note that he says that *sin* should vanish from the earth, rather than sinners."

Even today I sometimes feel neglected by my father. He can still sometimes be distant. He is a man of great responsibility, supporting some of his siblings and their children who are less fortunate, and the immense burden can sometimes show. I always want to retaliate. I'll show him, I think to myself. Now I am in England, I am, thank God, blessed with my own family. I'll have to learn to live without him. And then my brother always reminds me how harsh I too can be in my judgments, and what right do I have to judge him anyway? And this is an occurrence that transpires with regularity.

Truth be told, the pain I must have caused my father when I showed him all those years ago that I did not need him never dawned on me. I only found out what this hurt really feels like very recently, when I was on tour promoting my book *Kosher Sex*. I had been away from home longer than ever before, but justified my absence by telling myself that I was earning money and a reputation that would benefit my family. I was into my third week of not having seen my wife and children when I called Debbie in London and asked her to put the kids on the phone. All my girls came running. "How are you Tatti (Daddy)? Are you having a good time?" Then I asked for my six-year-old son, but he wouldn't come. He couldn't be bothered to speak to me. He was playing on his computer. When my wife finally pried him away from the monitor and persuaded him to talk to his father, the talk was perfunctory and empty. Images of the cold indifference I showed to my father so many years earlier flashed before my eyes. The Talmud says that the way you treat your parents is the way that your children will eventually treat you in turn. And here I was, the living fulfillment of that prophecy.

It then struck me that my son was learning how to occupy himself in the face of a father who constantly traveled. He was learning to live without me. His computer was becoming his principal companion. I was being replaced by Sonic the Hedgehog in my son's life. I honestly felt a pain that I have rarely felt in my entire life. Nothing, absolutely nothing, had hurt that much. I called back. Again my wife forced him to the phone. "Tatti, I'll speak to you when you get back—that is, if you ever get back," he told me.

Moments later I had to do a press interview, and I could barely concentrate. I thought about how I would have to change. But more importantly, I wished somehow that my son could understand. How could he know that, even if I was absolutely wrong for neglecting him, at least in my mind I was doing it all for him and his sisters? When Debbie and I married, we did so without a penny in our pockets. Our first year of marriage was tough and stressful for both of us, with the specter of empty bank accounts and unpaid rent constantly looming before us. I promised Debbie that I would work exceedingly hard so that each of our children would be given at least a bit of money with which to start life. But how could my son know that? As we judge our parents unfavorably, Uri, do we ever think to ourselves that at least in their minds they have the perfect rationalization for why they're doing what they're doing?

But the other thing I felt at that moment was how much my father must have suffered, and still suffers. Who could know how awful it must have been for him?—his children living in Miami, growing up without any manifest desire to speak to him. Who cares that in our minds he brought it upon himself? Here is a human being in agony. And that human being is my father!

I have since come to know, Uri, that I have no right to judge any man or woman because I am the worst person I know. I know how hypocritical I can sometimes be, how selfish and self-centered, and how I often treat people in a manner in which I hope no one will ever treat me. Who am I therefore to judge?

You spoke to me about your dreams, Uri, namely, how you had a dream that you saw yourself as a lifeless corpse in your father's apartment. When I was twenty years old, I wrote a book about dreams. The great writers on dreams say that one of the rules of a dream is that you can never see yourself die in a dream. But just as in so many other things, here again, Uri, you break all the rules. One of the rules of dream interpretation is that you can never interpret a dream unless you know the person inside and out—much like a doctor would be a fool to diagnose and prescribe medicine to a patient without knowing his full medical history. But here I will venture a guess as to what your dream means.

We are the product of our parents and have so much of them in us, whether we like it or not. We must therefore connect with them, whether we like it or not. Like a tree cut off from its roots, when we are cut off from our parents, we wither. When we are angry at our parents, we can know no peace. Your dream, Uri, means that in the tragedy of your broken relationship with your father, something of you dies as well. You are dead in his apartment, because he is dead in your life. And in the fragmentation of your parents' divorce, something of you is fragmented as well. Believe me. I understand this. My parents' divorce was the defining moment of my life. This is the meaning of your dream having taken place specifically in the apartment where your father lives with a wife who is not your mother.

The ancient Rabbis of the Talmud labeled honoring one's parents as the most difficult commandment of the entire Bible. So often we feel that our parents have wronged us, and we feel justified in disliking them. But the Torah says that our opinion on the matter ultimately does not much matter. The fact that we have an opinion at all, the fact that we can live, breathe, and think is entirely due to them and their sacrifice. The fact of our existence is enough of a reason to show them honor and respect. By commanding us to show honor and respect to our parents at all times, the Bible is attempting to inculcate gratitude within us at all costs.

Although your father is no longer alive and you cannot be reconciled to him, you can be reconciled to his memory. Rather than remembering the negative things about him—and no human being is perfect—you can focus on the positive things. You can remember the love and attention he showed you. Focus on the light rather than the darkness. Set your sights on the rising dawn rather than the falling sunset.

My friend Cory Booker once told me that when he was five years old, he thought his father was Superman. He was sure he was perfect and loved him for his perfection. Then one day, his father lied to him. He was devastated. He had discovered that his father was only human, and Cory was so incredibly disappointed. But then he thought to himself how he now loved his father so much more. Because amidst his imperfection, amid his capacity to lie, amid his own inner pain and confusion, he still mustered the courage and made sacrifices to love his children and be a decent father. The love of a perfect person is no big deal. It comes without struggle. But the love of an imperfect person is always special, because the person showing it has to fight for it.

There is one final memory I have of my parents and their divorce. It is a very painful memory, that of the divorce itself. My parents were separated for three long years before they finally decided to go to a rabbinical court and formally obtain a *get*, the Jewish bill of divorce. Through an ironic twist of circumstances, my siblings and I were present when this happened. The rabbi issuing the divorce was the father of one of my schoolmates. I remember how he gave my father the bill of divorce and asked him to witness it and hand it to my mother, thereby bringing their sixteen-year marriage to an end. My father, who up until that time had never shown any of us weakness or tears, began to hyperventilate. Soon, he was sobbing like a baby. "I never wanted this," he cried, "I never wanted any of this. What will I now tell my mother in Israel? What will I now say before my father's grave?" And with that, he handed the divorce document to my mother and ran from the room. It was first time I saw him as a vulnerable human being, and I loved him more than ever before. I still remember how me and my brothers walked my father down the road to see a cheap karate film in an effort to comfort him. It was also then that I came to understand the full tragedy of what had transpired in my family and how, ultimately, placing blame on any one party just aggravated the wound.

Having failed with the movie, my brothers and I chased after my father and tried to comfort him at a local restaurant, while my sisters did the same for my mother. But he just sat in stony silence, repeating his words like a mantra, "What will I tell my mother in Israel? What will I say at my father's grave?"

It was then that I decided I could not risk the regret that I too might feel after it was, God forbid, too late. I had to try and be a good son now, so that the terrible cycle of pain in my family would finally be brought to an end. I am still trying that, Uri, and every day is no easier than the previous day. But with forgiveness and reconciliation, life is certainly much clearer and more joyous. I have a strong and loving relationship with my father now, and I am less lonely as a result. It is not I who must forgive him for what I thought to be his inadequacies as a father. It is he who must forgive me for ever judging him as his son.

> With every best wish, your loving friend who admires you for the person you are, but especially the wonderful father you are,

Dear Shmuley,

I am fifty-two years old. My daughter is sixteen. Every week she is auditioning for stage-shows, going to photo shoots—she will be either an actress or a model. Natalie is very beautiful. She is also studying hard for her GCSEs, the exams that mark the end of her basic schooling. I look at her, still a child and too vulnerable to walk in the world without her parents' protection.

Sixteen years old. She is barely younger than my girlfriend was when my first child was born.

I met Damalis in Cyprus, in the early Sixties, before my military service and long before I met Hanna. My stepfather was no longer alive—with the money he left us, I had helped my mother to purchase the Pension Ritz in Nicosia. Damalis and her parents ran the bakery where, very early each morning, I would roll up on my bicycle to collect the bread for breakfast.

My love for Damalis was instant and impetuous, an uncontrolled eruption, very different to the love that followed for Hanna. Hanna and I knew we were right for each other, and we both knew it would be wrong to turn our friendship into a commitment until years had passed—perhaps many years. We did not marry, in fact, until 1991.

Falling in love with Hanna was thirty years of growth, like a tree that is an invisible seed at first, and then a tender shoot, and a wavering sapling, before it strengthens and puts out branches, and blossoms.

When I fell in love with Damalis, it was like a bomb-blast. One moment, normal life—the next, devastation. Noise and confusion. And pain, lots of pain. But the explosion seemed to blow my heart right out of me. I did not care for anyone or anything except this blistering emotion that felt as if all the skin had been stripped from my body. Even to be touched by anyone but Damalis was screaming torture.

Damalis was the prettiest girl I have ever seen, with immense gray-green eyes and ginger, curling hair cropped tightly round her head. Her hair was dark brown soaked in rust-red, the color of a flint stone when you break it open. Her eyebrows arched up naturally, so she had a perpetually quizzical look, as if she was constantly about to burst into mocking laughter. She did laugh a lot—she loved secret jokes, jokes no one in the world could understand but her and her lover. Her mouth was small and bowed. I will never forget how I saw her the first day: she walked up the steps from the ovens at the back of the shop in a white smock. I could think of nothing but kissing her. She saw me staring, and she stared back. Her face was full of laughter she could barely control. Later, I found out it was the look she always wore.

We started dating that night, and I found out very soon that, though Damalis looked and acted twenty-one, she was barely seventeen years old. I was not quite a virgin—there had been a German dancer in the pension, who called me into her room to "help me with the buckle of this damn bikini!" And then there was a prostitute called Lola. Damalis, though, was my first lover.

She told me she was not a virgin either, but I have never been sure if that was the truth.

After a few days, Damalis told her father and mother about me—some of it, not everything. I had never been treated with such open dislike and hostility. Her parents wanted to string me up, and all that stopped them was Damalis, hanging on my arm, telling them how nice and kind and funny I was. Once that ordeal was over, we ignored their disapproval. When Damalis and I were together, we ignored everything but ourselves.

If Damalis' father had known that day that his daughter was already pregnant, he would have tried to kill me—of that I'm certain, because that's how it would be today with me and my daughter.

Her father didn't know, and, as the weeks passed, I think Damalis had no idea either. She was so young. If she did, she hid it completely. I saw nothing different about her body— some pregnancies happen that way. When she had four months to go, she told me.

We were on a borrowed Lambretta, a motor-scooter I could occasionally get for an hour or two from an older friend. I remember we were actually riding it, not parked and chatting, but scooting through Nicosia at 30 m.p.h., Damalis with her arms tucked under my jacket and her hands against my shirt. She pressed her cheek against my shoulder and spoke in my ear: "I'm having a baby."

I braked hard and turned round, shouting at her: "What?" She said it again, and I could see how suddenly frightened she was. It wasn't pregnancy that was frightening her—it was me. She hadn't seen me angry that way before—scared angry. I know how I must have looked to her, because I saw my father turn that face on my mother so many times.

I accepted without question that the child was mine. Neither of us wanted her to have an abortion. The idea that a baby was inside her, our baby, fully formed and two-thirds grown, was deeply shocking, and moving. This little person had sprung into life because of our irresponsibility—my irresponsibility. A girl her age is not mature enough to see how actions must have consequences. A man who is running the family business, even at seventeen, should be more adult. I owed my child a duty.

Damalis did not want an abortion, but she certainly did not want to be pregnant, she did not want her parents to find out, and she did not want to be a mother. How was she to live with a baby? So we agreed to have it given away.

The man who owned the scooter had a friend, an old doctor who owned a tiny clinic. His name was Nikolas. Damalis came to live in the Pension Ritz, to her parents' disgust. I took her to Nikolas' clinic each week, and when her waters broke, I took her there in a taxi, and Nikolas delivered the child. Nobody knew but my mother.

Nikolas called me into the room, a one-bed closet used for gynecological examinations, and Damalis was sitting up in a bloodied cotton nightdress. They had wrapped the baby in a light blanket, and it was feeding from a bottle—Nikolas would not let Damalis breastfeed because he was about to sever the mother-child bond. He took the baby from her arms, and before he walked out of the room, he placed the bundle in my arms. A little face, tightly wrinkled and scarlet with blotches, was circled by the woolen hem. One dark lock of hair straggled over the forehead. It was a boy's face. Our baby was a little boy. I stood and stared, aware that Damalis was sobbing and that I should comfort her. But I kept holding on to the child. Nikolas tried to lift it from me, but I pulled back. More firmly, he took the baby. For a moment, I held on, with my arms reached out to it, and Nikolas stared me straight in the face. I had a powerful sensation that I was looking into the eyes of a grown man, and I remembered that my duty, as a father now, was to be a man too. Damalis wept silently as Nikolas closed the door, and then her sobbing became uncontrolled. I tried to hug her, but she would not let me.

Damalis and I stayed together for a short while more. We almost never talked about the baby. Sometimes I would lie awake, knowing that she lay awake too. We fell apart in the end. After the birth, we couldn't ignore the world anymore.

Two months after the birth, I could not control my agitation, and I went to Nikolas—I had barely spoken to him since the day of the birth. He had done everything you could wish of a friend, and now he belonged to a piece of my life I could not bear to face. When I strode into the clinic and demanded to know, quite rudely, aggressively, where our baby was living now and whether he was being properly cared for, Nikolas was calm. No, he was not *my* baby boy, and yes, he was well cared for. And loved, very loved. A Greek family had adopted him, and the child would grow up in a healthy, outdoor community, with plenty of food and good schooling. And the best thing I could do was forget him.

"You are not his real father," Nikolas said. "His real father is the man who chose to bring him up. You are his accidental father. So leave it behind, because that accident is over."

I have never left it behind. I have never spoken about it either. Upon my return to Cyprus, it would haunt me. In my mind, I would visualize myself, driving slowly on my scooter, staring over a wall, looking for a boy playing in a farmyard. I am certain I could see him with my inner eye. My son looked exactly as a boy who was to be born almost two decades later would look—like my son and Hanna's. Daniel.

I went back on one other occasion. The boy would have been a little older than Daniel is today—thirty-three or thirty-four, I think—and I was in Cyprus for a TV show. I made some excuses to get away from people, and drove out of Nicosia on my own. When I saw the farm in the distance, I stopped. I got out of the car and stared through the heat-haze, as if a tall, athletic, grinning version of myself would come striding out of the mirage. And then I got back in the car and turned around. I had no business turning up at that family's home just because I happened to be in Cyprus and I happened to have been wondering about my boy for more than thirty years. Like Nikolas said: in my boy's life, I was just an accident that occurred a long time ago.

I still wonder. There are spells of my life when I think of him every day, and days when I think of him every hour. I don't know what happened to Damalis. I loved her, but I think of our unknown child far more often than I think of her. I am glad I have told this story to you. I wish I had told it to Hanna, if not at the time, then at least before I married her. It was on that hot road, between Nicosia and the farm, when I knew the time had come to let go.

With my love,

Dear Uri,

I am flattered that you have chosen to take me into your confidence and divulge to me this secret you have borne all your life about your son. It must have been quite excruciating to have bottled this up all these years. It reminded me of some of my own dilemmas, because there are things that every cleric has to confront, not all of which are easy.

Every rabbi, priest and minister is caught in an insurmountable "catch-22." They have to have an understanding of human dilemmas so that they can offer advice—yet they can never experience the same dilemmas. The world rewards denial, rather than truthfulness, in its leaders. Of all the complaints that I have heard about rabbis, the one that I hear most is that "They're just not sufficiently down to earth. They don't understand my problems." But the moment they hear that their rabbi is a real beer guzzler, instead of going out and partying with him and getting to know him in a human way, they are appalled. Why doesn't he guzzle scripture instead?

We are both Jews, Uri, yet we come from different worlds. You write of your experience with women prior to marrying your beautiful and lovely wife, Hanna. Yet for me, it was the opposite. In Yeshiva we never spoke to—much less, dated—unattached women. To be sure, I had the most wonderful friends in the rabbinical academy, yet I was lonely and missed the nurturing and comforting presence of a woman. So I romanticized marriage. I was going to meet the woman of my dreams and live happily ever after. God was very kind to me and I met Debbie and married at the tender age of twenty-one. I loved being in love and thought that it was total. That it came with no distractions.

So you can imagine my horror—and excuse me for sounding so naïve—to discover once we married that I was still attracted to strangers! A few days after our wedding, I went to a shopping mall in Sydney, Australia, to buy a camera. Lo and behold, I actually noticed that other women were still attractive. I was deeply depressed. I felt there must surely be something wrong with me. I did not feel I loved Debbie any less. I was still walking on clouds and was thrilled that she was my wife. But was this not betrayal?! Still noticing the comeliness of strangers?

In my book, *The Jewish Guide to Adultery*, I finally managed to see how to overcome my anger at God for making love so imperfect. For it is precisely this attraction to others which forces us to constantly choose our spouse anew, thereby guaranteeing the freshness of our marriages. When a man comes home to his wife on a daily basis, notwithstanding the temptations posed by all the people whom he daily encounters, he is telling her, "I have married you anew today. In my eyes, you are the winner of a daily beauty pageant." If he were not attracted to strangers, then he should be choosing her only once, long ago under the wedding canopy, and the marriage would have a stale quality to it. And yet, this romantic insight which I published in my book drew ferocious fire from my rabbinical colleagues. An angry rabbi called me: "You are a disgrace to the Rabbinate. How can you admit to finding other people attractive?" "But was there anything untrue about what I said?" I asked him. And his response: "It's certainly not true in my case. My wife is the only woman to whom I am attracted. To me, looking at any other woman is just the same as looking at a block of wood." He may have been telling the truth. But as another friend of mine said, he may also just be a very bad carpenter. Now, the mere fact that rabbis feel the need to deny or obscure what to everyone else is obvious is deeply troubling. In essence, Uri, rabbis can never confess. And if they can never confess, how can they ever better themselves? Perhaps this is why I find so many of my colleagues choosing to bury their shortcomings.

Of course, clerics have egos, and one of the reasons that religion today is really up a creek is because it hides this fact and thereby dissuades honest and ambitious people from entering its ranks in the first place. It's as if religion is subtly telling its prospective clerical candidates that if they have any form of personal ambitions then they are unfit for the Rabbinate. Worse, people's unrealistic expectations—that their parish priests should have less inclination for sin than a doorknob—are based entirely on a false understanding of the purpose of religion. Too many people believe that religion is about either transcending human nature or suppressing it. Freud was right then! Religion demands that you repress your innate desires and instincts and instead adopt what is foreign to the needs and desires of the body. But this foolish approach to religion is what has traditionally made it about as appetizing as lizard liver.

The real message of religion is that every single one of us is born with an innate nature. And we mustn't be upset at ourselves for having it. It's not a bad thing at all. In fact, it's a darned good thing to have a nature—so long as it is channeled in the right way. Use your human nature to other people's advantage. Never stamp it out. Surely, a wife doesn't want a husband who is an unfaithful Lothario. But neither does she want a husband who is as dead as Elvis the moment the bedroom lights go out. The solution is that he should be very passionate, but specifically and only towards his wife. We all have these passions, even clerics; the key is that they should be channeled toward noble and life-affirming goals.

Once, I was sitting with a Jewish student who was new to Oxford from the United States. It was Friday night, the Sabbath, and our custom is to drink a *L'Chaim*, a toast to life. Well, OK, that night we drank many *L'Chaims*. I poured some Smirnoff into the glass of the student beside me and said, "Come on, man, say a *L'Chaim*. Say a toast!" He looked at me in disbelief. "I don't know if I can respect a rabbi who says 'man,'" he told me. "Let alone one who polishes off a half bottle of Smirnoff!" But a rabbi is not someone who never drinks. Rather, he is someone who drinks for reasons other than just getting drunk. Perhaps to rid himself of inhibitions that make him feel distant from the people around his table so that he can truly welcome them warmly. The reason I say *L'Chaim* on the Sabbath is to make it holy and celebrate the greatest blessing of all—that I am alive to celebrate another Sabbath!

Which brings me to the subject of your adopted son, Uri. All of us want to treat our children as the Sabbath, as something holy and special. But your son has become to you like a missed Sabbath. Rather than having all your children around your Sabbath table, feeling whole and complete, you have a child who is missing from your life. Who is this child to you, who on the one hand is your flesh and blood, but on the other hand addresses someone else as "father"? Parenthood consists of two components. There is first the issue of those who give the child his life. Only then is there the second issue of who nurtures that life and raises it into adulthood.

Which is more important, nature or nurture? As Jews, we are in a good position to answer this, since the Jewish people are unique among both the nations and religions of the world in that we are both a nation and a religion. Even atheist Jews who never observe the Sabbath or Passover are as Jewish as Abraham and Moses, so nature would seem to triumph over nurture. On the other hand, one of the many things that

Judaism attempted to reverse in the ancient world was the phenomenal emphasis on blood in general, and in having the correct blood in particular. Along came Judaism and sparked a revolution, standing all these ideas of race and blood on their head. Judaism proclaimed that men and women should be judged by their actions rather than by their lineage. Nobility of birth was a poor substitute for nobility of spirit. The son of the king will be judged by the same standard as the son of the maidservant. Blood was only one aspect, a highly insignificant dimension of a human being. But a far more important aspect was how that individual treated others. The result is the Western world as we know it, where the privileges of kings and princes have long been abolished, and democracy rewards all people according to personal merit.

In terms of your son, he will always be yours on one level for, after all, he has your blood. But he belongs to his adopted family on a deeper level. They have raised him and called him "son," and he owes them his allegiance. If, God forbid, you discovered that Daniel, to whom you have been the most exemplary father, had been caught in a mix-up at the hospital and was actually someone else's boy, would you not still love him as your son? And would you not expect him still to treat you as his father?

But there is more. As rabbi to the Jewish students at Oxford for nearly a dozen years, I saw many of my students struggle with the issue of adoption. I honestly never knew at first that it was such a big deal for them. At my elementary school in Miami, there were several kids who were adopted. But it never seemed to bother them. My two first cousins in Miami were adopted, and yet did not feel compelled to find their biological parents. Yet, when students reach a more mature age, it does seem to begin to haunt them. The desire to know their biological origins creeps up on them, catching them unawares.

One of these students was a brilliant and beautiful Rhodes Scholar from Texas. She was not Jewish, but she used to come to all our L'Chaim events. Although she had no intention of converting, she got so into Judaism that she actually set up a Talmud study group, which I taught once a week. One day, she told me that she was adopted and had decided, after ten years of deliberation, to seek out her real parents. The mother who raised her felt hurt and rejected by her decision and pleaded with her to let old ghosts lie. But she felt that closure would not be brought into her life until she found out her true biological origin. It took her two years, but she finally got her biological mother's address. The woman was working as a social worker in upstate New York. Jessica just turned up on her doorstep. There is no happy ending to this story because her biological mother had had her when she was sixteen years old, and had never mentioned it to the man she eventually married. Her mother was horrified and coldly told her to go away and never come back. Jessica returned to Oxford more depressed than ever. Her studies suffered commensurably.

I went to her and told her that she was being self-indulgent. Home is the place where you feel most loved. Jessica was amazingly fortunate in having two very loving parents, even if they weren't of her actual blood. Uri, you have the most amazing family. Few men have wives who are as devoted as Hanna is to you. And few fathers have children who are as devoted to them as Daniel and Natalie are to you. This is your home—the son who you have never known is a distant relation by comparison. But because you were kind enough to take me into your confidence, Uri, I will reveal to you something that I have not discussed with anyone before—not even with my own wife. You may dismiss this as inconsequential, but it is something about which I too feel the need to unburden myself.

Because of my parent's ugly marriage, and because of the lower-middle-class family I was a part of, I grew up wishing that I could have been born into a different family. I used to fantasize about it all the time, and this attitude later spilled over into my married life as well. I dated Debbie for three months, and I knew from nearly the first instant that she was the girl I would marry. I knew that she was perfect for me, that she complemented me completely. But that scared me enormously as well. She complemented me because she was everything I wasn't: compassionate, immensely humble and unassuming, and totally devoted to other people with no need nor desire for recognition. She exuded a humility and a selflessness that at once humbled and startled me. Because Debbie's essence was quiet and good, I knew that she wasn't going to help my career in an overt sense. That she wasn't going to give speeches for me, or edit my books. Her main strengths lay in different areas. I loved her because I knew that through her kindness and goodness she would bring redemption into my life, make me feel appreciated even when I wasn't performing, and teach me to value the more subtle and precious things in life that will never appear in a newspaper article and will never get one one's own TV program.

And, truth be told Uri, I spent the first six months of my married life deeply regretting that I had married her. So many of my other friends were marrying girls who were more extrovert, louder, less shy, more entertaining. They were marrying the kind of girl that you could bring your CEO home to, the kind that could keep important company entertained and laughing for hours at the dinner table. Why didn't I get the same? The women they were marrying also came with all the bells and whistles I craved. They had pedigree—their fathers were famous rabbis or they had money. Debbie had neither. Her one asset was that she exemplified the biblical woman of Valor as described by King Solomon. She was beautiful and God-fearing and was a paragon of kindness. But who cared about that? I was insecure and wanted someone who would raise my status. I was convinced that I had married down. Debbie was more in the mold of my own family. Too ordinary by far.

And yet, in hindsight, I know that God exists, and that He led me to a wife whom I, in my own superficiality, would never have chosen. I now respect and cherish my wife infinitely more than I do myself or any other woman. She is everything that I one day hope to be: secure, kind, courageous, loving, and devoted.

When Debbie and I first married, we really had no money and I couldn't pay my rent. My eldest brother, Bar Kochva, found out about my plight and began paying our rent every month until we moved to Oxford. He even gave me a credit card and told me, "Here, make sure your new wife always has the nicest clothes to wear." Similarly, whenever we visit Miami, my sister Sarala, who, thank God, has six kids of her own, knowing that we have no family in England to ever look after our children, immediately takes them all off our hands and insists on looking after them for the one or two weeks of our stay. "I'm gonna look after the kids, Shmuley. You and Debbie are on holiday. Go and rest and give your wife some time."

What I am trying to say, Uri, is that my family is perfect for me. My brothers and sisters, to whom I have remained very close, would do anything for me, and they are the best friends that I have. All it took was for me to see the blessings. For me to show the gratitude. God is good, but it takes maturity and insight to appreciate His blessings. This is where my home is, where I am loved. It is now a source of deep shame to me that I could ever have been embarrassed by my family, and I attribute it to my arrogance and insecurity. My only consolation is that I now appreciate them immensely and do everything in my power to be devoted and loving toward them.

And speaking of blessings, I thank God every day for a friend like you who exhibits the quality of a brother: someone who loves me unconditionally.

Hoping to be your brother and comforter always,

Dear Shmuley,

Kosovo is in the news. It has been in the news for weeks. I am writing with a TV muted and flickering next to my desk as thousands of people are herded into fields of deep mud to wait for food handouts and inadequate medical aid. The reporters have been comparing Milosevic to Hitler, and the Serb army thugs to the Waffen SS. They're talking about war crime trials. It is impossible not to feel implicated—for eating as I watch families starve, and for being dry and warm as I watch families freeze, and for paying taxes as our governments spend billions to answer violence with violence. War makes us all criminals.

In my career, I have met two men whose lives have pivoted on war crimes. One was a Nazi scientist. The other was a Nazi-hunter.

I was introduced to Dr. Werner von Braun by a Nasa astronaut, Captain Edgar Mitchell. Ed was the man who stood on the moon and tried to send back telepathic messages. He taught me to hold a seed in the palm of my hand and will it to sprout. I was escorted to Dr. von Braun's office, where he had masterminded the U.S. space program, and while he held his gold ring in his fist, I bent it psychically. "I have no scientific explanation for this phenomenon," he remarked.

I was not aware until later that von Braun had also designed the V1 and V2 flying bombs that killed thousands during World War II. When Germany was defeated, his team was very close to creating atomic weapons. He had worked enthusiastically for the Führer, and I believe he deserved to stand trial—if not for his scientific work, which had murderous intent, then for his use of Jewish slave labor. Instead, he was brought to the U.S., with dozens of other active Nazis, to have his slate wiped clean before setting to work on America's nuclear missile research. If the Axis powers had defeated the Allies, von Braun would have been their guiding genius. If the U.S. had bombed the Soviets, von Braun again would have been the key player. Such a tide of evil which that man barely failed to release.

The list of ex-Nazis on the U.S. payroll makes unbelievable reading: Klaus Barbie, Franz Alfred Six, Emil Augsburg, Otto Skorzeny. The Americans ran a clandestine program called Operation Paperclip. Its objective was to detach incriminating files from scientists' dossiers and clip new, bland documents in their place. This bypassed President Truman's edict that no known Nazis were to be employed. Werner von Braun had been an SS major, but this fact was conveniently lost.

Meanwhile, Germans who had risked everything to oppose the Holocaust, such as Oskar Schindler, were abandoned to business failure and bankruptcy.

A dozen years later, I met Simon Wiesenthal. His focus and concentration were inspiring, and his genuine humility shamed me—he really had no interest in fame, recognition, or money. He was obsessive about tracking down Nazis. He told me how disappointed he was in the new generation of Israeli politicians, especially the men behind the Mossad. They did not care deeply enough about the past, he believed. Justice for the dead millions was not a sufficiently high priority. The politicians, of course, argued their case from a mirror position—they were elected to care about the future. The past could not be changed, and the future must not be allowed to repeat it. If millions of man-hours were spent on breast-beating, the future would arrive in chaos and perhaps be even more dreadful than the past. Despite the constant labors of Wiesenthal, we closed the door on Nazi war crimes.

And then, when it was finally safe to turn the key, when there were only a very few living skeletons on the other side of that door, we opened it.

It seems to me a hate-filled justice that can callously extract the best minds from the worst regime, and leave the rest to skulk until all but a few of the old Nazis are dead. Then the courts can pick off the tail-enders with a great show of forensic precision.

A seventy-eight-year-old retired British Rail ticket collector was recently jailed for life by a judge at London's Old Bailey.

Fifty-five years ago, this half-deaf, half-blind man had been a Belarus police killer, joining in a systematic extermination of Jewish villagers in the Ukraine. They were the same villagers he grew up with. Anthony Sawoniuk was the name he went by at his trial. With a Serbian name, he could easily have fitted into a Kosovo hit squad. Mass murder does not change with the decades—probably no different to the slaughter of townships by Genghis Khan or Attila.

Sawoniuk was convicted on two token charges involving eighteen Jewish murders. The court heard stories from a succession of witnesses of how the twenty-three-year-old thug slaked his lust for blood by slaughtering women in the most humiliating conditions, by killing babies and old men, and those he recognized and those he had never seen before. No one wasted any sympathy on him. Nothing that is done to him now could bring a tenth of the terror and anguish his victims suffered. He deserved to be tried and convicted and sentenced to life imprisonment. But why wait till he is a seventy-eight-year-old diabetic with a heart condition?

Sawoniuk is the only ex-Nazi to be prosecuted under Margaret Thatcher's War Crimes Act. After the war, he was admitted to Britain, given a government job, paid by public money, and pensioned off at sixty-five. British taxes kept him, in work and in retirement, for more than five decades. Then British taxes, $17.5 million of them, put him on trial. During those decades, tens of thousands of war criminals lived out their lives in peace—a peace won by Allied soldiers and their families.

In Austria, Dr. Heinrich Gross is accused of nine murders at a children's hospital in Vienna during the war. His crimes, if the allegations are true, seem horrific beyond human understanding. The Austrian parliament has examined claims that hundreds of youngsters died in a euthanasia program that targeted the disabled, the bed-wetters, the illegitimate, the hare-lipped, and any particularly good-looking child who caught the doctor's eye as he did his rounds as head of Am Spiegelgrund Children's Clinic at Steinhof in 1944. The nine charges relate to nine brains in his private collection, of children aged ten days to fourteen years, which all showed signs of poisoning. Investigators believe he may have kept children's body parts for decades, using them in research that earned him an honorary cross and a top salary as one of Austria's leading neurologists and forensics experts. Dr. Gross is eighty-four. In 1951, he was cleared of one count of manslaughter. If guilty, he is one of the vilest monsters of a vile century. He has also been paid throughout his life from public funds and granted one of the most privileged and rewarding existences imaginable. Would such a monster feel remorse throughout his life? Would his days be guilt-laden and his nights be writhing torments of nightmare? I do not think so.

The condoning of war crimes has been a long, sick episode in postwar justice. It leaves depressingly little hope that mankind is really fit to mete out punishments and keep the moral balance. But it leaves still less hope that God is fit to do so.

We have been created not only capable of the most horrific acts, but also able to live with their memories. Regret and shame do not weigh a man down into the dust. For many, perhaps, the knowledge of unthinkable crimes that have gone unpunished is exhilarating. It bestows an extra layer of power on the criminal. The crime could not be prevented—the victim was powerless. Now the crime cannot be avenged—still the victim is powerless. War criminals do not live in fear of God. God hardly seems worth fearing. God did not intervene in Am Spiegelgrund Children's Clinic. Is there any real reason to fear divine retribution fifty-five years on?

Does God's justice operate like human justice, leaving the defenseless to be slain and the murderers to lead long and well-rewarded lives until, at the very end, a show of retribution is made? Is that how God works? A world without rules and a reckoning without consequence? If that is the true nature of

God, I am no longer puzzled that atrocities are allowed to happen. I am only amazed that anything good ever manages to shine through.

Yours with deep sadness,

[signature]

Dear Uri,

I have no idea why God allows so much evil and cruelty to run over the earth with so little visible retribution. Why are rotten people allowed to get away with indiscriminate wickedness? Looking at a world seemingly devoid of justice, the Psalmist cried, "Rouse yourself! Why do you sleep, O Lord? Awake, do not cast us off forever! Why do you hide Your face, ignoring our affliction and distress?" (Psalms 44:23). At times, it appears as though God is asleep and permits the wicked to get away with their crimes. I sympathize greatly with the tone of despair in your most recent letter. As we witness how evildoers flourish without restraint or retribution, it snuffs out our belief in fairness and justice. Why be good in a cruel world if the good do not seem to be rewarded and the evil do not seem to be punished?

The subject of God's silence in the face of cruelty and injustice is a common motif running through biblical and rabbinical literature. We expect God to be both the Judge of the world and its policeman, ensuring that the good guys triumph and the bad guys get locked up behind bars. We feel abandoned when God refuses to show his hand and redeem the innocent. The Jewish tradition was never to let God off the hook when it seemed as though He was abandoning the world, allowing it to become a jungle in which the mighty triumphed while the meek perished.

The pain you express in your letter, Uri, was echoed thousands of years ago in the cry and torment of God's great prophets. In the same way that there was a modern-day Holocaust, which you mention, Uri, there was also an ancient holocaust. When the Romans destroyed the Temple in the year 70 C.E., they also murdered hundreds of thousands of Jews in the process, a monstrously high percentage of all Jews alive at that time. The rabbis who watched were appalled that God allowed this to happen and that the Romans escaped unpunished.

The silence of God in the face of injustice opens ever deeper questions. Why should we not take justice into our own hands? The Bible declares that we may not take revenge. If that is so, then at least God should have been fair. If He commanded us not to take revenge, then at the very least He should have said that there is no need to take revenge because I will always enact retribution against the wicked. But every day we see the most wicked people—liars, snakes, human vermin—prospering and living in mansions, while kind and decent folk struggle to make ends meet. We see the strong oppress the weak. There is even a common belief that we must be ruthless if we are to get ahead—and it seems that this describes many big businessmen to a tee.

I struggle with this question every single day of my life. You hear that someone has defamed or slandered you—both you and I are controversial figures—and you immediately want to retaliate. All human beings find it difficult and challenging to rise above wanting to dish out to others what they dish out to us.

Uri, I too am a great admirer of Simon Wiesenthal and was privileged to host him in Oxford, where he lectured to more than one thousand students. I have also visited Wiesenthal in his documentation center in Vienna on two occasions. All he has is his trusted non-Jewish assistant Rosemarie and the files and documents with which he pursues the greatest criminals in the history of the world. And yes, if you read his book, *Justice Not Vengeance*, you really do get the impression that there is lit-

tle justice in this world. For every one Nazi criminal that Wiesenthal catches, ten thousand get away.

The classic argument for the pursuit of goodness is that the good will be rewarded in the world to come, while the wicked will be punished. Well, a lot of good that will do! Who cares that Hitler is rotting in Hell somewhere? Does that notion bring any comfort to a mother who has watched her children turned into lampshades and ash? And what kind of message is religion sending to people with this poor response? With this weak argument, aren't we really capitulating and admitting that in this world you can get away with murder? Aren't we saying, "Don't worry about being a lowlife fiend because it isn't going to catch up with you until the next world anyway"? Doesn't this just encourage people to behave indecently with the assurance that not until the next world is there any fear of retribution?

I don't have the answers to all these questions. I can't explain God's silence. I can only challenge it. But I do know why it is important to continue to be a good person even in a cruel and hideous world. A very important verse in the Bible reads: "The secret things belong to the Lord our God, but the revealed things belong to us and to our children forever, to observe all the words of this law" (Deuteronomy 29:29). God has his mysteries. But that has nothing to do with my visible need to believe in and affirm justice. God has a lot of explaining to do. But that doesn't change my responsibility to try and be a good and moral person. In the face of God's seeming silence, it is we who must step into the breach and combat injustice while promoting compassion.

There is only one strong reason why we must always be good even when it seems to make no real difference. The reason is this: it is what we all most deeply desire. For when we sin and behave cruelly, or cheat or lie or steal, we are not sinning against society. Rather, we are sinning against ourselves, for what we all want more than anything else, is to be good and decent people.

Believe it or not, even the Nazis, the greatest beasts of all times, also wanted to be remembered as good people. That's why they made such an important point of covering up their crimes, blowing up their crematoria and dismantling so many of the death camps while they still had the opportunity. And do you know that many people on death row leave testaments justifying their crimes and murders, showing that they had never done anything wrong and were simply "misunderstood" by a cold and indifferent society? Murderers are not proud of the fact. They usually have a rationalization or cover for their crimes. Even the world's worst criminals engage in PR once the end is nigh. When the war is drawing to a close, and the game of life is almost up, we all sit down and try to either cover up or explain away our misdeeds.

If any of us were asked to write our very own eulogy, what would it say? How do we want to be remembered? If a guy works on Wall Street, would his eulogy read something like this: "He was a dedicated man who got up at the crack of dawn to sell Japanese futures. His commitment to making money was such that he rarely ate lunch, and even after work, his beeper told him of the goings-on in markets across the world. He loved his parents, but had little time to visit them, but he did at least find the time to attend his grandmother's funeral in between meetings. He made sure always to use the Stairmaster for at least thirty minutes before he went to sleep, and he never, ever missed a New York Yankees game"!

I suspect that most of us would only laugh at this image. Rather, all we want is to be remembered as decent and loving people: "He had a law practice of only medium size, but was scrupulously honest in dealing with all his clients. No matter what the financial hardship, he and his wife's Friday evening Sabbath table was always brimming with guests. He worked hard to grant his family a decent standard of living, yet he always spent time with his children and did their homework with them at nights. He only ever had kind words to say about

anyone, and he lent money to those in need. He forgave slights and rarely bore grudges, and respected his friends' confidences. He did his best to clothe the naked, feed the hungry, and, if he lost his temper with anyone, he was always the first to apologize. And he made his wife feel like she was a queen."

Happiness is predicated on inner and outer harmony. Since our innermost desire is to be good, we cannot be fulfilled unless our outermost actions reflect that desire. We can't let the world corrupt us, Uri. We still have to be the wonderful people we always planned to be. In essence, the wicked have robbed themselves of the great joy of making a positive difference in someone else's life. The wicked will never know happiness because happiness presupposes having your inner and outer self—your internal and external desires—in total sync and harmony. But since the wicked do not accommodate their innermost desire they're always at war with themselves. Notice, Uri, how one of the universally admired qualities of the saints is their inner and outer serenity. When we think of righteous and saintly figures, we always focus on the peace that surrounds them. The Dalai Lama, the Lubavitcher Rebbe, and Mother Theresa immediately come to mind. The same is not true of the Hitlers and Pol Pots of this world, who are always surrounded by dark noises and turbulence.

There is a final consideration about taking revenge. Once a good friend of mine, a wealthy jeweler, was robbed at gunpoint in his own home. For two full hours, he had the horror of being tied with both his hands behind his back as his wife was taken upstairs. He thought they were taking her there to either rape or murder her, but fortunately it was only to have her open the safe and give them all her jewelry. They survived the encounter, but were severely traumatized. When I sat with him the next morning trying to bring him comfort, I asked him how he would feel if the police didn't catch the perpetrators. He said to me:

"There is little chance they will be caught. But it doesn't matter. You see, Shmuley, there are only two kinds of people in this world. Winners and losers. We are the winners. Those scoundrels are the losers. The greatest revenge is knowing that they will always be losers. They can wear my gold watch, but it will bring them no satisfaction. For me, it is a statement of hard work and achievement. For them it is a statement of theft and deception. And they will always live in permanent envy of people like us. It is not me who is in fear of them. It is they who fear me. Every day, they look at the house that I live in, thanks to my own backbreaking labor, and they ask themselves, 'What can we take today that belongs to him so that I can be like him?' I control them. I am the image of the person they want to be, but are too corrupt ever to become. I own them. They may have momentary victories. But they go back to the same feeling of emptiness that pervades their entire life."

The Nazis had a momentary victory over us, Uri. And in their moment of triumph, they took away one out of every three Jews in the world. But just remember: it is they who are today on the run; it is they who are pathetically hiding away with secret identities, afraid of their own shadows; they who are rotting in their graves; they who live and cower in fear. Moreover, it is they who have children who are ashamed of them and in most cases deny ever having been related to them. And it is they whom the Almighty will indeed one day punish at the time when "the whole earth shall be filled with the knowledge of the Lord, like the water, of the sea which cover the ocean's floor."

Yours in great hope,

Dear Shmuley,

I hardly need to write. How many times have I phoned you this week? Twenty? How many times have you phoned me?

You were never off the phone. On Wednesday, I think, you rang me on the main house line and on my cell phone at the same time. And then tonight you were kind enough to share your Sabbath table with my whole family. We have talked day and night. You were worried about problems in your organization and with dwindling finances. You are concerned with the constant attacks against your character which have been intensified ever since you published *Kosher Sex*. It's been a tough week for you.

But you made it tougher on yourself. I've been telling you this endlessly—Shmuley, stop worrying, don't let them get to you, you'll give yourself a heart attack; take a step back, take three steps back. Take it easy. Did you listen? For a few seconds, maybe. Long enough to take a deep breath, thank me for my generous words of wisdom, and launch into another cascade of anxiety.

So yes, I have to write. Light one of your Cuban cigars, the ones as thick as my forearm, and clamp your mouth shut around it. Breathe these words right down with the smoke.

You have been afraid. Ever since synagogues around the country began canceling speaking invitations to you because of your authorship of the book, you have been living in fear. You have been villified and slandered. So OK, that's more people in the world who don't love Rabbi Boteach. There are enough of them, after all—you were never afraid of taking people on.

For once in your life, Shmuley, you are Sir Galahad—virtuous on the inside, armor-clad on the outside.

Except Sir Galahad's knees never knocked in fear. All week, you have been aware of a tin tattoo, a metallic little drumming as your armored knees rattled against each other. You have been so ashamed of your fear that you let it run into panic. You saw your fear, and it terrified you.

That kind of fear almost finished my career. It cost me millions of dollars, and it held me up to ridicule across America. When I went on *The Tonight Show* with Johnny Carson in 1973,

I was so much in the grip of fear that my hands were trembling. You can see it on the video as I try to dowse for water hidden in metal canisters. I was stupid with fear, sick with fear, almost blind with fear, that on TV, before America's biggest TV audience, I would be exposed.

No one has ever unmasked me as a fraud, because I am not a fraud. The powers I claim to possess, I really do have. I can read images in your mind, I can bend metal by rubbing it lightly, I can move a compass needle by staring at it, I can sprout a seed in the palm of my hand. These abilities have been demonstrated to scientists in their laboratories—first to Puthoff and Targ at Stanford Research Institute, later to Byrd at the Naval Surface Weapons Center, to Hasted at Birkbeck in London, and to Hawke at Lawrence Livermore. All these tests yielded positive results, under conditions that totally ruled out trickery. To prove me a fraud, you would have to disprove every one of those tests, and innumerable others.

To a skeptic, that counts for nothing. Skeptics know better than the scientists. Though they don't have the scientific training, the laboratories, or the experience of the tests themselves, skeptics have something more important. They have certainty. Unshakable certainty that paranormal physics are impossible, paranormal experiments are all rigged or flawed, and Uri Geller is a fake. Sometimes, if they want to seem magnanimous, they say I am a very good fake. One or two have gone so far as to call me the greatest fake in the history of conjuring (well, thanks for nothing). A few who really dislike me say I am not a very good fake at all. One, a Canadian conjurer called Randolph James, who goes under the stagename of James "The Amazing" Randi, says spoon-bending is the kind of child's magic trick he's seen printed on the back of cereal boxes.

Johnny Carson was a skeptic. And The Amazing Randi was one of the conjurers he used to police me on his show.

In 1973, I was riding very high—riding for a fall, I can see now. At the time, I thought I was going to be a superstar forever, getting bigger and bigger with no limits. All I had to do was carry on blowing minds. There were billions of minds in the world, and millions of new ones were born every day. I could keep it up for ever. Already in the States I had bent spoons for Barbara Walters, Mike Douglas, Jack Parr, Tom Snyder, and Merv Griffin. Carson was bigger than all of them, but then that was the logical progression. After I'd torn the skeptic's badge off Johnny Carson's jacket, whose mind would I blow next? They would have to give Richard Nixon his own talk show, I said, and we would see if the President of the United States would dare to let me read his mind. I was really riding for a fall.

I knew it, too. I would not admit to the fear, but it was all over me. My white knuckles were getting whiter, my vertigo sent the whole of America spinning around me. Everybody told me Carson was serious about his skepticism. He wasn't just cynical, he was certain—Geller was a fraud, and he would love to hand me my biggest ever audience…and humiliate me.

He did that. Or I let my fear do it to me. What I feared most was what happened. That was inevitable. In the hours before that show, I feared exposure so deeply that I thought of nothing else. I was totally focused on humiliation. It was as if I was praying for failure, praying with the greatest intensity my mind could muster. Nothing else intruded on my concentration. It was failure, failure, failure all the way to the cameras. And my prayers were answered.

Everything failed. The spoon didn't bend. I couldn't tell which of the metal cylinders on the coffee-table contained water. I tried again and again, and the people in the auditorium were howling with laughter when Johnny rolled his eyes up. Of course they laughed; he was funny. And I was hilarious. Hilariously weird. Hilariously hopeless.

For a few months, I beat myself up over my performance on *The Tonight Show*. I was angry all the time, and I took it out on the people around me. I couldn't focus—I started one thing, switched to another, broke off to complain to a reporter that

Carson had set me up, gave up on that rant to sit and sulk for hours. I was a whole lot of fun to be with. Dozens of friends, including three or four really good, close, dear friends, tried to sympathize and share my troubles. Like most people who are obsessed with their own stardom, I didn't make the effort to reach out in return. I didn't try to understand what our friendship meant to them or how I could take a little sting out of their own fears. Other people's fears meant nothing in my misery. The Carson debacle had cost me a lot of credibility in America's eyes, and I was doing nothing to repair the damage when I sulked and ranted. All I could think of was the opportunity missed. The millions I would have made if Johnny's spoon had snapped. The book deals, the movie contracts, the big, big bank account.

What I didn't know then, what I spent the next twenty years learning, is that life is not a one-shot gamble. Nothing is make or break. When something goes wrong, you should mark it down to the losses. When something goes right, you have to celebrate. Put a mark on the credit side. But never imagine you've won the game of life with that one success. And don't let the fear of failure obsess you, because nothing fails like fear.

Fear is raw loneliness—fear that no one can feel just the way you feel, think just the way you think. Fear is the idea that you live and die entirely on your own and that the pain you feel is 100 percent your own pain. That is the only fear in the world, when all the details are stripped away. That's the fear that has obsessed you all week—that your life will be shredded and no one will feel it but you. Your wife will suffer if you are destroyed, but she has her children and her own life to lead. Your children will suffer if their father is crushed, but they are young—they'll survive, they'll grow into their own lives. All that pain will be yours alone to bear. That's what you fear.

The way to switch off fear is to share someone else's. Think yourself into their thoughts when their minds are beset with nightmares. Feel as they are feeling, suffer the pain that they think is theirs only. I have tried this week to share your thoughts and agonies. I have smashed my fist down on the shining surface of your panic, to shatter your concentration, even if it was only for a couple of seconds. I had to break that focus on fear, to keep you from praying yourself deeper into loneliness.

You didn't know it, but every moment you were sharing your fears with me, you were easing my own prayers. When the mind is focused on a friend, it cannot be pointing inward. The harder I tried to share your burden, the lighter my own heart became. Long from now, when we have both forgotten exactly why this week seemed such a crisis, I will still be grateful to you. You will be less grateful to me—you were only aware of my friendship for fragmented moments, while I was aware of it all the time. That is the essential lesson of fear. For the loneliness to be broken, it is never enough to receive friendship. What matters is to give it.

Be strong,

P.S. Shmuley, look at the photograph attached to this letter. It was waiting on my e-mail when I returned from your home tonight. Look at the note that came with it: "I got a tumor in brain, and physicians said there isn't nothing to do. Please help me. I have seven years old, don't ask me to think hard on you because I am at Hospital (Emergency Care Unit) and I have not strength or age to do that. Help me. Mafalda."

Shmuley, do you think you have troubles?

Dear Uri,

I found your last letter immensely profound and enlightening. You have a talent for lifting me up whenever I feel down and defeated.

Your letter also brought to mind images of the great Rabbi Israel Baal Shem Tov, founder of the Jewish Hassidic movement. The Baal Shem, as he was known, maintained that the best way to help ourselves through a problem was to help someone else first. By showing love and concern for others, we demonstrate that our problems never have the power to overwhelm us. Love and compassion make us so much larger than we would otherwise be. I thank you, therefore, not only for comforting me but for saving me from the suffocating silence of my own selfishness.

I was also very moved by what you said about life not being a one-shot deal. This is a lesson whose truth becomes more apparent as I get older and which goes right back to our understanding of righteousness. To most people, the righteous man is someone who never contends with evil. He only entertains good thoughts and always seeks to help people. But the Cabbalists said that the truly righteous person is one who struggles to do the right thing amidst a predilection to do otherwise. Life is not about one big victory, but rather about always being engaged in the battle. Those who struggle are much more interesting, much more real, and much more righteous than those to whom everything comes naturally. So I thank you as well for your excellent point about life consisting of the sum total of our actions, rather than resting upon a single occurrence.

But that does not mean that we do not live in fear of a single episode derailing us. You and I are public figures, Uri. Editors will do anything to try and find that one thing that will sell their newspapers for a week, even though it might destroy a life forever. Their reporting of the controversy that *Kosher Sex* engendered in the Jewish community was designed to further ignite that furor. It takes great skill and wisdom to know what to do in these situations, and it was sobering to discover over the past few weeks that these were qualities I mostly lacked.

I have indeed been gripped by fear, and I am not proud of it. I had never expected that a book that I had written could, on the one hand, save so many marriages and, on the other, create so many enemies. The Talmud says that of all the crowns available to mortal men, the crown of a good name is the most precious of all. It is said of Alexander the Great that he decreed that he be buried with his hands outside his coffin in order to teach his soldiers this valuable lesson: although he had conquered the entire world in his lifetime, his hands were empty when he departed. All we really have in this world, Uri, is our name and our reputations. That is what is everlasting, and when people impugn my character, I take it to heart.

Uri, I have always been a controversial figure and have spent much of my life shaking up the Jewish establishment. I have faced scorching criticism and never flinched. But when they try to say that I am a fraud, that the rabbi who writes about sex only does what he does in order to promote himself, the pain is real. I have discovered that my skin is not half as thick as I once supposed. You see, Uri, our critics want to rob us of the only human virtue that really matters: being real. They are not saying that we are bad people, or that we are stupid people, or that we are misguided people. They are saying that we are not people at all. We are not real. We are fakes. They are attempting to rob us of our very humanity. And when someone rips your heart out and tries to replace it with a heart of plastic, it hurts like hell.

So, yes, I have lived in fear, and I don't like it. There are few emotions that make life as unpleasant as does fear. To live in fear is to have your life made into a nightmare of anxiety and worry, and so those who live in fear witness the diminishment of their humanity. To fear is to shrivel prematurely, like in old age. Notice that advanced age and fear (or worry) have two things in common: they both sap our energy and they both leave lines on our face.

Coming back to the Baal Shem, another reason that your letter made me think of him was that he became my hero as a young boy of ten, when I learnt his own approach to fear, and how he had come to fear none but God. The Baal Shem was orphaned as a boy of eight. Left with the prospect of being totally alone, he resolved that the first thing he would conquer was his fear. He got into a routine of walking nightly through the terrifying Eastern European forests all by himself. With shadows haunting him and bloodcurdling howls piercing his heart at every turn, he continued to walk until he had become a part of the forest, and feared nothing within it. To me, there was something immensely noble in this action. My God, what a life to lead! A life free of fear.

For someone who has always found fear to be the most degrading and humiliating of human emotions, this was wonderful. And now it seems even more so. Because there are only two motivating forces in life, Uri: love and fear. Up until now, the world has principally used fear as the engine of human advance and historical progression. Religions have told us that if you don't believe, you're going to go to the eternal Bar-B-Q. Governments have told us that if you don't obey, then you're going to go to the gulag or the concentration camp. Teachers have told us that if we don't try harder in class, then we're going to get demoted. And husbands have told wives that if you don't lose a few pounds, they're going to find a younger, more delectable dish.

And it's worked, Uri. It's worked. People are afraid so they pay their taxes, students study for exams, and wives continue to go on diets. Fear drives the entire system, and it all works. Except for one very important thing. It has no joy. People aren't happy. They go to church, but do so as a matter of rote. They pay their taxes, but shed tears as they write the checks. They study at school, but complain how much they hate it. And they continue to marry, but think about strangers when they make love to each other. Fear can make you move forward, but never with a smile on your face. Joy, on the other hand, makes you feel light, like you can float. Fear places an unmanageable burden on your back, and you walk as if encumbered by the weight of a nine-hundred-pound gorilla.

Like many of the people who come to me for counseling and guidance, Uri, I am riddled with fears. Some are rational. Most are ridiculous. But I have been able to reduce them all to a single idea. There is really only one human fear. And that is the fear that we don't matter. That we aren't special. That we aren't unique. That if we didn't wake up from our sleep tomorrow morning, perhaps no one would even notice!

Think about it. A child fears things like noises in the night and monsters. When that happens he goes running into his parents' room. Why? Because to the monster he doesn't matter. He'll just eat him and get on with his business. But Mommy and Daddy hold him in their arms when he cries. To them he matters. So Mommy and Daddy are the perfect antidote to his terror. The greatest fear of a business or professional type is the fear of failure. Fear of failing has forever been the great male fear especially. A woman who stays home and looks after the family entertains the fear of losing the love of the man she adores or that her kids will go off to college and not need her any more. At root, all of these fears are the same. They are all based on the fear of losing our dignity and becoming insignificant. Of not being unique. Of being less than ordinary. This is why we all fear death. We're afraid that tomorrow morning we won't wake up. And still the world will continue to function happily without us. There was nothing special while we were alive if there is no trace of us left after we are gone.

Take away a man's dignity, Uri, and you make him into your slave. Without dignity he becomes indistinguishable from an animal or a thing. Purge him of dignity and you have robbed him of his will. And that's why you can enslave him. Because he is already dead on the inside. A man has got to be able to point at something and feel pride. "You see that? I made that. It's mine." "You see that child over there? Well, he's *my* son. He's mine." But a slave can say none of those things. His work, even his children, belong to his master. To be free you must have dignity. Fear is the ultimate imprisoning emotion and it robs us of our dignity. What on earth can counteract it?

The overwhelming majority of people fight this fear through professional achievement, amassing status and wealth. "Here, I'm gonna prove that I matter. I'm not just part of the indistinguishable morass. Look at the kind of car I drive. The kind of clothes I wear. The house I live in." If you make a lot of money, then people notice you and take you seriously. If you become a famous model, then cameras flash their bulbs at you. If you become a president of a country, then all its citizens salute and respect you.

The problem with this is manifold. It is just not a solution. By distinguishing yourself in other people's eyes, you become a slave to public opinion. You have now set the locus for your importance outside of yourself and have empowered others to determine your self-worth. You will be condemned to a life of misery since you are dependent on other people's whims. You only exist when they crane their necks in your direction. Otherwise, you have vanished.

Others counteract fear through love. They get people to love them, and this makes them always feel important. No doubt, this is a better solution than the shallow pursuit of money, status, and material objects. But it suffers from the same defect. You are special only because people notice you. There is nothing intrinsically unique about you. And if they forget you—and love always fluctuates and wanes—you go back to being a big zero.

Still others maintain that you have to love yourself. Only then can you feel special and important. But who are they kidding? Find me one person in the world who takes himself so seriously that being in a relationship with himself is sufficient and he never requires anyone else's approval. As Socrates said, man is a social creature. He cannot feel significant unless he is connected to and impacts something outside himself.

To counteract this deepest of human fears, that we ultimately don't matter and are of no consequence, we must first
identify its root cause: the reason that people feel so naturally
inadequate is that they feel the weight of the infinite pressing
against them at all times. We feel God's presence about us and
then feel our own worthlessness. The cause of this feeling is
that God is significant and we are insignificant. God is eternal
and we are mortal. God is all good and we are flawed.

The only way to deal with this is by connecting ourselves
with God. People with a deep spiritual core rarely experience
the same fears as their secular counterparts. Pious men and
saints of all religious denominations have one thing in common,
whether or not they have wealth: they all demonstrate a phenomenal nobility of character. What empowered millions of
Jews to lay down their lives for God? And what empowered
Christians to be eaten by lions? It was the fact that they felt
connected to and loved by God. Since they were connected to
the greatest and most special being, they felt great and special,
and they had no fear connected to the all-powerful. They did
not feel powerless. Attached to the infinite, they did not feel
limited. And anchored in the eternal, they had no fear of the
transient. They did not fear death because the fear of death is
based on the anxiety of ceasing to be. But connected to God as
they were, they knew that they could never cease to be. Our
real goal must be to remain connected to the source of all life
at all times. Only then can we know no fear.

But there is also something we humans can do to enhance
the dignity of all human beings and help them counteract their
fear. We can simply take them seriously and make them feel
like indeed they are special.

Every time we take someone's opinion seriously, listen to
them intently, or compliment them on how great they look, or
show gratitude for some favor they did for us, we give them dignity and enhance their humanity. The highest form of charity is
to give to someone without his knowing, so that he doesn't feel

indebted and doesn't lose his dignity. For me, Uri, the very definition of goodness is the act of enhancing human dignity at all times. Even if you feed the hungry stranger, but make him feel like a lowly parasite, you have not done a good deed.

And so, Uri, I too must learn to find my dignity in areas other than fame and attempting to write bestselling books. This is the main reason that I am so ashamed of the fear that you point out I have exhibited over the last period. In reality, it betrays my disconnection from God. Being afraid of public attack over your convictions is an indication that you have empowered others to determine your dignity. And the essence of human strength is to leave the determination of your worth firmly in the hands of the Creator.

The ancient Jewish sage Hillel once said, "Those who seek fame, end up losing their name." The ancient rabbis further said that "those who pursue renown, it runs away from them. While those who run away from renown, it ends up pursuing them." After my American book tour, Uri, I came back pursuing renown. I never expected to write a bestselling book, and the explosion of *Kosher Sex* on the American scene was like a dream come true. But the negative publicity and attacks on my character upon my return reminded me that you are never important because the newspapers say you are. Rather, you are important because when you walk into your home at night there are children who run up to you and hug you, and there are friends—like you, Uri—who are on the phone already, holding on the line, to offer support and encouragement. There is one more thing that I learned about fear this week, Uri, and it is this: you can only be frightened when you are alone. Fear is predicated on a sense of abandonment. Walking down the street alone is frightening, while doing so with a group of friends is not. Because, when we're alone we feel vulnerable, and when we have friends, we feel unbreakable.

I once told you that I would be your herald to the world. Everyone knows that you can bend spoons in someone's hand.

But they don't know that you can also break the darkness of people's hearts, dissipate the gloom that has accumulated in their minds. You can indeed make a seed sprout in your hands (I have witnessed it myself), but more important than that, you can cause hope to grow and flourish in people's souls. And although you can read people's minds, what is more important is that you can heal their hearts. I know that you have helped to heal mine.

Your formerly frightened friend,

Dear Shmuley,

As I walked through customs control at Lisbon airport to appear on a Saturday night show on Portuguese TV this week, the man with a gun at his waist asked politely why I was travelling on a Mexican passport and why it was registered to Uri Geller-Freud. I explained the Mexican practice was to add to a man's surname his mother's maiden name, and my Berlin-born mother was related to Dr. Sigmund Freud. And I also told him that passport cost me $950 million.

I could have been rich in Mexico. I have never seen wealth like the endless shelves of gold and gems and jewelry and cars and carpets and Jacuzzis and chairs and cabinets and candelabras and fine clothes that lay in the president's massive storehouses, guarded by elite commandos with orders to shoot to kill at the first suggestion of armed robbery. I was confronted by a temptation out of ancient myth, an offer that seemed to come directly from God—"You can have everything you ever desired, Geller. I'll give you more clothes than you could wear in a hundred lifetimes, more cars than you could drive in a hundred races, more money than you could spend in a hundred centuries. You can have sex with more beautiful women, in more gorgeous palaces, than any man ever dreamed of. Reach out your hand and it is yours."

You think I'm fantasizing, but I swear I am only telling you about the face of this temptation. Behind the mask lay greater temptations, of magnificent and lush corruption, more complex than I could begin to comprehend. Only after twenty-five years, and a long study of the depths to which a man's nature will sink, am I really aware of the intensity of God's diabolical offer.

One illustration: I was dining in Mexico City with a cabal of business men. They told me of their undying admiration for the President's wife, Señora Carmen Romana de López Portillo, who happened to be my closest friend in Mexico. They told me of the intricate brooch that they had commissioned, at a cost of tens of thousands of dollars, from an internationally famous jeweler. They followed me to the washroom after our meal, and I was handed a leather pouch, so heavy that I almost dropped it on the shining white floor tiles. Under the bright strip lights, I peeled back the paper-fine calfskin, and a flash of brilliant yellow flickered about the room. I glanced around me. Among the urinals and handbasins of a Mexico City restaurant, I was holding an ingot of solid gold.

I slowly slipped off its protective sleeve and examined the underside. The metal felt warm and soft enough for me to have dug my fingers into it, like a living organ. The imprint of a Zurich bank was clearly visible.

That single bar could have bought fifty schools or ten million meals for the city's poorest urchins, the uncounted children who lived by scavenging. Its value was nothing compared to the boundless wealth that was overspilling the racks in the presidential warehouses.

I called the President's wife by her pet name, Muncy. She had seen me on a Televisa show one night in the mid-seventies and arrived with twenty bodyguards at my suite in the Camino Real hotel as I was preparing to check out for the airport.

Muncy picked up the phone and cancelled my seats. Then she demanded a private demonstration and had me delivered to her villa by motorcade, with bike outriders screaming through the choking traffic and thick smoked glass shielding me from the dirty realities of Mexico City. In the drawing room of her home, she had her cook open a canteen of solid silver cutlery on the sofa beside me. "Bend that fork," she commanded, extending a fingernail so red it could have been dipped in blood, "and the set is yours." As I lifted the fork, its prongs writhed together, like panic-stricken eels. The stem sagged. Holding it only by my thumb and forefinger, at its spatulate end, I held out the fork to Muncy. The neck snapped and Muncy shrieked. Then I closed up the canteen carefully and said with a smile, "Your offer is very kind, but I must refuse: I am afraid the collection is incomplete."

She was not quite the president's wife then. Her husband, José López Portillo, was professor of political science at National University and Mexico's president-in-waiting. The country knew what was coming to it, and already Muncy was treated like a woman born to save or condemn the lives of millions with a crook of her finger. She was not a cruel woman, nor an insensitive one. But she was capricious, and she wore the mantle of power like an actress wears a fur coat to conceal her nakedness.

We traveled the country in her Sabreliner. This private jet was built like a fighter—I once ordered the pilot to execute a barrel roll, and he poured a glass of water before leaning into the maneuver, and as the Sabreliner twisted a corkscrew path through the sparse air above the Gulf, not a drop of water spilled from the tumbler. Muncy took me to Palenque, where the Temple of the Inscriptions within the Great Pyramid was thrown open for me, and I examined the 1,300-year-old sarcophagus of King Pacal, with its walls patterned with carvings of an ancient astronaut astride a blazing UFO. We flew to Guanajuato where, in the Museum of the Mummies, I saw 150-year-old bodies preserved by the mountain's unique soil and now on show, staring with empty eyes at the ghouls and fun-seekers who come to gawp at them.

And I performed for her friends. One such was Jorge Dias Serrano, director-general of Petroleos Mexicanos, who was present when I dowsed for a tiny phial of oil concealed within the presidential offices. I found it, buried within a flowerpot, and Serrano invited me to inspect several possible drilling sites, first by dowsing over maps, then on helicopter flyovers. I told him which sites felt rich, and his engineers asked dozens of questions. Later, I got paid.

I was made a treasury agent, which gave me a license to swagger with jewel-studded silver pistols at my hip or in holsters at my shoulders and to fly in and out of the States as often as I wished, with full diplomatic privileges. No one searched me, and I could carry what I liked. I was given a golden ticket on AeroMexico—free flights wherever I wanted, whenever I wanted. If a flight was full, someone got turfed off. If a flight was about to leave, it got held until I was aboard. Nobody but the president of the airline and the president of the country possessed golden tickets, and Muncy probably had to threaten a senior director with imprisonment before I could join the club.

Muncy took me to the warehouse soon after she officially became Mexico's first lady. The gifts from polite nations and corrupt citizens were still being poured into crates, but already my benefactress knew where to find what she wanted from those infinite racks of riches. She pulled down a bone chest, its arched lid patterned by engravings of an orgy, with Inca-style bodies knotted in fascinating invention. She pushed it open—it had not been padlocked. In the white interior lay a hundred glistening watches. I saw the Rolexes first, with their bracelets like caterpillar tracks and their gilt frames burning. They were molten drops of unabashed power. I tried to hold back my hands. Beneath the Rolexes were smaller, more discreet time-pieces, with platinum dials and rows of sapphires on the hands.

Muncy said, "Take one." I reached in without answering. I was struck dumb by this sight. Perhaps the value of all the watches was less than the price of the gold bar that had been placed in my hands a few nights earlier, but so much gold seemed meaningless to me: it was like seeing ten thousand of the most exquisite meals scraped onto one vast platter. But the bone box of watches was different. I could comprehend this. I was a connoisseur of what people wore to express their power and their wealth. I knew how many senators and congressmen could be adorned with these potent symbols. I believed in the advertisements that said a man was no more than the watch he wore.

I did not take a Rolex. I wanted Muncy to wonder whether I already owned one. I picked up something much smaller, much more delicate, much less obvious. Later I discovered it was a platinum Vacheron Constantin, worth at least 50 percent more than the most extravagant Rolex.

I never slept with Muncy. She treated me like a lover, or an adored pet, with open shows of public affection. She touched me, kissed me, flared with violent jealousy if I flirted for even a moment with another woman. But she did not bed me. There was an agreement, thought and never spoken, from the first hour when we were alone together in the Hotel Camino Real, with only her twenty bodyguards outside the door. We could love, but not make love.

This fine distinction was wasted on the Mexico City gossips. We did not care—Muncy lived in a realm of power and wealth infinitely distant from all of her enemies. Her husband had brought peace and prosperity to a privileged sector of the country, oil was being drilled, revolution had been castrated. Muncy was untouchable. Then the tide turned, and the President's ground began to slide away from him. Reports appeared, hinting that Muncy had made unwise friendships. Then it was suggested I was an unwise friend. Then a photograph was published of us dining in a prominent restaurant, though the caption suggested we were indulging in unfettered and bestial passion.

I received a warning from one of Muncy's bodyguards, a man I liked. I believed it came directly from the president. It advised me to leave Mexico before I was imprisoned, or killed. One hour later, I used my golden ticket for the last time.

I did not take the gold bar with me. I had handed it back, in the washroom, rather than promise to deliver a business card to the president's wife. I did not leave Mexico with huge reserves stealthily stored in numbered Zurich bank accounts. I had refused all Muncy's offers of money gifts. In Mexico, I lived on the proceeds of corruption and corporate theft, executed on a scale more vast than the Third Reich's looting or Marcos' bloodsucking. I wallowed in wealth while, in every city where our Sabreliner landed, tens of thousands of children were starving. And I never once spoke a word, never hinted that Muncy's storehouses were killing millions by their obscene inactivity. Never tried to grab a handful of diamonds and hurl them into a crowd. What would that have achieved?

Sometimes journalists visit my home today by the Thames, where original Dalis hang on the walls, gifts from the artist, and huge televisions and hi-fis stand in every room. They ask, "How can you claim to be a spiritual man, and be so affected by wealth?" And I think, "You should have known me when…"

I still have the Vacheron Constantin watch, and I still have one of the guns, a traced silver Colt, which I keep in a New York strongbox. I no longer want to handle it, but I would not like to give it away. It represents the arsenal I might have owned.

Jorge Dias Serrano, the head of PeMex, went to prison for his part in a corruption ring that embezzled $9.5 billion from the Mexican oil boom. I might have stipulated, before I began to dowse for that oil, a 10 percent stake in that boom. Even if I had collected only 10 percent of what was creamed off, I might have pocketed $950 million. If I had been allowed to collect. If I had not succumbed to a heart attack, or an unexpected suicide, or a mysterious disappearance. Instead, my payment for finding oil was a passport. I got the right to travel as Uri Geller-Freud, of joint Mexican nationality. And I got to live to enjoy it.

In deep friendship,

Dear Uri,

Ah, the lust for cash and celebrity. We are all infected by the plague. But given the choice between the two, I have always wanted to be famous rather than rich.

One of the things that you and I—and ultimately all people—have in common is the desire to be recognized. That elusive spotlight is something that I have been chasing throughout my life. From an early age, I have been conscious of my desire for recognition. I have seen it as my Achilles' heel, ever since I had a fairly quick taste of fame and the world's great celebrities at an early age.

When I was twenty-two, I founded the L'Chaim Society in Oxford. Because of the prestige of the university, and thanks to some strong international contacts we had, I was quickly able to secure some of the biggest names in the world to come and lecture on our behalf to the students. At twenty-three, I booked President Reagan. Unfortunately, after six months of preparation for his visit and the expense of tens of thousands of pounds, he cancelled just one week before he was due to arrive. But we quickly bounced back by booking Mikhail Gorbachev, just after he left the presidency of the Soviet Union. Then, in quick succession, we hosted everyone from Boy George to Diego Maradona, Javier Perez de Cuellar, Jon Voight, Leonard Nimoy, professor Stephen Hawking, Yitzhak Shamir, Benjamin Netanyahu, Elie Wiesel, Simon Wiesenthal, Shimon Peres, Jerry Springer, and Bob Hawke, among many others. Since I acted as host, I became friendly with many of these people. They invited me to their homes, and I could take endless pictures with them and drop their names at cocktail parties.

From twenty-three onward, I was writing books, some big, some small, and being courted by TV producers. At thirty, I published *Kosher Sex*, which I never expected would sell to anyone outside the Jewish community. Amazingly, it became an international bestseller and was translated into eleven languages. I appeared on the leading TV and radio shows in the United States, Britain, Canada, Australia, Israel, and South Africa.

Yet as my star rose, I was having less and less time for people. It bothered my wife enormously. She felt I was being seduced by the glamour and was gradually losing my bearings. Things came to a head, and Debbie and I had an argument. I was in the midst of the British book tour for *Kosher Sex*. A couple whose marriage was crumbling had had two meetings with me, and they requested a third. But I had no time. From morning to night, I was doing interviews—and selling books. I was on the phone being interviewed by a magazine when Debbie came into the room and told me that the distraught wife was on the phone to talk to me. I made a hand gesture to Debbie, as if to say, "*Cosmopolitan* magazine is interviewing me, and you want me to speak to this woman who never leaves me alone about her marriage. She can wait!" My wife walked out of my office in disgust. Later that night, she refused to speak to me. "You're becoming someone I don't recognize," she said.

I felt bad about what had happened and went to discuss it with a famous friend of mine who once worked helping people and now had his own television show. "Stop feeling guilty," my friend said to me. "These people who want your time and never pay you for it or deliver a positive message to show you zero appreciation, they're the selfish ones, not you. You don't have to accommodate every parasite in the world just to appease your Jewish guilt. You have every right to pursue and advance your career. Besides, what would God prefer? That you address two people in the privacy of your office, or deliver a positive message to a million people through the pages of the *New York Times?*" I was happy to have the corroboration of his logic, extreme as it may have been, and went and told Debbie that I had a powerful and wise ally, who backed me up. But she would have none of it. "You're just being selfish. I respect you when you help people. Not when you sit in front of a TV camera."

This is something that I have struggled with a great deal, Uri. But it is a battle that Debbie is winning and I am losing. The ancient rabbis of the Talmud said that life is about three things: *Torah, Avodah,* and *Gemillat Chassadim—* studying God's divine teachings (values), worshipping the Creator through prayer, and finally, acts of loving kindness. There is no mention of having your own TV show, and I can't fool myself into believing that that's what it's about. Because I have seen so many times in life how great an impact you can have on people's lives simply by being there for them, I cannot believe that any form of similar gratification could be had by being successful, famous, or rich. We are all bitten by greed and the desire for wealth. But I have already, at this young age, discovered its emptiness.

I watched a father struggle to build up a big business, losing his family in the process. When my mother was going through her terrible divorce, with all the accompanying pain, I remember how it was a poor black woman who worked with her in a Los Angeles bank who called her constantly, making sure she was OK. Once, after my parents had a particularly bad argument, I remember that this woman came over and offered to take my mother to her house for the night. When my mother refused to leave her children behind, the woman insisted that we all go to her tiny house in the middle of the black ghetto. This she did for a Jewish woman whose only connection to her was that she worked in the same bank and she was in distress.

I have realized that there are two aspects to my relationship with the subject of relationships. The first is the glamorous side of appearing on television talk shows and offering advice to the viewers. The second is giving up the glamour and sitting with couples whose marriages are crumbling—cajoling, persuading, pleading against all the odds to give them hope that they have a future together if they can just forgive each other, redeem each other, and move on. When I see couples who are still together because of the time that I gave them, I never ask myself why I am alive. But the same degree of self-esteem rarely follows a television interview. In fact, the reverse is true. I usually finish an interview feeling anxious and hoping that I did OK.

At Passover time about five years ago, when we were living in Oxford, I received a call from acquaintances whose marriage I was trying to salvage. They said to me that they had given up, and the next morning they were going to their respective lawyers to file for divorce. I asked them to wait for me, because I would drive to London and be with them in ninety minutes. "But it's already eleven o'clock at night!" they protested. "Too bad," I said. "I'm already out the door and on my way." I drove to their home and sat with them the entire night.

The husband was screaming, "This woman drives me crazy." "This woman?" I said, "*This* woman! Do you remember who this woman is? This woman is the mother of your children, you ingrate! She is the woman who supported you for four years when you went through medical school. She is the woman who went to the gym three times a week to look beautiful for you. She is the woman who stood by your bed and nursed you when you were sick. So stop speaking about her as if she is some stranger." And I gave it to his wife as well whenever she got really negative about her husband. We argued throughout the night. It was now early morning. I finally turned to them both and I said, "There are only two kinds of people in this world. The great people and the mediocre ones. The great ones are in complete control of their lives. They set out to do something and they achieve it. The mediocre ones allow every passing wind to steer them off course. They make a lot of money, achieve great professional success, but they sink in the most important area of life: their personal lives. Their kids grow up scarred and disillusioned, having watched the relationship responsible for their very existence dissolve before their eyes. Their kids go through life feeling that nothing ever really works. The parents' action has shown them that the world is broken and there is no one who can fix it. When you marry, you intend to be together for the rest of your lives. But now you have been blown off course. So, you have a choice. You can forgive each other and move on and be two of the great people, or you can allow your past and your problems to overwhelm you, and you can sink to the level of all the other ordinary people who professed love only to watch it wear off. Just another two people whose dreams all vanished into thin air."

At that point, I witnessed one of the most moving events of my life. The husband got down on his knee, as if he were proposing anew, and said to his wife, "You are the most beautiful woman in the world. You are my wife and my shining light. I have destroyed my own soul by hurting you. I am nothing without you, and I am asking you to come back to me so that I can have happiness again." The wife was in tears. She turned away and wouldn't accept his embrace. "Please, honey," he pleaded. "Please accept me back as the man who wants to dedicate his life to you. I am an imperfect man, and the only thing going for me is that I have you." And with that she fell into his arms, and it was I who had to run into another room to conceal my own flood of tears. Now, can you compare that kind of achievement with the ephemeral star of celebrity?

Another friend whom I encouraged to persevere with his marriage now tells me how thankful he is. How much he owes me. "I am only married because of you." "Nonsense," I tell him, "you owe me absolutely nothing. It is I who owe you. Because you made me feel like the messiah." OK, so not *the* messiah. But a little messiah, nonetheless. A guy who can make a difference.

All of us, Uri, are born to be the messiah. There is a part of the world that only we can redeem. And our objective in life is to devote ourselves to finding the areas and the people where we can make a difference.

But I lament just how much it has all changed now. How all the young people to whom I serve as rabbi are only interested in making money or being recognized by strangers while they sip coffee at Starbucks. Human beings have lost the ability to experience the human depth-crisis. All of us need to wake up one morning and ask, "Why was I born and for what purpose am I alive?" Answering that question is the beginning of finding real meaning in life. But rather than be shaken by that all-important question, we simply paper over the human depth-crisis with meaningless distractions, like money, objects, and material ambitions.

In an earlier generation, rabbis and priests had to rail against money superseding everything else. Money used to be the most important thing in life. To be sure, people did other things besides hoard money. But they seemed to put money before everything else—before marriage, before family and children, before health and hobbies, and certainly before religion. But times have changed. Today, there is nothing *but* money. Money is not the most important thing any longer. It is the only thing.

Several times a week, Uri, I drive between Oxford and London and while away the time by listening to, among other things, the great political speeches of the twentieth century. And when I listen to the great speakers of yesteryear—Churchill, Roosevelt, Kennedy, MacArthur, Adlai Stevenson, Martin Luther King Jr.—and compare them to today's instantly forgettable political speakers, I realize that something monumental has changed. You can't compare any of even President Clinton's outstanding speeches to Martin Luther King's "I Have a Dream" speech, or to Jesse Jackson's address to the 1984 Democratic Convention, or to Kennedy's "Ich bin ein Berliner" speech (which actually translates as "I am a doughnut"). The reason? There are no great themes left to address.

Every political speech delivered by a Western leader today is about inflation, the economy, and a single European currency. And how inspiring is that going to be? How good can Clinton be as he discusses a balanced budget or how he will lower interest rates? How inspiring can we expect Tony Blair to be as he discusses the pros and cons of European monetary union? In short, money has overtaken everything, and it is an uninspiring world as a result. Without fail, the great speeches I listen to in the car are remarkable because they discuss grand, majestic themes: Kennedy screeching for democracy and human freedom, King appealing for equality and the purging of racism, Churchill affirming how "we will fight them on the beaches." The boredom of today's political rhetoric has to do with the simple fact that we have forgotten the world's great themes. The result is stultifying listlessness.

Once upon a time, a man needed only to sell his soul in return for extraordinary wealth. And that's what you were asked to do in Mexico, Uri. Then, as wealth increased and the stakes got higher, our humanity had to be thrown into the deal as well. If we wanted to get ahead, we were told, well, we had to be ruthless. But today, the ultimate price is required and paid on demand, that being life itself. People work themselves to the bone, morning, day, and night, and in the process, forego the extraordinary multicolored diversity of human life and emotion in exchange for a single monotonous emotion, greed; and a single dull color, green.

I have discovered that in the process of trying to accumulate as much money as possible through the banking profession, people become utterly boring. They have no hobbies. You meet them for dinner, and you hear first about whether the Dow was up or down. Later in the evening, they tell you about Alan Greenspan and interest rates. And for dessert? They play prophet and tell you the exact direction of the markets in the coming months. Could you imagine their confusion if they stood at Sinai and heard "I am the Lord your God who took you out of Egypt!" No doubt they would say, "Well, this doesn't bode well for Egyptian markets at all. Tomorrow I will immediately short all the Egyptian stocks I own."

I do not claim to be immune to the lust for wealth. We all work for money, we all need it, and perhaps we all love it. But surprisingly enough, it does not have the capacity to excite and fire our deepest imagination. This is why those who earn a lot of money are also the ones who think of elaborate ways to spend it. This is how they get their kicks. They have little other stimulus besides making money and spending it. They're bored. And the more consumed they become, the more boring they become. An elderly multimillionaire businessman recently told me that the difference between today's generation of entrepreneurs and his own generation is that the new guys have no hobbies. Sure, they read a bit, play a little golf here and there, watch TV, and go out with friends. But they don't enjoy this half as much as making money. There is nothing that engages them so much as talking stocks and shares and new investment opportunities. The result, he contends, is that they become monoliths. Worse, he says, since they can never disengage or learn to think outside of the box. They can never approach their business from an entirely new perspective and take the imaginative, long-term view that business requires. The world's all-encompassing lust for riches is leading to internal collapse and external dullness.

In the Bible, God commands the Jewish people to go out of the slavery of Egypt every single day. A great rabbi named Joseph Soloveitchik once explained, Uri, that there are two aspects to slavery, which need not always coincide. The first is political slavery whereby a man is reduced to a chattel, a form of private property, an object belonging to an owner. The slave's body and skills belong to his master by virtue of a legal system that totally degrades his status. He is a "thing" and is subject to the whim and caprice of his master's will, to physical coercion, exploitation, and humiliation. The second type of slavery is typological, a mental state of servility rather than a physically imposed enslavement. This is when a man is enslaved from the inside. When he cannot be what he wishes or do what he wants. This second state of slavery is far worse than the first, because it is easier to take the man out of prison than it is to take the prison out of man. Juridical slavery imprisons only his body while typological slavery imprisons his mind.

This second type of slavery reaches its apogee when we open our eyes at the age of forty or fifty and discover that we have ended up becoming something that we never planned to be and perhaps may even despise. Once, when we were political slaves in Egypt, Uri, the Almighty Himself redeemed us from servitude. Today, when we are typological slaves, when we are incarcerated by our lust for wealth and prestige, it is we who must redeem ourselves from the restrictive clutches of materialism and egoism. If we fail at this, then we will never have lived, but merely existed. But for those who seek it, help is provided in attaining liberation. For deliverance from the poisoned air of a suffocating selfishness is the ultimate purpose of religion. Religion's goal is to unlock our goodness, release our selflessness, and empower us to lead truly honorable lives.

That modern day man is utterly lost without work and something to strive for, that he is confounded by excessive moments of leisure that render him ill at ease, is best demonstrated by the obsessive nature of today's career-oriented society. Professional success is a mania that leaves virtually no time for contemplation and enjoyment of the transcendent aspects of life. We accumulate clients instead of acts of loving-kindness. A case in point: look what we have done to the Sabbath. Sunday used to be a time for church and family. Today all the shops are open, and it is like any other day of the week: a time to indulge in further consumption. The prayer hall has been replaced by the shopping mall, the cathedral by the stadium, contemplation by consumerism. The Sabbath was designed as a day when we could withdraw from our constant exertion of mastery over creation and discover humility, dependency, and a common bond with all living things. But we have forsaken God's day in favor of further acquisition and impressing the boss with overtime. We all must return to a more spiritual life, Uri, because it is specifically a holy way of life that gives humans something to strive for after they have made their money and built their reputations.

There are only two things in this world that are really interesting: God and man, because they are the only two things that possess infinite depth. We tire of everything else all too quickly. We cannot watch even the most sensational film more than a few times, but we can have endless hours of conversation with the same person, because that person is infinitely creative. On days like the Sabbath, we dedicate large amounts of time to cultivating human friendship and company, and enhancing our relationship with God. By doing so, we cultivate a deeper dimension of our personalities so that, instead of being two-dimensional individuals who offer clichéd opinions lifted from glossy magazines and insipid television talk shows, we cultivate that most pivotal of all personality traits: depth. Those with depth have a third dimension that affords them a broad inner expanse so that acquaintances and friends always find something new in them, making them exciting, unique, and fresh.

For nine years now, Uri, I have asked Oxford students what they plan to do after graduating. Inevitably, I hear the same response: I'm going to be a banker, a doctor, a lawyer. I then point out to them that I never asked what they were going to *do*, but rather what they were going to *be*. One does not *become* a doctor. Rather, one *practices* medicine. Neither does one become a lawyer. Rather, one engages in the legal profession. But today we have mistaken the art of being for the art of doing, so that our entire existence is summed up by our capacity for production, rather than our innate humanity.

Incurable insecurity, Prozac, and lithium are the reward for a generation that has learned to define its very being through material and professional success—productivity—rather than through being God's children, whose value is therefore immutable and immeasurable. No wonder, then, that we thirst endlessly for more money, bigger homes, faster cars—anything that will obviate the inner feeling of worthlessness that haunts us at every turn. Since we have failed to develop vertically by acquiring more depth and sublimity, we compensate by increasing horizontally, through acquisition and consumption.

When I chose to become a rabbi, Uri, I knew that I would never be rich. And if it were said that sour grapes and jealousy of those more materially well-off than me have prompted the sentiments I have articulated in this letter, my response would be "guilty as charged." I am absolutely jealous—of all those who have forty more zeros at the end of their paycheck, for instance. I have always loved money and luxury. I have always been pretty spoiled and tried to surround myself with nice things. But if such riches will rob me of knowing the redemptive quality of prayer, the serenity of the Sabbath, the pleasure of a great book, the mind-opening sensations of transcendent thought, the serenity and innocence of a child, the beauty of marriage, and the purity of human love, then I prefer to remain envious. May God bless us all with riches. But may He especially bless us with the enlightenment to know what to do with those riches.

And may God bless you too, Uri. Even without $600 million, I will be taking your phone calls (albeit for a brief hello).

Hasta la vista,

Dear Shmuley,

I suppose I am above China now. I look down from the triple-thickness porthole that slices my view of the planet into a distortion of pressure-proof slits, and I can see the greatest nation on earth, teeming with more than a thousand million people. They speak languages I will never hear, much less learn, and they worship gods I will never comprehend, and many millions of them will possess astonishing psi powers, and none of them has heard of me, or you, or Judaism. Don't let anyone tell you it's a small world, Shmuley, because it is not. It's a vastness. And I am skimming over the vastness in an ANA 747, heading back from a series of TV shows in Japan.

There is an egg-like object in my pocket. I think it is made of metal, though I walked through the metal detectors at Tokyo International without triggering the alarms. It weighs about three ounces. I haven't looked at it for years, but I felt a last-minute compunction to bring it with me on this trip. It was given to me by John Lennon. And it was given to him by…

We were eating in some restaurant in New York City. John started talking about UFOs. I didn't bring the subject up, though my autobiography had appeared by then, and all the controversy about alien voices and lights in the sky was destroying my public credibility. He said he believed life existed on other planets, that it had visited us, that maybe it was observing us right now. It told him what I thought.

We have never discussed my belief in alien intelligences, Shmuley, though it has a direct impact on my religious beliefs and on all religious concepts. Maybe twenty thousand feet above a truly foreign sector of the planet is the right place for me to start telling you about it. Maybe. But that's not the story. The little metal egg is the story now.

John took me to a quieter, darker table, lit a cigarette, and pointed its glowing tip at my face. "You believe in this stuff, right?" he asked me. His voice was so earnest and so cynical at the same time; he was like a priest trying to convert a sinner when he knew that no one, nobody on the planet, would ever believe in the same god that he did. He knew exactly where his spirit was at, but his mind was hopelessly lost. I think that's why he needed Yoko so much.

I looked at him, stinging the air round my face with his cigarette, and I said: "You know I believe in 'this stuff,' John."

He said: "Well, you ain't fuckin' gonna believe this. About six months ago, I was at home, in the Dakota Building. I was asleep in my bed…and suddenly, I wasn't asleep. Because there was this blazing light 'round the door. It was shining through the cracks and the keyhole, like someone was out there with searchlights, or the apartment was on fire. That was what I thought—intruders, or fire. I leapt out of bed and pulled open the door. There were these four people out there."

"Fans?" I asked him.

"Well, they didn't want my fuckin' autograph. They were, like, little. Bug-like. Big bug eyes and little bug mouths and they were scuttling at me like roaches." He broke off and stared at me.

"I've been high, I mean right out of it, a lot of times, and I never saw anything on acid that was as weird as those fuckin' bugs, man. I was straight that night. I wasn't dreaming, and I wasn't tripping. There were these creatures, like people but not like people, in my apartment."

"What did they do to you?"

Lennon swore again. "How do you know they did anything to me, man?"

"Because they must have come for a reason."

"You're right. They did something. But I don't know what it was. I tried to throw them out, but when I took a step towards them they kind of pushed me back. I mean, they didn't touch me. It was like they just willed me. Pushed me with willpower and telepathy."

"And then what?"

"I don't know. Something happened. Don't ask me what. Either I've forgotten, blocked it out, or they won't let me remember. But after a while, they weren't there, and I was just lying on the bed, only I was on the covers. And I had this thing in my hands. They gave it to me."

"What was it?"

Lennon dug into his jeans pocket. "I've been carrying it 'round ever since, wanting to ask somebody the same question. You have it. Maybe you'll know."

I took the metal, egg-like object and turned it over in the dim light. It seemed solid and smooth, and I could make out no markings. "I've never seen anything like it."

"Keep it. Too weird for me. If it's my ticket to another planet, I don't want to go there."

I did keep it, though I didn't get it checked by scientists or examined by journalists. It was too weird for me too. This was more than a decade before alien abductions became a subject for books and newspaper interviews. In the mid-seventies, just seeing a UFO was enough to get you locked away. I put John Lennon's alien gift on a shelf and secretly hoped it might one day be my ticket to another planet.

Shmuley, this is twenty-four hours later. I'm back in England, back at home, and something so strange has happened that I wonder whether you will believe me.

We pulled into the driveway just after 5 P.M., and my mother let the dogs out to greet me, and I told Hanna I would walk with them before I ate. The evening was hot and close, with the air so tightly packed over the river and the meadows that every slap of waves from a passing boat sounded like the report of distant gunfire. The dogs loped along beside me, too hot to run. I was stooping to pick up a stick for our greyhound, Jon-Jon, to fetch, when I saw a stone glint on the ground and scooped it up. I am not a collector of pebbles, but I wanted to look at this one.

It was egg-like and heavier than I had expected. There were no markings on its surface, just a smooth, enigmatic egg—identical to the one John Lennon gave me in New York and which

I had just carried with me to Japan. I searched in my pocket for the original, to reassure myself they were two separate objects, and held them up together. The one still stained with Berkshire mud was perhaps an eighth of an inch smaller.

It is impossible for me to believe this has happened by chance. Nor can I imagine this is the hand of God. What sort of God would trouble to drop pebbles at my feet, while allowing children to be born with agonizing handicaps in the hospital a few miles up the road? And what sort of chance can arrange for these baffling coincidences to erupt and outrage all the laws of physics and mathematics, while still imposing sober and predictable odds on roulette tables and lottery machines all over the world? God does not play pranks, and the Geller Effect cannot mutate mathematical laws. Something else put that stone in my path and drew my eye to it.

I believe there are many levels of intelligence between us and God. Some call them angels. Some call them aliens. They observe humankind, and sometimes they interfere. Sometimes they whisper lies to us, and sometimes they drop hints of truth, and sometimes, for fun or as proof that they exist, they offer frivolous signs. I used to think I had been picked up by a mischievous baby alien, on board some spaceship on the far reaches of our solar system. Perhaps its parents were not watching it carefully. Perhaps today was its birthday, and for a special treat it would be allowed to play with a human. That human was me. The baby alien picked me up and molded my mind, implanted one or two bizarre and attention-grabbing skills that other humans didn't have, and set me back down. Perhaps my life lasted a few seconds to the baby, whose mothership was traveling at close to light speed. Perhaps it gave me an inquisitive poke every moment or two.

Now that my own children are grown, I am more doubtful that this baby alien ever existed. I do not feel like a plaything any more. I believe now that these strange echoes of other intelligences are like momentary glimpses of God. Moses once prayed that God would reveal himself in all his dazzling glory, and God permitted him to see, through a crack in the Sinai rocks, for one split instant of a blinding moment, the hem of God's robe. Not Yahweh's face, or the back of his head, or the back of his gown, but merely a thread at its swirling edge, for a fraction of a second. Anything more would have burned Moses up like a billion-megaton hydrogen bomb.

Dreamlike meetings with strange figures in doorways, an egg-like stone that appears in a pop star's hand, the twin stone that materializes at my feet—these things are glimpses of the hem of God's robe. They are all we can understand of higher intelligences. To know more would be to burn out our brains.

There is more that I wanted to tell you, but I am tired. I have not slept for thirty-six hours, and the last time I lay down I was nine thousand miles away. I wanted to tell you about the night John was killed, and how I thought of him when Princess Diana died. I have been thinking about his declaration that "The Beatles are more famous than Jesus now," and how he was telling a brutal truth. I wanted to talk to you about Elvis Presley, who became an immortal God and died anyway. But I must sleep first.

Love Is All You Need,

Hello again Uri,

Love is all you need? If love was all you needed, then all parents and children—who surely harbor love for each other—would get along like a house on fire. Unfortunately, all too many do set the house on fire—with their arguments, misunderstandings, and mutual invective and abuse. No, love is the most important thing that we need. But like all main courses, it needs side helpings in order to make it usable and special.

A T-bone steak is fantastic (although I can't comment since it's not kosher), but who eats it on its own? No, you need some vegetables and a good wine to make it all go down.

The same is true of love. One of the tributaries any loving relationship needs is differentiation. People have to remain autonomous and distinctive individuals, even amid their love for each other. Which allows me, finally, to disagree with you.

Let me first address your point about alien life forms from my own perspective. While we agree on so many things, Uri, here we will go our own separate ways. For me to believe in intelligent life outside this planet, I have to ask one simple question: why is it seemingly nowhere to be found? Is the universe inhabited only with shy aliens? Are they all in need of therapy to boost their self-confidence? Are there no Martians with a bit of *cojones* who can come out from behind the mask of their planet and introduce themselves properly, like smack in the middle of New York City? Why is it that everybody who claims an extraterrestrial visitation has almost always been alone at the time, in some godforsaken desert, with a camera that can only capture blurred and shaky images? The witnesses usually have no or little corroborating evidence, other than really fuzzy photographs of things that look like flying soup bowls.

And if we do believe the testimony of some solitary individuals who claim to have proof of having met aliens and invited them to dinner or tea, I don't see why we shouldn't also believe in all the new religions whose protagonists claim to have had some great divine revelation that only they could see and only they could verify.

About seven years ago, Uri, a young man came to see me at my office in Oxford. He was very neatly dressed in a dark suit and wore a badge above his lapel that said "Elder Oaks." He explained that he was a Mormon missionary from Utah on assignment for two years in Britain. He offered me a free copy of the Book of Mormon and offered to discuss it with me. He was in the business of making Mormon converts. Now, I have a policy of never turning down anything free. But here I was more cautious. In fact, many Jews would have asked him to leave the office. After all, he was trying to convert a rabbi, for goodness' sake. But I held my cool because I understood him. He was a young man, passionate about his beliefs, and he wanted to share them, from his perspective, out of the goodness of his heart. I was impressed with his earnestness and wanted to show him my respect. I calmly said to him, "Look, I've got to be honest. I don't think you're going to get very far with me because I'm one of those guys who gets paid to be Jewish. My whole living is being a rabbi. And if I convert to Mormonism, I'll be out of a job. But, that doesn't mean we can't be friends." I then asked him to sit down.

"Tell me," I asked him, "it must be really rough when you go out missionizing on the streets. I can't imagine that everyone is sympathetic. You must have some real horror stories." He sighed, and at that moment, he almost cried. "You're a mind reader," he told me. "Just last week, some guy spat at me, and the week before that someone kicked me."

"Well, you're in good company," I said. "One of the things I try and do here is get the Jewish students interested in Judaism, and they don't always respond in the kindest way either. So we're kindred spirits, you and me. And I just want you to know that I'm here for you as a friend. My office is right in the heart of the city. And if you are ever frustrated and fed up, I want you to come up and talk to me. Use me as your punching bag."

And that's how our friendship began. Brock started coming to my office nearly every day, and we became the closest of friends. I would serve him falafel and hummus, and he would tell me the most interesting stories relating to his proselytizing efforts. I was therefore fairly saddened when a year later, he came to my office and told me that he had completed his tour of duty and was returning to the United States. "But what are you going to do," I asked him. "Well, I'm going to go to the

United States Air Force Academy in Colorado. You see, my father is the supreme allied Air Force commander in Europe of all NATO Air Forces, as well as commander-in-chief of the United States Air Forces in Europe. So, like him, I want to be a pilot."

My jaw dropped and cracked the floor upon which I was standing. What an incredible kid. All this time, and he never told me. What character. What humility. Wow! This kid was just as humble as me!

We got his father to come and give a lecture at Oxford, and General Robert Oaks reciprocated by inviting me and Debbie to his headquarters at Ramstein Air Force Base in Germany. Through Brock, I met many other Mormon members, especially a young student by the name of Mike Benson, whose grandfather, Ezra Taft Benson, was actually the president and prophet of the Mormon Church. Mike also became one of my closest friends, and he even became an officer of the L'Chaim Society. Mormons are in many ways like Jews, Uri. They are immensely devoted to their families and have many children. They are very charitable and take immense pride in their tradition, and I have really come to respect the family orientation of the Mormon tradition and many other highly valuable tenets of their tradition.

So why am I not a Mormon? It's not only because I was born a Jew. Rather, Uri, Mormonism is based around the belief that Joseph Smith was approached by the angel Moroni who taught him how to decipher ancient tablets that he found in upstate New York. But, while I cannot deny that this is true, why should I put my faith in one man's claims to the truth? Maybe the highest truth was also revealed to Mary Baker Eddy who founded Christian Science. Perhaps she ascended to the loftiest prophetic heights. But again, this is the claim of only one person. Maybe these were very sincere and good people who simply had a dream and thought it was real. Maybe they ate too much chili and had indigestion. I'm not trying to poke fun. I respect all religions that lead to a moral and ethical lifestyle and Mormons, with their immense commitment to family and charity, are some of the people I admire most. But how do we know they are true when only one person claims them to be true?

And here I want to point out two immense differences between the Jewish religion, to which you and I pay allegiance, and all other religions of the world. These differences do not make Judaism better, or worse, than any other world religion. But they do make it different.

Every world religion is based around the idea of an individual revelation to a single person—a prophet or a saint—or to a small group of people. Most of Jesus' miracles took place only among his small group of apostles. Mohammed was spoken to individually, and the Koran conveyed to him, by the angel Gabriel. And the warrior Prabudda was spoken to by the god Krishna in the Bhagavad Gita. What makes Judaism different is that it is the world's only religion that claims a collective revelation to an entire assembled nation—not just the prophet Moses—at the foot of Mt Sinai. According to the Bible, there were at least two million people gathered at Mt Sinai, all of whom heard and received the Ten Commandments. Now, for our purposes, it's not important whether or not this is true. I know that there are many who would deny it, while I, of course, affirm it as a central staple of my belief. What *is* important is that the Bible even claims this.

What the Bible is trying to say with this claim to a collective revelation revealed to an entire nation is that there are two kinds of truth: individual truth and absolute truth. Individual truths are conveyed only to small groups of people, and they often apply only to that group of people. But collective truths apply to all humanity and are therefore revealed to all humanity. Even those who are not Jewish must live by the Ten Commandments. They cannot steal or commit adultery or covet the property of their neighbors. And this is why the Ten

Commandments have far transcended the Jewish sphere of influence and have become the moral framework for all the Earth's inhabitants.

Moreover, the fact that the Bible claims a collective revelation to millions of people is significant, because it could easily be refuted. When only one person claims to have seen something, then it is either true or not true. But when a book claims that two million people saw something, well, that's another story altogether. You have to have a lot of courage to make a claim like that, because it is so easily refutable.

You ask me to believe your story about finding the metal egg-like object outside your home in Sonning, just as John Lennon asked you to believe a similar tale. And, of course, I believe you. You are a man of the highest intelligence and integrity. You have no reason to lie, and you can easily distinguish between fantasy and reality. But there is a difference between believing someone and embracing their beliefs. I believe your story with all my heart. But how will it change my life or have any practical significance for me? When I choose to believe in God, although the belief may be abstract, it still affects my very being. For example, if I believe that God gave me life and unconditional love, then I have a responsibility to use that life to spread unconditional love. But of what practical significance is it to me that you found this object? Or to you, for that matter? It is wondrous and miraculous, to be sure. But how should it change any of our lives? What real meaning does it have?

If these beings are visiting us secretly, covertly, leaving behind trinkets that are useless to us because either they are nothing special or we are too dumb to understand them because they are meant for a vastly superior intelligence, then of what value is it to us that these aliens exist at all? Why are they hiding? Why is everything done so covertly? The fact that aliens who confound us by their inconspicuousness may or may not exist is about as useful to my life as the existence of the tooth fairy or the Loch Ness monster.

Until the first Europeans visited the New World in the Americas, why should a Seminole Indian have cared one way or another if there were other humans across the Atlantic? But once they invaded his territory and stole his lands, you bet he cared. So, I come back to my first point. If these aliens don't even have the decency to show themselves, why should we be so preoccupied with their existence? Even as a rabbi, Uri, I don't delve into a deep understanding of the angels. They have their realm, and I have mine. And it is existence here on terra firma that I find so much more intriguing, by comparison.

You will accuse me, Uri, of being pedantic at best, and petty at worst. You will tell me that I am being overly logical and sourly cynical. But there is a reason for my cynicism about extraterrestrial life. I believe that there is a scientific conspiracy against the human race in advancing the unsubstantiated belief in alien life. I am amazed that almost no men of science believe in God or angels, yet they can believe in alien life forms on a different planet. They are not prepared to accept that God fills the infinite expanse of space, but they are prepared to believe that life forms radically different to ours travel through space at the speed of light. Indeed, most scientists deny the existence of God. In fact, they deny the existence of the entire spiritual realm. Yet they will spend millions of dollars on giant radio telescopes to try and find other life forms when there is not a shred of evidence that they exist.

I am pleased and privileged to be a friend—most surprisingly—of professor Richard Dawkins, the celebrated author of *The Selfish Gene* and *The Blind Watchmaker*, and the world's most famous atheist. At the beginning of each Oxford academic year, our L'Chaim Society stages a science versus religion debate, and most years, Dawkins participates. Through these many encounters, which I inevitably chair, professor Dawkins and I have become friendly. Once, in what can only be described as a backhanded compliment, he said to me, "You know, I don't really understand it. You seem to be such an intelligent guy. So how can you believe in religion when there is absolutely no proof?" And while I disagree with his conclusions, his premise is correct. God cannot be seen, and that's why Dawkins is complaining. But, and this is the all-important *but*, God can be experienced. And yet, isn't it odd that so many world-class scientists, who are absolute atheists, believe in the existence of extraterrestrial life, when there is so little, or at least such scant evidence?

Like I said, it's a conspiracy. You see, Uri, the Ptolemaic universe posited the existence of the earth at the center of our universe. This meant that man was the crown jewel of creation. He was literally at the center of existence. Of course, when Galileo embraced Copernicus' system of a heliocentric universe, the Catholic Church opposed it because they thought it would denigrate the position of man. Suddenly, we were only just one tiny inhabited planet—not even first, but third in the universe—revolving around the sun. Man was cast from the center to the periphery. Man wasn't so special after all. But Copernicus was right, and we live with the facts, whatever the consequences.

But I see in the continued emphasis on extraterrestrial life an attempt to denigrate man further. Whereas religion tells us that man is the highest creature in the universe, empowered by God with the intelligence to serve as a moral agent capable of choosing between right and wrong, the alien life advocates would have us believe that we are all a bunch of dummies and that there are life-forms out there that are a gazillion times smarter than us. This denigration of our specialness relieves us of the responsibility for leading exemplary lives suffused with holiness and moral purpose. While we humans trudge along in our unimpressive, gas-guzzling motor vehicles, aliens, we are told, are infinitely more technologically advanced and have space-ships that move at warp speed. Doesn't this sound like the parent who tries to give his kid a guilt trip for not doing well at school by pointing out how Johnny down the road is so much smarter and more accomplished than their son is? Those who tell us that humans are so underdeveloped, so under-evolved, desecrate the majesty of man. They are telling people that they don't matter as much as they think they do. The contrast with the message of religion could not be greater. These traditions tell us that man was created in God's image. There is nothing higher than that. And there is nothing more important that intelligence can confer upon any organism than the opportunity to serve as master of its own destiny—to do the right thing, amidst constant temptation to do otherwise.

The whole preoccupation and obsession with alien life forms seems to me to be driven by an innate boredom. We hardly understand what it means to be human any more. We all lack direction in our lives and live in a state of moral chaos and ethical confusion. And yet, we are still more interested in beings with perhaps ten heads or six pairs of eyes, when our own eyes seem focused on all the wrong things.

But then, Uri, returning to what I said earlier, there is a second and more important point that distinguishes the Jewish faith from all other religions of the world. You tell me that you believe that there are any number of intelligences between ourselves and God. I agree. I wrote about this extensively in my very first book, *Dreams*, in a chapter discussing how, according to the Jewish mystics, the celestial spheres, or what are known as *galgalim*, can interfere with our dreams and send us clairvoyant messages of the future. Furthermore, Judaism of course recognizes the existence of angels, conduits of the divine will.

Yes, Uri, for some life is lived in moments of dreamlike states in which we see figures in doorways and mysterious egg-like stones that serve as glimpses of God's radiance. But I would contend that the real magnificence of God and the small perceptions of His glory are more readily found in what we would normally dismiss as the everyday details of life, the mundane threads that are mostly trodden upon as we reach for those things we perceive as higher. God's real glory is found in the "trivial" things we so often take for granted. His infinite light is seen in the innocence of a child, the purity of human love, the pleasure of a kind deed, and the enlightenment that comes through the pursuit of knowledge. God is found in the colors of the rainbow, the mistiness of an early dawn, the refreshing vapors of a morning dew, and the white brilliance of a fresh blanket of snow.

We can't make the mistake, Uri, propelled by this great age of space exploration, of getting bored with the earth and exchanging the profundity of all that goes on around us in favor of the mysteries of the heavens. This is the mistake that is usually made by teenagers and others who approach the subject of human relationships with insufficient maturity. What they want is a fireworks display rather than steadily glowing embers. They think that real love is kissing in airport terminals and writing long treatises of poetry to one another. They get turned on by the big things of a relationship and have no time for the small things. Having children together is seen as a nuisance that will prevent romantic and spontaneous weekends in Paris. No doubt, overtly passionate and romantic encounters are profound and valuable expressions of love. But real love is found between a husband and wife who love each other, who work hard to support each other every day both financially, morally, and emotionally. Real love is found when a wife is thirsty at night and a husband volunteers to go downstairs and bring her a glass of water. Real love is found in a mother and father who sit by the bedside of their child with a high fever, waiting and praying together that the life they have jointly created recovers to see another day. This is the stuff of which real relationships are made. Those who focus only on the splendor of birthdays, anniversaries, and Valentine's Day, ignoring the sublimity of the everyday, are those who end up divorced. By rejecting the fabric of existence, they end up as loose threads that have slowly come undone.

You mention, Uri, how Moses was allowed to see God's mantle from behind. That is true. But notice that the Bible, which begins with the action of Creation in Genesis and continues with the great miracles of Exodus, slowly tapers off. The miracles become less frequent. And as the Bible moves on, God begins to vanish. By the time we get to the books of the Prophets—the second section of the Hebrew Bible—God can no longer be seen. Only heard. He has gone from being visible and has become an intangible calling, a disembodied voice. By the time we read of the great prophet Elijah, God has become a still small voice. Later, after the Bible canon closes, God cannot even be heard directly. There are no more prophets. God lives on as the source of all inspiration. In our time, He is invisible and can only be experienced. In the book of Esther, the reader must peer between the lines to see that it is God who has brought salvation.

But there is a profound message here. God is trying to teach us to find Him in all our ways. He is just as present now as He was in the days of Moses. But when God appears at Mt. Sinai, or when He splits the Red Sea, we might make the mistake of thinking that He is not present at any other time or place. He is only at the top of mountains. He only makes appearances in magnificent volcanic eruptions and in swirling tempests. He can only be found in burning bushes, in grand plagues of locusts, or glorious battles in which a small David can defeat a giant Goliath. So God teaches us that we must always find Him in everything. He is found in the blinding splendor of the sun, in majestic snow-capped mountain peaks, in the kindness of sharing our meals with strangers, and in the complexity and design of human intelligence.

The great Rebbe Menachem of Kotzk once asked his students where they thought God was. One said that He filled the heavens. Another added that He pervaded the earth. The Rebbe told both that they were wrong. "God is found," the master said, "wherever we let Him in." The Rabbis of the Talmud said that every day a voice goes forth from the heavens. It is the voice of the Almighty calling out to man: "Open up your hearts for me even as big as a needle, and I will open for you a portal as big as the earth and as wide as the sea."

All we need do, Uri, is open the door and bring Him into our lives.

Written by a friend whose love is not alien and
whose devotion is not foreign,

Dear Shmuley,

I was in New York, at my apartment on 57th and First Avenue, when I heard John Lennon had been murdered. I ran to wake up my secretary, Trina, who was a devoted fan, and we sat beside each other, trying to take it in. It was a senseless death, and it left the world even more fragmented. I kept thinking of Elvis, whose death had also torn a piece out of my life. I met Elvis once, in a trailer home in the Nevada desert outside Las Vegas, and what he told me about UFOs left me shocked and uneasy. But now, when I think of the night Lennon died, what I remember most clearly is 4 A.M. in a Berlin hotel gym, pedaling angrily at insomnia on an exercise bike and watching CNN. It was August 31, 1997, and the first screen subtitles said Princess Diana had been injured in a car accident.

I grieved for Diana that day as bitterly as if she had been a daughter of mine. The pain possessed an unusual quality—she was someone I knew and loved intimately, with a love I had not suspected until she was killed. And yet I had not met her, and I was aware I was not grieving for a real friend. I discovered she meant a great deal to me, but I may have meant nothing at all to her—that is not a friendship. Coming to terms with this fact was almost as painful as accepting that she was gone, and that the world was incomplete again.

What I felt for John Lennon was close to this pain. We had met, and the meeting was profoundly important to me—but I have no idea what it meant to Lennon. Perhaps he had forgotten it. His child had been born, he had made his first record in five years—his life had moved an infinite distance from that restaurant in New York, though both of us still lived only a few hundred yards away. I grieved for him as a friend. So did millions who never met him.

On August 16, 1977, my brother-in-law Shipi's birthday, we were walking out of a hotel in Bel-Air when the concierge said breathlessly, "Have you heard the news? Elvis is dead." For a few moments, reality crumbled. It did not seem possible that a man who had been so young such a short time ago was now gone beyond aging.

These people we hardly knew, they were such fundamental figures in our world. John Lennon, though he regretted it soon after, said it best: "We're more popular than Jesus Christ now." Everyone today can understand what he meant. As he protested a few weeks later, when Beatles albums and pin-ups were being burned across the Bible Belt, he hadn't intended to claim that his songs meant more than the New Testament—it was just that people listened to what he wrote, and they had stopped listening to what Jesus said.

Stars become gods. It is not hard to understand. Stars live mythic lives, recounted in fables told daily on the front pages. They appear in nightly visions, on TV. They feud, make love, and dispense riches upon humanity. Beverly Hills is Olympus and Hollywood is Homer and the Beatles are still bigger than Jesus Christ. I have always resisted the urgings of promoters and agents who wanted me to claim divine power, to throw a god's robes around me and declare that spoons were the weapons of the immortals—but I have tasted the superhuman strength of TV, when I've appeared before early-morning cameras to urge national support for the England football team. I like to stand outside Wembley stadium, holding out my palm to the camera, and order the viewers: "Touch the screen! Come on, touch the screen! Stand up, don't be embarrassed, don't hold back, you're doing this for England! Step up to the TV and put your hand on mine and shout out, 'Win, England, win!' Touch the screen!"

And more than a million people will do it. They will do it and know, with a faith beyond any scientific reasoning, that their energy is being channeled to England's footballers. They know it is a tiny burst of energy, and the players use energy in megawatts every minute of the game. But those hundreds of thousands of hands can help. They link together, and in their vast numbers, they create something vast.

If a rabbi could unleash such power. If a priest could step before a camera and inspire a few moments of unreasoning faith. If an imam could wield this weapon. If God still possessed this divine power.... But Lennon was right The Beatles could provoke that reaction just by stepping off a plane. They were bigger than Jesus Christ, and when one of them died, we mourned as if a god had been killed.

I believe this is the reason that you, and I, and so many other people, desire fame. It is not a Freudian urge to be loved and valued by our fathers, though I have been told this many times by psychologists. It is a desire to be gods. To be all-powerful and to be immortal.

You must not be ashamed of your impulse to fame, Shmuley. It will make you a different man from the one Debbie married, though I know she will love him just as much. It will give you less time for individuals, but that is only because there are a limited number of hours in the day. With a million hours in every day, we could get everything done. Our task is to make choices—about what we do with every day, with those very few hours. Your instincts lie on the path to fame. Don't ignore your instincts—they know more than you do. Become a god, because you desire that power for the very best of reasons. You want to help people. To help them, you need power. Fame bestows power. Do not be afraid of it.

When I met Elvis in 1975, he was probably the most famous man in the universe. He heard I was in L.A., on a shopping trip from New York, and he asked me to pay court. I drove from Los Angeles to Las Vegas, and then an hour further into the desert. We reached an aluminum Airstream trailer, and a man stepped out in a plain white suit.

No rhinestones, no pearls. Just a belt buckle as big as a license plate. And he gave me a spoon and asked me to bend it, and when I did, the god-like reserve fell away. He was a Tennessee truck-driver who could not believe his own eyes. I held the spoon at the base with my fingertips, stroked the middle three times and held it out to Elvis. As he took it, the metal curled. I was brimful of energy, despite an uncomfortable drive, because I was standing next to a living god and talking to him as an equal. The spoon bent upwards, and Elvis poured out stories to me as if I was his confessor. He told me of his mother, whose love had meant more to him than everything. He was at Graceland, his mansion, when the phone rang at 3:30 A.M.—"I knew what it was before I answered the telephone." His mother had died, on August 13, 1958. Elvis believed he would see her again.

We were a short drive from Area 51, the U.S. military base where many believe that captured UFOs have been dismantled and probed by scientists who take the technology they can understand and translate it into modern products: transistors, microchips, holograms. In 1975, before the X-Files and the fascination with aliens, Area 51 was a deeply-kept secret. But Elvis talked of it openly—the craft, their construction, their pilots, and what it could all mean to mankind. He was in no doubt that UFOs came "from the stars," or that injured extraterrestrials had been taken prisoner from damaged UFOs and interrogated by CIA agents. Elvis's status as a god-human gave him access to every level of national intelligence—the President would be as proud to entertain Elvis Presley at the White House as a senior USAF operative would be to provide a tour of Area 51's most secret bunkers. As we talked, I had a strong sense that this honest, forthright man felt guilty to be keeping back a good many secrets.

He died in 1977. I saw the photographs, and I accept he is dead. The "god" part of him is immortal—Elvis will always be the King. But the human part died. I am 99 percent convinced of that...99 percent. Just 1 percent doubt.

In the Blessed Name of Elvis,

Dear Uri,

I have sometimes wanted to be famous, but I have never wanted to be a god. I find being human challenging and rewarding—enough.

This does not mean that I do not wish for immortality or that I do not fear death. Nor does it mean that I do not want to be all-powerful, which I would probably enjoy. Less so does it mean that I do not wish to have the secrets of the universe revealed to me, because I would love to know those things that no human can fathom. What it does mean, Uri, is that if I were to be a god, none of these things would have any value to me because I had not earned them. I might have infinite knowledge, but it wouldn't be *my* knowledge. I might have power, but it wouldn't be *my* power. And I might have everlasting life, but it would not be *my* life.

Uri, I do not shy away from your offer to be a god because I am shy or humble. Rather, it is because I believe that to be fully human is to be more than a god. It is to have all the god-like features but to have actually earned them, instead of having been granted or given them. To be fully human is to have worked and struggled to be special. Like any other human being, I have been endowed by my Creator with certain gifts that I can choose either to deny or develop—to use for the common good or exploit for selfish ends.

The ancient Greek gods were powerful, but they were not majestic. For majesty is a luster that can only be achieved through struggle. Witness how the royal family in Britain has ceased to shine as in times of yore. Having the right blood is a beginning, but having the right stuff is the crowning glory.

Many people today have little respect for struggle. Perhaps it is because we have been blessed to be alive at a time when few in the Western world struggle for basic sustenance, when diseases are being curbed and life is being prolonged. We want everything to be easy. We expect instant gratification and instant results. And when the going gets tough, the tough get going—and quick. Look how easily people quit on their marriages today. We all live in the disposable society. Our motto is, "If it's broken, don't even think about fixing it. Just throw it out." How can Western society continue to call itself structured, civilized, and ordered when one out of two marriages ends in divorce? Why is it that diplomats try and prevent fighting between nations, but clerics do not seek to prevent fighting between men and women? If one out of every two businesses in Europe went bust, a state of emergency would be declared. But when one out of every two marriages goes bust, no one utters a peep. If something doesn't produce immediate results, we discard it without a second thought. Take your computer whose hard disk has crashed to an engineer and the chances are he'll tell you it isn't worth paying to have it fixed. Throw it out and get a new one. And that's what we do with our relationships as well.

Hence, we all want to be gods. We all want to just lift a finger and make things happen. We want a magic wand in our hands. And, what do you know? Today we have it. It's called the remote control. That's my theory as to why we all so love television. You just lift a finger and it all happens. You don't even have to get up. Just raise the remote and an entire universe of hundreds of channels and millions of stories and fantasies opens before you. Like Michelangelo's depiction of the Creation in the Sistine Chapel, we create whole universes with nothing but the flick of a finger. Meanwhile, inertia takes over and you become a couch potato. Isn't that a god, Uri? A powerful couch potato?

Thankfully, there are some who do not shy away from the battle, but gird their loins in strength and rise to the occasion. They fight to be better people and struggle to win understanding. They toil to be exemplars of altruism and selflessness. They labor to expand their minds and broaden their horizons

In my time as rabbi to students at Oxford, I have witnessed two kinds of parents. The first type complains when their children don't meet their expectations. They look dejected and disappointed when their children come home with a second-class degree. These aren't parents, but aristocrats. They want victories, never defeats They are not raising children, but the future nobility. The second type of parent revels in the struggle and celebrates the triumphs and the defeats—because even when it is a defeat, it is *their* child who is defeated. And they would rather have their own child who is defeated than someone else's child who is victorious. They are simply thrilled to be parents. They accompany their children to the mountain tops, but also they never abandon them in the valleys. They take pride in the fact that they never give up. Children are an intrinsic blessing, and every blessing involves a struggle.

In November 1990, a father called me up and asked if I could assist his thirty-five-year-old son, who had been born with motor neuron disease. The man had always been in a wheelchair, could not hold his head up, and used a tablet with letters on it to move his elbow and thereby communicate. When I met the father and son, I was moved first by the young man's intelligence and determination to lead a normal life. But I was just as inspired by his father, who knew what every sound meant and was infinitely patient with his son. As they were leaving, the father pulled me to one side. "I really need your help," he told me. "Last month, my son attempted suicide because he feels that he is useless. He's out now after three months in the hospital. We need to find him something to do or he'll try it again. He has told me repeatedly that I am a monster for allowing him to live when I should have let him die as a baby. Please, I need your help."

I was amazed therefore to receive a phone call from the boy's uncle later that night. "Please Rabbi, whatever you do, don't help my nephew. I know this is going to sound horrible, but it would be a blessing if the boy were to die. What kind of life does he have anyway? He's a burden both to himself and to his family. My brother worked hard for what he has. But every penny has now gone into his son's medical care, and there's never going to be any improvement. They all deserve better than this."

Here are two brothers. One wants be a god; he wants an easy life and he wants control over life and death. The other just wants to be a father—not a father in heaven, just an earthly, human father who is distinguished by one thing and one thing only: he never gives up on his son, even when his son gives up on himself. Which would you rather be?

A god can make miracles happen and disrupt the ordinary. But human beings can find the miraculous in everyday situations, making the ordinary extraordinary. The gods of old are beings who control whole planets and worlds, but human beings can surpass even that, because they can exert control over themselves and their inner world. The men and women who have impressed me most in my lifetime are those who have developed their humanity to the highest possible degree. They are the wisest, most compassionate, most empathetic people I have met.

Hence, like you, I revered Diana, Princess of Wales, because she tried to ameliorate the suffering of millions worldwide. It was her humanity that we all most admired, and our ability to instantly identify with her made her the icon of our generation. and do you know what it was most about her that established her as our symbol. It was the fact that she was the paragon of someone with everything and nothing—simultaneously. A princess, on the one hand, who lived anything but a fairy tale life, on the other. She was the most famous woman in the world and perhaps the loneliest as well. She was also a silent spokesperson for a generation far wealthier than any that has preceded it—but one that suffers from depression more than has any other generation in history.

The greatest scourge of this generation is loneliness. Through our teens and early twenties, we are conditioned and encouraged to nurse our every professional ambition. We study and work hard to become a material success, only to discover that reaching the mountain's summit is not as important as sharing the view with someone you love. Diana, as the ultimate example of this uncontrollable sadness, earned a place in our hearts. Her isolation and forlornness reflected our own, and we identified with her suffering. Diana was emblematic of a generation possessed of everything save the one thing that makes life livable—love.

And yet, amidst this all-too-visible suffering, she never allowed her own pain to block out that of others. Although consumed with her own insecurities, she never allowed this to get in the way of feeling another's plight. Diana taught us that there is nothing wrong with being inconsistent. Even imperfect people can contribute to the perfection of the world. She found value and self-worth through alleviating the pain of friend and stranger alike, and became our heroine, a shining example of someone who never became so caught up in her own pain that she became deadened to the plight of others. The anguished din of her own heart was never so deafening that it drowned out the faint stirrings of someone else's sorrow.

Many modern-day psychologists tell us that we have to get our own house in order before we can contribute to other people's lives. A lot of people I know actually refrain from entering into a relationship because their therapists have told them that they can't love someone else until they love themselves. This kind of misinformation is robbing the world of so many good works. In Diana, we discovered someone with eating disorders and who had made suicide attempts who still contributed vastly toward the welfare of other people. While she spent much time ensconced in an all-consuming darkness, she still held aloft a candle of hope. Had she waited until she had sorted herself out, she would never have given inspiration to the millions who adored her. All of us know that we're imperfect, but while we're prepared to admit our faults, we don't consider ourselves to be bad people. We are not indifferent to the plight of strangers. In Diana, we found someone who, while far from perfect, still had enough confidence in herself to believe she could make a difference.

The ability to be famous and still remain earthy is something achieved by a select few. To an extent, I understand the arrogance of the famous. You go out to dinner and people drive you crazy for an autograph. You walk on the streets and people follow you. After a while, even if you are nice, you feel like telling them all to fly a kite, and very few people can avoid this. But some do. I remember when we hosted Argentine soccer idol Diego Maradona at L'Chaim a few years back. He warmly welcomed every person who approached him for an autograph, especially children. He also held onto the hands of his two little girls wherever he went. He wouldn't let go. He even insisted they sit up on the stage where he delivered his lecture.

Simon Wiesenthal was perhaps the most humble celebrity figure I have ever encountered. The legendary Nazi hunter arrived to speak for us in 1993, when he was well into his eighties. I was dragging his luggage off the belt at Heathrow airport and it all nearly came apart in my hands. The suitcase certainly wasn't Louis Vitton. In fact, it was junk, but he didn't care. He spent his money finding Nazis, not on himself. We put him up in a beautiful suite at Oxford's best hotel. He protested at what it must have cost us. "Isn't there just a room somewhere in this city with a bed?" Later, when he called his wife in Vienna to inform her that he arrived safely, he apologized to me for the expense.

Even Jerry Springer was uncompromisingly polite and humble when we hosted him at our London branch in March 1997. He refused to accept any money from us and told me that he simply wanted to help us because we were a Jewish charity, and his parents had escaped the Holocaust. Hundreds of people swarmed around him to get his autograph and he signed every single one.

Have I ever felt envy, being around these famous people all the time? Of course I have. But I do not believe that it is true, Uri, that we human beings crave fame because we want to be gods. I believe that we crave fame mostly out of insecurity and a lack of identity. And we are all infected by it. So even while I am envious of all these people, I am ashamed of my envy. Why do I want to be them? I should be happy being me.

For eleven years, I have hosted some of the most celebrated men and women in the world. And I have noticed something fascinating. So many famous people are themselves name-droppers. They tell you, "Last night, I had dinner with so-and-so," "Tonight, I'm on Concorde back to New York because I have breakfast tomorrow with so-and-so.' It's almost as if they want to be famous in order to feel special. But a void remains at the core of their being. One that can't be filled. So even when they become famous personalities, they're still convinced that they're only special because of who they know.

There is a commandment in the Bible that orders us not to lie to other people. Now, the ancient rabbis said that a truly pious person is someone who not only fulfills the law, but goes beyond the letter of the law. Not only do they not lie to others, but they don't even lie to themselves.

I cannot lie to myself, Uri. I know what the source of the search for fame is, Uri, and it is not always altruistic. It is mostly fueled by insecurity. I've told you this a thousand times: those who are not given enough love or stability when they are young end up with a weakened sense of identity. They become special and important when someone recognizes them in a restaurant or when they see themselves in a newspaper. This is not to say that there aren't healthy permutations of fame. Indeed, we can use our ambition and our search for glory for a lofty purpose. We can see our ambition as a raging bull, and we can harness all kinds of positive causes to it. I thank you for telling me not to fear my search for fame. I agree. I shouldn't fear or feel ashamed of it. But I should seek to redeem it. And that's what I have chosen to do. I have chosen to try and become known for good things, like promoting ancient Biblical values, offering students a home away from home, and saving people's marriages and strengthening their relationships.

But, isn't it odd, Uri—just to prove my point—that so many of the celebrities you have met are so utterly lost? Are they really gods? Or are they somewhat broken individuals whose entire identity belongs to those who control them? Can you imagine what it's like to host your own TV show, and to await the daily Nielsen ratings which are released at 4 P.M. in the afternoon? Can you imagine the insecurity caused by having a fickle public determine your value? Elvis was king because he was crowned by the people. And as the people began to forget him, he became an increasingly sad and lonely figure. Toward the end of his life, this was an emperor with pretty strange clothes. His marriage broke up, he lived on an endless stream of pills and drugs, and he couldn't control his eating. Of what was he king? Was his fame a blessing or a curse to him? One wonders, had he remained a Tennessee truck driver, would he have lived to a ripe old age instead of being cut down, as he was, in mid-life? I am convinced that the prime reason that Hollywood has a disproportionately high level of drug use is that the average celebrity lives in pain and seeks to numb the pain with substance abuse.

Just after releasing his autobiography, *Take it Like a Man*, Boy George spoke to our students about life. One arrogant student stood up and said, "Who are you to lecture to us? Your own life is a mess. You were a druggie for so many years. You're gay and have had a string of broken relationships." George looked at him and said, "And who are you to judge me? Do you know what it's like to be twenty-three years old, step off a bus in Manhattan, and have thousands of people immediately surround you for your autograph? And who is to say that under circumstances like these, you wouldn't have made far greater errors?" (By the way, did I tell you that I thought Boy George was highly intelligent? I had a wonderful time with him, and he really is quite deep.)

Much of this comes down to what we discussed in our last letter, about seeing God's mantle. We've got to go beyond promoting the superficial things, like fame, over the real things, like character. We've got to make the ordinary special rather than always chasing shooting stars. A healthy society is one in which ordinary people are treated like celebrities, and everyone is famous. The secret to finding fulfillment in life is to make the natural miraculous, the ordinary extraordinary, and the everyday unique.

This is exactly what God has been saying for thousands of years. I roll out the stars against the backdrop of the dark heavens to illuminate your night. I create the sun to shine upon the earth to give you warmth. I endow you with life and intelligence and have made you masters over all the animals. You are the jewel of creation. And all I want is to be acknowledged for it.

God also wants to be treated like a celebrity. He also wants a microphone. He wants people not just to worship Him, but to take notice of Him. To listen to Him. He wants people to recognize Him and give him credit for his wondrous acts. He is tired of being ignored.

And that's why He gave us the Bible. So that He could star in His own book. And so that we can use that book to discover that fame and fortune, while nice, are only valuable when God remains the ultimate star. When goodness and virtue still remain our ultimate goals. The world has seen many small gods in the past, Uri. They all ended up in the same place—deep in the earth. But the world has only ever witnessed one true God. And it is time we accorded Him his rightful place—deep in our hearts and at the center of our lives.

There is a final point I wish to make about Elvis. According to his biographers, he was forever haunted by a single question he could not answer. And his inability to answer that question is what led to his burnout and implosion. The question was: Why did God give this all to me, and what am I meant to do with it? Elvis was a candle that first burned brightly and then too brightly. The result was that his light was later diminished, until it was extinguished. Had he understood that God had given him the great light of celebrity in order to shine it on those who felt neglected, making them feel like they were the center of attention, he might have retained the inspiration to lift himself out of the abyss of despair.

Wishing both you and me a significant extension on the normally allotted fifteen minutes,

Dear Shmuley,

About ten years ago, many of my closest friends were lawyers. I was fighting legal actions—it seemed like I was fighting thousands of them, suing people all around. I tied my brain in knots and battered it flat with a two-ton file of affidavits. I won, mostly, following countless months of grinding tension, but after the long struggle, I felt no euphoria, only exhaustion. I look back and realize there was one bonus, which has always paid out at tough times in my life—I discovered some real friends.

One was Joel, a New Jersey lawyer. He had a wife and three children and a ruthless attitude—he wanted more than just to win the case, he wanted to win it laughing at the other guy's expense. He had a talent for voices and outraged us with impressions of the lawyers on the other teams, of the people we were suing. He once rang me at 3:00 A.M., using my own voice, claiming to be me and demanding to know who I was. I was stumbling around, trying to wake up, terrified this was some kind of paranormal backlash from all the stress. It just didn't occur to me this was a joke. When I insisted I was the real Uri Geller, he swore he'd sue me as an imposter and slammed down the phone. I sat on the end of the bed, trying to make sense of it, and Hanna put an arm around me. "You had a nightmare?" she asked.

"I think I'm suing myself," I told her.

"Of course," she said. "You're suing everybody else in the world—why not yourself also?"

Then I saw the joke. Joel had a serious message for me—I was driving myself insane in this legal frenzy. That wasn't the advice of an attorney, it was the counsel of a friend.

You can imagine, a man like this—successful, talented, and funny—had a wonderful family. His wife forgave him everything, and his children were all brilliant. The two girls both went to Yale—one's a university lecturer, one's a lawyer. Their younger brother was expected to follow them.

He was a great boy. I'll call him Alan, because that's nothing like his real name. I met him in New York when he was sixteen and a total Giants fan, full of the prospect of a trip to the Super Bowl, raving about his hero, Jeff Hostetler. Six months later, he came with his father to my home in England. I knew the Giants had beaten the Buffalo Bills 20–19, and as he climbed out of the car, I seized his shoulder, grinned, and said: "How about those Giants, hey?"

He said, "Yeah," like he had to humor a dumb grown-up. That was it. Just, "Yeah." And I had believed the Super Bowl meant so much to him.

His father walked the dogs with me later, and he wasn't joking when he told me: "I want you to speak with Alan. He's just not our boy, you know? Something's happened to him."

"I hate to make this suggestion but, it's possible, have you thought...?"

"Drugs? Sure I've thought that. I've confronted him. I don't believe he's lying—I'm a lawyer, I should know. He's clean."

"So what is it?"

"Ask Alan. He'll tell you. I can't explain it."

Alan was sitting in our family room, alone, when we got back. Everyone else was in the kitchen. Alan was not watching TV, not reading anything, not looking out of the window. Just sitting. I gave his father a push towards the kitchen and went to be with the son.

"Are you happy, Alan?" He just stared at me, and I repeated the question, forcefully, like I was ordering him to answer.

"So what's to be happy about?" he replied.

"The Giants, maybe?"

He looked at me for the first time. "That made me see reality," he said. "The Giants won. And it was meaningless. I thought I would feel great, but I woke up the day after, and everybody was expecting me to be so happy. I wasn't. All I could think was, the team has got it all to do again now. Everybody's talking about next year already. They won, and the next day it was history."

"And it's in the history books," I protested. "Super Bowl XXV, New York Giants."

"Yeah, it's history. You can never go back to it. It's dead."

"Could happen this year too," I prompted.

"Then it'll die again."

"Well, you know," I said, puzzled and missing the point, "it's only a game. Sport is just sport. Don't take it too hard."

"Everything's the same," he answered. "None of it means anything. I go to school, Dad wins a case, you go on TV or whatever you do—next day it's gone. Who cares who won last year's Super Bowl? Or the year before, or Super Bowl V? So who cares who wins it this year? Only the idiots who don't realize that nothing matters in the end."

"Come on, Alan! You've got to live for the moment. Live for now! If history doesn't matter, you have to admit that what you're feeling right now, this second, is even more important."

He lay back in the sofa and said, "OK, I admit that." But he wasn't admitting anything. He just wanted me to leave him alone.

"Let me tell you what matters to me—my family. My children. And you matter to your family. Your parents love you, so do your sisters. Your dad is worried about you."

Alan was shaking his head. "I know, they've told me, but can't you see there's no point to any of it? Listen," he asked me, "did you ever know your great-grandfather—your father's grandfather?"

"No—so what?"

"That's what I'm saying. So what? Do you care if he was happy, if he led a good life or whatever? I bet you've never thought of it once in your whole life. He probably thought he loved his children, but the next generation won't even spare a thought for him. Dead people are history. Everything's history as soon as it happens, and that's what makes it pointless."

"You're a Jew. You can't change that, and you can't pretend it's meaningless. You're part of a culture that is living history."

"All of it based on a lie," he said.

"What lie?"

"God. God is a lie."

"Alan, you know, the only thing that's pointless is this stupid argument we're having. There is a universal energy, we call it God—that's undeniable."

"I can't believe in that," he said slowly. "And there's nothing you can say to make me believe in it. And if I pretend to believe it, if I delude myself to give my life some meaning—that would just prove what I told you. It doesn't matter what you do, or what you think, because no one cares for long."

I had two more long talks with Alan. They were both like this. I tried to think of everything that could make a difference. Love, art, stupid TV, health, pain, religion, UFOs, self-respect, hedonism, philosophy, Yale, parents, children, college girls. I told him I would kill him to be seventeen again. He told me maybe he would save me the trouble.

Alan kept on believing that nothing mattered. He took his final exams, without caring what his grades were, without even caring whether he turned up for all the tests—because whatever seemed important to other students was only an illusion, and he could see through it. He didn't get his offer from Yale, but his grades were good enough to get him to another college. That summer he drove his father's BMW off the highway and into a wall. He was such a good, well-brought-up boy, when they cut him out, he was still wearing his seat-belt.

I remembered Alan when I read your letter, Shmuley, and you asked me: "Are there no Martians with a bit of *cojones* who can come out from behind the mask of their planet and introduce themselves properly, like smack in the middle of New York?" That's the denial of a skeptic, the unanswerable Nothing that deadens every argument the way a vacuum snuffs out a flame.

It's dangerous to try and think our way through the universal mysteries. We end up asking facile, sarcastic questions and getting stupidly depressed when we can't answer them. Why doesn't God appear on TV? If he's all-powerful, why won't he answer my prayers and deposit a million dollars in my bank account? How come aliens don't rule the planet since they've got all this amazing technology?

I try not to think my way through. I just accept the facts and keep my brain open. Tens of thousands of New Yorkers have had encounters with other intelligences, with types of life which do not seem human. Hundreds have written in detail of their experiences. Some have produced independent evidence to corroborate their sightings and experiences. A few have collected their findings in books—the artist Budd Hopkins, for instance, the thriller writer Whitley Streiber, and the Harvard professor of psychology John Mack. All New Yorkers. All talking about their experiences, all of them unable to convince you, because they don't have the proof. They can't present the world with any captive aliens right now. But I'm willing to believe it's possible—it's possible the facts are right, it's possible these intelligent and highly respected people are telling the truth, it's possible there are other species out there in the galaxy. It's very, very possible.

Joel phoned me the night after his son's car crash. Alan was in a coma, and not expected to survive. He asked me to pray for the boy, and I promised I would, but I knew that only a powerful will to live could wrench a comatose accident victim back to consciousness. And that was missing in Alan.

Joel phoned again the next day, and I was braced for bad news. Instead there was hope. "The boy's toughing it out. He's still out cold, but the doctors say his immune system is fighting back. That's a positive sign. He wants to live."

We all made tapes for Alan—my children sang songs, and I yelled every motivating word I could think of into the microphone: "Live, Alan! Come on, you're alive! Keep fighting! You can beat this! You're a winner! Fight it! Wake up and win! Come on, live, live, live!" His whole family, his schoolfriends, everyone talked to him in his coma. Joel had the breakthrough idea—he got a tape of the Super Bowl radio commentary, the Giants just edging the Bills, and he got quarterback Jeff Hostetler to read a short, personal message to Alan at the start of the tape. While that tape was playing for about the thirtieth time, when the coma was almost a month old, Alan regained consciousness. It was two months before he was allowed to go home, but he left walking. Three years of physiotherapy lay ahead, three years of guts and determination, three years of hard work that took him at last to college.

During his final semester he married a girl, the daughter of one of his tutors, and their first child was born around Passover last year. I flew to New York for the wedding, and Joel said to me: "Thank God the Giants won the Super Bowl that year. Think about it. Who would ever guess something like that could matter that much?"

With deep affection,

Dear Uri,

When I was fourteen years old and studying in Los Angeles, I read a story in the newspaper about a young girl named Angela. We were almost the same age, she being just two years older than me. But she was in the newspaper and all over the evening news, and I was not. You see, Angela and I had radically different approaches to life. Her approach made her famous, or at least just once. Journalists described the horrible way in which she chose to die. She called her parents into her room and then, as her mother walked in, she stuck her father's pistol into her mouth and pulled the trigger. But before she did all this, she first chose to say good-bye. OK, not directly. She left a letter, the full text of which her parents chose to publish in the newspapers in order to dissuade other children from copying her example.

You will have to forgive me, Uri. Many years have passed, and I do not quite recall the exact words she used. But I certainly remember the gist of what she said because it made an indelible mark on my young psyche. Angela said that she was taking her life because it was pretty unimpressive anyway. Nothing really mattered, so why go through the drudgery of existence? She said that she woke up in the morning and went to the bathroom. Then she got dressed and went to school. She returned from school and watched television, after which she did her homework. And the next morning, it started all over again. So she took her life because death seemed so much more exciting by comparison. Angela was a young girl, but inside she had grown old and saw only a pattern characterized by predictability, monotony, and meaninglessness.

I of course never met Angela, Uri, but at the time, I felt close to her. Hers was the kind of action that challenges all adolescents, as life quietly whispers in their ears: "Hey, why don't you do the same? Haven't you heard about the absurdity of life? Aren't all the grown-ups around you a bunch of hypocrites anyway? Don't you know that nothing really matters? Things come and go and nobody really cares. Nothing really changes. Everything stays the same. Everyone only ever cares about themselves, and all the air around you is putrid and foul. And no one will really notice you anyway. Therefore, you don't really fit in."

My first brush with suicide was therefore from a great distance, but unfortunately, with the passage of time, it was to come ever closer. As a rabbi at Oxford, I came across a tragic case, a brilliant young student from a mining family who had excelled in her A Levels. She came first in Science in the whole country. Boy, did she show all those kids from the pompous public schools like Eton and Harrow. If only her Oxford professors hadn't made such a big deal out of all that when she arrived at the university at the tender age of eighteen. Sadly, they weren't that smart. She hadn't been in Oxford two days before several of her tutors had told her what big things were expected of her. The next day, they found her hanging from the lamp fitting in her room.

But nothing hurt more, Uri, than the most recent suicide to have crossed my path. One of the reasons that I can converse well with you in Hebrew is that I studied for two years in rabbinical school in Jerusalem. I lived in a dormitory, but I had a very special uncle who looked after me. He was my father's younger brother. He would drive up from Be'er Sheva once every two weeks to give me pocket money and take me out to lunch, and I would travel to his house every other weekend. He was a surrogate father to me. We would walk to synagogue together, arguing about life and religion. He scolded me for not taking care of myself. He was concerned that I didn't exercise or have a healthy diet. He was a serious man, and I took pleasure in being one of the few people who could make him laugh.

Last summer was the last time I saw him. We met in Tel Aviv over breakfast. By now, he was a completely different man—bitter, miserable, and obsessed with a business deal gone wrong. The problem was that the deal was in the family, and he felt abandoned by his own siblings. They all told him to get over it. In our last meeting together, even I abandoned him. He wanted me to involve myself in the altercation. I felt it wasn't my place. Besides, I couldn't be bothered. I had my own things to worry about. Part of me was even upset that he could use these very infrequent meetings to discuss business rather than catch up. I guess when he finally needed me, I wasn't up to the task.

Four months later, when he felt abandoned by absolutely everyone around him, he walked out onto the main highway outside Be'er Sheva and stood in front of an oncoming truck. My brother called me from Los Angeles to tell me he had gone missing. My wife and I pulled out a book of Psalms in the middle of the night, hoping that God would listen to our prayers and my uncle would be OK. But God didn't listen any more than I had listened to my uncle's entreaties. Another uncle went that night and identified the body. And all of us in the family had to live with the knowledge that there was so much we could have done to prevent this act of desperation.

My uncle's action cut me up and terrified me. I loved my uncle, Uri. Truly I did. But I also mourned him for selfish reasons. With a suicide so close, with it happening in my family, it struck me that anyone is capable of it. My friends, my uncle—maybe, God forbid, even me. After all, how can any of us know if something will happen in life that will push us over the edge?

I know what your friend Alan was going through, Uri. I know because I was there. After my parents' divorce, I became a cynic who did terribly at school and who distinguished himself primarily by being the class jokester. Life whispered in my ear, "Why even try when the odds are stacked against you? You'll make friends but they'll just gossip about you. You'll smile at strangers, but they'll just walk right past you. You'll love people and ultimately, they'll just leave you." So I embraced the carefree life of meaninglessness. I became a high priest of nihilism, a poor student who lived on a diet of junk food and junk television.

Children of divorce, Uri, become politicians. They learn how to give each parent just enough love without upsetting the other. You are well aware of each parent's deep hurt and guilt over not keeping the family together. Each one wants to fault the other for the break-up. Witnessing their pain, you learn to indulge them. Let them get away with believing that everything was the other party's fault. It brings them comfort. You understand that your parents represent two rival factions. You're careful not to compliment the other faction in front of the parent you're currently with because that would cause pain and portray you as more devoted to the other party. You begin to say what people want to hear. I too became a politician. I felt like a yo-yo, torn constantly between dual allegiances. Passover with my father, the Jewish festival of *Sukkot* with my mother. When I was with my father, I found myself becoming more attached to him. When with my mother, the same thing happened with her. Life was an emotional roller coaster. After a while, I decided to stop playing the games and just fall deeper into myself.

I never contemplated suicide, Uri, and I never drove a car into a wall, although with the way I used to drive my moped, sometimes it came mighty close. But whatever my internal torment, I never thought of hurting myself, God forbid. That takes courage and my particular brand of cynicism was immensely cowardly. No, I took the easier way out. Rather than killing my body, I suffocated my spirit. I killed off the part of me that aspired to be anything or develop my potential. I slowly sunk to the bottom of my class and looked for attention wherever it was doled out.

But then something happened, something rescued me. I'll tell you what it was. Someone came along and made me believe in the sun again. I befriended a young rabbi in Miami who showed me how I was special. He entered me into a competition in which young boys were tested as to how much of the Bible they could study by heart. He inspired me to study, and to my surprise, I won three years in a row. This while I continued to be a terrible student in school. I joined a Jewish choir that went on tour to various cities in the United States. We sang Jewish songs based on scripture and the book of Psalms. When I asked my choirmaster how I could become a soloist, he told me it wasn't dependent on how richly I hit the notes but on how deeply I felt the words. I started studying the words of scripture and their beauty resonated in me. King David, through his beautiful Psalms, was teaching me to discover God as a comforter, as a healer of shattered hearts:

> O God, you are my God, I seek you, my soul thirsts for you; my flesh faints for you, as in a dry and weary land where there is no water. So I have looked upon you in the sanctuary, beholding your power and glory. Because your steadfast love is better than life, my lips will praise you. (Psalms 63:1–3)

A year later, I was given a solo song that I sang on a stool so tall I could barely clamber up onto it while on stage in front of a thousand people. We made records. I felt special. People would stop me on the street and tell me how much joy my singing brought into their lives.

The principal of my school, a truly noble and righteous man named Rabbi Alexander Gross, started taking me to retirement homes on Friday afternoons before the Sabbath. I would sing for elderly people whose children and grandchildren had sent them there so as not to be burdened by parents and grandparents who needed constant care. They were lonely and frail and, for two or three hours a week, I became their grandchild. They lavished presents on me. I was only twelve years old, and at first, I too felt they were a burden. I hated the way they pinched my cheeks and fussed over me. But after a few weeks, they began to give me purpose, and I waited the entire week for those visits. One Friday afternoon, a woman named Martha, who was over ninety, had a hunched back and no teeth, called me over to her just before I started to sing. She told me that she had put it into her will that she wanted me to sing the *Kaddish* at her funeral. "Only then," she stuttered, "will I feel that my *neshama* is still alive." Two weeks later, Martha's *neshama* fluttered away like a butterfly, and I was there to help it ascend still higher.

It was largely through these visits, Uri, that I slowly began to feel that my life could make a difference. And that's ultimately what rescued me from that cynicism. I began to believe that my life was precious rather than worthless. I felt that God had placed me on this earth for a purpose, and I reveled in trying to live up to His expectations. Even today, I struggle to recapture that sense of mission. But I know it is always there, just waiting for me to tap into it and connect. I know that it can always uplift me, if ever I am feeling down.

Many today mistakenly believe that depression is an emotion, albeit a negative emotion. But an emotion nonetheless. The ancients knew better. They declared that depression is not an emotion at all. Rather, it is the absence of emotion. Depression is more akin to numbness than unhappiness. When you are unhappy, you feel down, you feel bad. When you are depressed, you feel nothing. You become like a stone. Depression is when you have ceased feeling. Your friends come around and try and cheer you up. Come out with us to a movie. Or how about playing some football. At the very least, they say, sit up and let's talk about it. But you don't feel like talking at all. When you are depressed, all you want is to be left alone. You want your parents to leave you alone and your friends to go home. Most of all, you want life itself to leave you alone. Depression is the horrible state whereby a human being is converted from flesh to stone, from a being to a thing, from organic matter to an inanimate object.

As a rabbi to students, Uri, I have seen all too many people whose hearts have become like stones. And it often leads to suicide because once you have died on the inside, it spreads around your body like a disease, and you end up dying on the outside as well. To be sure, suicide is a big step. But not if you're killing that which is already dead. And that's how those who do it rationalize their actions. If I'm already dead, then I am only killing that which has already ceased to live. I am not taking a life. I am confirming death.

Worse, Uri, are those people like your friend Alan who embrace nihilism and make a philosophy of it, for they become the living dead. They wish to be profound in their despair, philosophical in their cynicism. Life is absurd and they can't figure out why everyone else can't see it. How dare you try and talk them out of their black mood. You are the one who is crazy. Can't you see? Are you blind? Can you honestly deny the meaningless of life, the ephemerality of existence, the transient nature of human relationships? Don't you see how God has distanced Himself from the world and abandoned us to the elements? Are you insensitive to the blindness of justice and the triumph of the wicked?

This is all so blatantly apparent that only one of three responses is appropriate. First, you can sink into madness and despair. You simply succumb to the absurdity of life and accept that the gods must be crazy—So why fight them? Choose insanity along with them.

The second response is to embrace the "Enjoy life today, because tomorrow we all die" philosophy. Live for materialism and pleasure. Give your life meaning by placing yourself at the center of an ever-expanding circle of material possessions, professional achievement, and success. And that's the philosophy that most people today have embraced. Watch as much television, buy as many clothes, take as many lovers as humanly possible. Because that's the only thing that gives life any meaning. Since life has no inherent purpose, at the very least, enjoy the sun while it shines.

There is one final response. Once you have discovered the meaninglessness of your own existence, then give it meaning by devoting yourself to someone else's existence. Once you have recognized the transient nature of your own being, reach out to the infinite and connect yourself with a higher being. And once you have discerned how all of your achievements mean nothing because they instantly vanish, then give them permanence by devoting yourself to acts of loving-kindness. The imprint you make on someone's heart is everlasting.

The only thing that makes our lives worthwhile, Uri, the only real response we have to your young friend Alan, is that every time we choose to undertake a caring act, we lend our lives significance. Because, while we will ultimately disappear, the mark we leave will be permanent. King Solomon, in his book Ecclesiastes, is the man who has everything—wealth, power, love—but can derive satisfaction from none of them. He speaks of everything as vain and unimportant. He seems weary of life, bored of existence. Nothing is challenging, and nothing is permanent. Read these verses and you would think that it was an older version of Alan talking. (Perhaps it was Alan, in a previous incarnation, centuries ago):

> All things are wearisome; more than one can express; the eye is not satisfied with seeing, or the ear filled with hearing. What has been is what will be, and what has been done is what will be done; there is nothing new under the sun. Is there a thing of which it is said,

"See, this is new"? It has already been, in the ages before us. The people of long ago are not remembered, nor will there be any remembrance of people yet to come by those who come after them. (Ecclesiastes 1:11)

On and on the book goes, growing ever more cynical. It only begins to grow lighter toward the end, until the penultimate verse makes sense of the entire book:

Now all has been heard; here is the conclusion of the matter: Fear God and keep his commandments, for this is the whole duty of man. (Ecclesiastes 12:13)

And this is what gives our life permanence. This is the only response we can give Alan. We must fear God, lead ethical lives, clothe the naked, feed the hungry, impart hope to the hopeless, because this is what life is all about. To expand our horizons, broaden our lives, and respond to the call of greatness. Notice, Uri, that when a body dies and decays, it sharply contracts. Conversely, when a body truly lives, it expands. Life is about development, growth, and spreading out. Specifically, the expansion of life comes in three dimensions. When we reach deeper, higher, and wider outside ourselves.

We must reach deeper into ourselves and unearth core human truths. We must reach higher than ourselves and latch onto God. And we must reach outside ourselves and connect with our fellow man. Through our good deeds, our charity, we will be remembered, because good deeds are everlasting.

There is a story, Uri, of a medieval Spanish king who had a rabbi as chief advisor. The various cardinals were violently jealous of the rabbi's influence and did all they could to undermine his credibility. They finally got him on fabricated charges of embezzlement from the Royal treasury. The king had his advisor arrested and placed in chains. When he was brought before the king and accused of treason, the king informed him that he had reluctantly confiscated all his property. "You shouldn't have betrayed me, my friend," the king said. "Now you have nothing left." But the rabbi turned to him and said. "Oh, yes, I have everything left. The good deeds I've done in my life, they are the only things that were ever mine in the first instance, and I still have all of them. The rest of the things that were in my possession—my house, my jewels, my land—why, they were never mine. Didn't you just take them away? And if you can merely snap your fingers and take them away, doesn't that prove that they were never mine, even while they were in my possession? But my deeds of kindness, they are indeed eternal. Not even death can take them away. I die knowing that I was a good and decent man, even if you currently deny it. It is enough that God knows it, for I was created to serve Him, the truest majesty."

And finally—for now at least, Uri, I'm glad to see that you've gotten a bit testy. I have finally provoked you. You are always such a cool customer. So now we're finally equal. True, I can't bend metal with my mind. But as a Rabbi, I have the power to get under your skin. It's what we Rabbis are good at. As a psychic, you have the advantage of knowing what my arguments are going to be before I even express them, and now I can counter by being a pest. Ah, equality at last!

You are upset at me, Uri, accusing me of taking a cheap shot in my arguments against the existence of aliens. You feel that my demand that they reveal themselves openly is the same kind of cynical argument that can be applied to God as well, namely, that He should reveal Himself and if He does not, then He does not exist. I agree. This is a cheap shot that superficial and overly materialistic people make against God. Since they lack spirituality in their lives, they are incapable of peering beneath the surface. They only accept what they see. They would deny the existence of love as well, since they can't see that either.

But I have to defend myself, Uri, because I think that you have made a fundamental error in your comparison. While God cannot be seen, his *effects* can be felt. No one has ever seen electricity, Uri, but we know it exists because when we switch on an air conditioner, a dead appliance suddenly comes to life. The same thing is true of the soul. Without it there is only a dead body. And that's how we know that God exists. He is hidden, but all his effects are felt. He is the soul of the Universe. It is self-evident that the infinity of space required an infinitely powerful Creator to design it. The incredible complexity of the human mind required a designer of the highest intelligence to fashion it. The eternity of the Universe requires an eternal origin. And the staggering diversity and color of all that exists demands an all-powerful artist to craft it. That's how I know God is with me, Uri, even when I don't see Him.

But the same cannot be said of aliens. Here, not only do we not see them, we do not see their effects either. What practical effect, of any detectable magnitude, or of any even infinitesimal benefit to mankind, can be attributed to aliens from outer space?

There is still one thing I don't understand, Uri. You are a humble man. You acknowledge that the extraordinary gift you possess is just that, a gift. You take no credit for it. You have written many times that the fact that you are the only person on the planet who possesses this gift confuses as much as it exhilarates you. Then why attribute it to aliens? Why not God? Why not give the credit to He who is responsible for all the other incredible gifts you have as well?

It was due to the extraordinary and miraculous gifts that God bestowed upon all humanity that Job, a man who suffered so much, yet never lost his faith in God, said, "yet in my flesh I will see God."

In God, we find eternity in the heavens, Uri, and through his children, our fellow human beings, we find eternity on earth. A single ray of human love and warmth is enough to dispel all the gloom and darkness of all the world's confused adolescents. Because, in the final analysis, I believe that young adults like Alan ask their questions simply to be heard. They want to know that we are listening. They want to know that we take them seriously. And they want to know that there is light at the end of the tunnel, and that the light isn't an oncoming train.

Gotta go now. My daughter Shterni lost a tooth, and I have to go put a dollar under her pillow.

Wishing you the vibrancy of youth and
the wisdom of old age,

Dear Shmuley,

It's close to midnight on August 16, a great day for conspiracy nuts. August 16 is the day Elvis faked his death—or did in fact die, murdered by the CIA—or was taken up to a heavenly planet by the aliens who spawned him. All three theories have been earnestly expounded to me, one by a Hollywood producer who claimed he was at Graceland that day in 1977. You can see I don't feel like taking any of this too seriously tonight. August 16 is also Shipi's birthday and, to celebrate, the whole family went to have dinner while we watched an Elvis impersonator.

During the show—when the King was collecting some floral tributes, after a really rockin' version of "Heartbreak Hotel"—a woman at the table beside ours recognized me. She kept waving and half rising from her chair and at last scurried across and knelt beside me. I tried to make her stand, so that I could also rise and briefly shake her hand before sending her back to her seat with an autograph. But she wanted to be kneeling, and gripped the arm of my chair and hissed in my ear: "I'm so glad it's you, Mr. Geller. Please help me. I know you can. I lost my wedding ring, you see, and it's breaking my heart. Please can you use your powers and help me find it?"

"I can't make it appear out of thin air," I protested.

"But can you psychically see where I've lost it? I don't mean I want to hire you to search my house, but can't you...don't you have any ideas?" She looked crestfallen. The band started kicking up "Blue Suede Shoes." "I've looked down the back of the sofa, under the mattress, in the glove compartment, and everywhere..."

"Have you looked in the shower? Where the water drains away?"

She stared at me. "I haven't," she said.

"That's where it is," I said with total confidence. The confidence was important—if I'd told her, "I think, maybe, it's possible..." she would have demanded more guesses. And they would have been wrong guesses, because my first suggestion had been sheer inspiration, said without thinking. I strongly believe I'm right that her ring really had slipped off in the shower and was wedged in the drain. Perhaps she saw it happen, though her conscious mind did not register it, and my own subconscious read her thoughts.

Driving home, Shipi and I started talking about other things I've been asked to find. Oil, diamonds, gold, relics, bodies, kidnap victims, Soviet missile silos. A ring is not the most trivial item I've been challenged to discover. One German billionaire once paid me a ridiculous fee to find out what happened to a $3,200 koi carp which dematerialized from an open-air aquarium (a heron ate it). We were approached last year by a team of treasure-hunters on the trail of $160 million in gold bullion, looted from Dutch banks as the Nazis retreated in 1945 and buried in fox-holes somewhere between the Rhine and Berlin. I liked that idea, but I did not want to trudge across Germany with a spade. If I'm going to roll up my sleeves and dig, it has to be for something more than gold. I want to discover something holy.

One friend of mine, an internationally renowned Holy Land archaeologist, has invited me to Israel. He believes he is close to finding the Ark of the Covenant. I had an idea it had already been found, in Ethiopia, by one of his colleagues, Graham Hancock—but a publisher has just sent me a book by two other Ark-hunters, Stuart Munro-Hay and Roderick Grierson, who say Ethiopia is crowded with Arks. The relics of that parched and war-torn land are really just replicas of the tablets Moses brought down from Sinai, carved centuries ago to serve as the focus for a reborn Christianity in Africa. The believers needed symbols of God, icons of the new religion, and the priests had to create them.

All my life, like every Jew and Christian and Moslem, I have been ruled by the words on those tablets. They shaped our world. But some of the words mattered more than others. "Remember the Sabbath day and keep it holy"—this is a cornerstone of my culture, a commandment that is also a pleasure. But, "You shall not make for yourself a sculptured image, or any likeness of what is in the heavens above, or on the earth below, or in the waters under the earth"—this goes against everything that gives form to our society. It is a commandment that seems to outlaw television, newspaper photographs, computer graphics, art galleries, Hollywood. It forbids stained-glass windows in churches and portraits of rabbis on book jackets. It denies us sketches by war artists and Leonardo da Vinci and our children and Rembrandt, beautiful nightmares by Picasso and Van Gogh and Goya and Dali.

We find out about our planet through images, far more than words—very often, there are no words for the images. We remember the anti-missile fire that blossomed over Baghdad as the Gulf War began, a vivid night-sky of fiery flowers, but we cannot remember one word that CNN's commentators spoke over the pictures. We saw the bodies of children being cradled as Ethiopia starved, and we saw the world's pop stars on stages both sides of the Atlantic, singing to feed the millions—but no one recalls what the reporters said about the famine, or what the rock gods said between numbers. The words didn't matter. The images were literally the difference between life and death for tens of thousands of people.

Images reach much deeper into our brains than words. Our conscious minds process the words, but images permeate every part—conscious, subconscious, unconscious. If I try and remember a conversation from my early childhood, I cannot...but the images rush my memory: the spark on my mother's sewing machine that knocked me across our one-room apartment, the glass that showered my cot from gunfire in the street outside, the light that hit my face in a deserted Arabic garden.

The priests of Ethiopia understood this power, as they made tablets that echoed Moses' own tablets—which were replicas themselves, because Moses broke the first set of commandments God gave him. He was in a rage when he returned from Sinai to find that the Jews had forgotten his words and were worshipping images. Maybe God should have accepted the inevitable at this point and scratched out the line about any "sculptured image, or any likeness." No one ever lived by it. Since the days of Exodus, there have only been nine commandments that count.

I love the idea of searching for the Ark in Israel. I would be seeking the Holiest of Holies within the Holy Land. It is a wonderful image for the inner search that I cannot put into words, the endless seeking of something especially clean and good and incorruptible in my own soul.

That woman tonight at the Elvis show didn't want to find her wedding ring because the gold had some value at a pawnbrokers. Money just did not come into it. She was desperate to regain the only symbol that could ever prove how perfect and wondrous her own marriage should be. Whatever had happened to this woman and her husband in the years since they pledged their lives to each other, the first day was always with them, in the shape of a ring on her finger. She carried newness and hope and perfection in a precious circle on her hand, her own Ark of the Covenant. I hope she found it again.

With deep affection,

Dear Uri,

I have my own story of pop star impersonators, albeit not Elvis. A few years ago, when my older brother and sister, Chaim and Ateret (who are twins) celebrated their birthday, we all went to a Miami beachfront hotel where they had drag queen impersonators of famous rock 'n roll and country music stars. Don't ask what a rabbi was doing at a drag queen evening, even one in a small, cheesy hotel. (My family made me do it.) The guy who did Madonna was almost indistinguishable from the real thing. He looked exactly like Madonna, albeit a muscular male version. We were sitting in the very front row when "Dolly Parton" came on to the stage. Well, it didn't take long for Dolly to notice that a guy who looked like a rabbi was sitting just a few feet in front of her. Right after the applause for the first song, Dolly came off the stage, made a beeline straight for me, grabbed me by the hair, and stuffed my face into her artificial mammaries. I tried to struggle free, but Dolly had a fearsome grip, and I soon found myself suffocating. Of all the horrible deaths imaginable, I never dreamed of going out like this! I determined that death by suffocation in silicone by a Miami drag queen would not look good in that week's obituaries, and I finally managed to push the guy away. Everyone laughed. Including my wife. But after that, I played it safe. For their next birthday, I took my brother and sister to an octogenarian bingo game instead.

My students at Oxford have great dinner-table debates about symbols and their power. Many students say they refuse to marry. Their reasoning is that marriage is only a symbol, and if you have real love you don't need symbols. They tell me that symbols are only external, and if you don't marry for each other but only for others, this public display is degrading to the entire relationship. "You see Shmuley, marriage is only a symbol and our generation has progressed beyond that," a girl from New York told me. I then asked her, "So why are you here at university taking a degree? Furthermore, why did you travel all the way across the Atlantic to get an *Oxford* degree? Isn't that also just a symbol? Why are you suddenly living to gratify the people around you? Your degree is a symbol to all around you of the status you have achieved as an educated adult. It's for people like future employers, not for you."

It seems that symbols have really only ever been respected by the ancients. Ancient peoples wrote and conveyed ideas in pictures, Egyptian hieroglyphics being the most famous examples. The ancients respected, embraced, and lived by symbols. But modern men and women, Uri, live by words. We talk rather than show each other symbols. Our language is verbal rather than pictorial. We take pictures only to remember past events rather than to communicate ideas. That's why we can't even understand our dreams since they speak to us in the language of symbols.

There are many advantages to conveying ideas in pictures rather than words. Notice that using words as a mode of expression always means proceeding from the details to the larger picture. Language is incapable of conveying the whole picture in one stroke the way an image would. For example, if I wanted to tell you what my childhood home in Miami Beach looked like, I would start by telling you that it was white and had two stories. Then I would tell you about the circular driveway, the brown front door and the large circular window at the front of the house. I would then tell you what the entrance hall looked like, and so on. As I gave you more and more details, you would slowly compose an overall picture of what the house looks like.

But there is one problem with the description. If I were to give ten people the most detailed description of the house—

down to the very last blade of grass—each one would have a different image of what the house looks like, because each person builds his own composite image of the home in his mind. That is why the spoken word can be so pleasurable. It invites the listener as an active participant in the story by asking him to amalgamate the description into one great whole, incorporating his own particular tastes and preferences. This is also why the movie version of a book is never as good as the novel. Because reading the novel allows me to choose my own representations based on my own personal tastes. And people would rather have their version of Don Vito Corleone over Francis Ford Coppola's any day (I say this even though *The Godfather* is my favorite movie of all time). But this is also the great weakness of the spoken word as opposed to the image: it detracts from the truth. There is only one way that the house looks, not ten different ways.

Seeing is believing. Seeing paints a direct impression on your mind. The viewer is totally passive in the face of what he sees. So seeing has the disadvantage of not involving the viewer as a participant, thereby risking a subjective edge to the item in question. Seeing has the direct advantage of being about the unadulterated truth. When you see something you can't misconstrue it. Images and symbols are not subjective, but objective. They mean the same thing to everybody.

That's why, when God gave the Jewish people the Ten Commandments on Mt. Sinai, a code of universal law by which all people were to live equally, He made sure that the entire nation were present to witness it. He didn't want them to hear about it from Moses. He wanted them to see it themselves. There can be no room for personal interpretation when it comes to laws like "Do not murder" and "Do not steal." These were absolute standards with which all people had to comply. The people were there to see the laws and have them make an indelible imprint upon them. Hence, after the Ten Commandments were given, God says to the people, "You have seen for yourselves that I spoke with you from heaven" (Exodus 20:22, NRSV).

This is why symbols are so powerful, Uri. Because they have collective meaning and leave no room for individual interpretation. A man and wife who show their spouse love will always be far more appreciated than those who just profess love. This is why, even in the secular age in which we live, people want to get married. There is nothing that can capture a couple's feelings for one another more than the fact of marriage. Marriage is a statement whereby, on the one hand, a man and a woman consecrate themselves to one another and, on the other hand, they give up everyone else and establish an exclusive relationship with one another. He becomes her husband, and not every woman's man. She becomes his wife and not every other man's potential sex partner.

In the Ten Commandments which you quote Uri, you'll notice that the first two commandments read, "I am the Lord Your God," and, "You shall have no other gods before me." What God establishes is a relationship consisting of primacy and exclusivity. He tells the Jewish people that He must be first in their lives, and that He must also be their only God. This too is the essence of marriage. To make your partner the one and only. To put your spouse first and to cordon them off in a protective pocket from all other competitors.

If someone is in a relationship, I have every right to ask them, "Is your relationship serious?" But if the couple were married, then the question would sound ridiculous because marriage is a universal symbol of very serious commitment. That is why marriage is the single most romantic thing available to two partners in a relationship. It is the only thing they can do for one another that establishes a universally respected set of rules concerning what they have every right to expect. A husband cannot later tell his wife that his one-night stand with another woman was "no big deal." It is a big deal because everyone knows that sleeping with a stranger when you're married is adultery. There is no other way around it. But if the couple are only living together, then he can easily say, "Hey, you're getting too possessive. I never agreed that we can't sleep with any other people. Besides, I didn't even love her. It was just sex."

And here is why people today fear symbols. They all want to be individuals. They are afraid of submitting their individual authority to a collective code of behavior. Submission to symbols requires conformity and is antithetical to the cult of the individual. They are terrified about being brought under the communal umbrella of a universal symbol which will deny or constrict their individuality. They don't want to be typecast, so they discard symbols.

The ancients, who had a far more collective identity than we do today—submerging their individual needs to the communal will did not fear symbols but welcomed them. They understood that symbols were the substance of life. For them, symbols were not empty representations. Nor were they merely things which stood for something else, with no intrinsic connection. Rather, for the ancients, symbols were a natural and organic outgrowth of the object they represented. A fire or flame was the natural representation of the soul because in the same way that a fire is full of life, reaching up and down, and also bright and burning with heat, so too is the human life force, capable of great vitality, passion, and warmth. Hence, the Bible says that "the fire of God is the soul of man." Unconfused, undistracted, and substantially more focused than we are today, the ancients were far more adept at homing in on the essence of a thing. Thus, they were able to create direct representations of things. They lived for pictures because the pictures captured the spirit of the item they were trying to render.

One of the most potent sources of human symbols, of course, is a dream. In fact, it was because of the recurrent dreams which I had in the wake of my parents' divorce that I took a strong interest in the subject and ultimately wrote a book about it. As a little boy, I would go to sleep far too late into the night, which made it difficult for me to get up in the morning. My mother would therefore take away my blanket and would freeze me out of bed. I would then go secretly to the laundry room and curl up on top of the drier where it was snug and warm. In my dream, however, I wasn't on top of the drier, but inside it, going around and around. And it was a large, dark monster, with eyes both in the back and the front of his head, who had put me in and would not let me out. Finally, I would break out and throw a stone at the back of his head. He then collected all the members of my family to ask who had thrown the stone. Remarkably, they all turned me in. Both my parents and my siblings all told him, "It wasn't us. It was Shmuley who threw the stone." He would then turn around and chase me, I would run away, and then I would wake up.

Now, it didn't take a rocket scientist to understand the overall message of the dream and my sense of abandonment on the part of my family. But till today I have not fathomed what the other symbols mean. That's why I became a student of dreams and also studied Freud. But while Freud is rightly credited with sparking a global revival in dream interest, he can also be forcefully criticized for propelling dream understanding back to its infancy by reducing all dream symbols to single, sexual representations. Freud seemed to miss the vast color and richness of symbols. He saw them only in black and white.

But here is where I want to address the central and powerful point raised in your letter, Uri, about the second commandment which forbids us to create molten images and false symbols. The exact verse reads:

> You shall not make for yourself an idol, whether in the form of that is in heaven above, or that is on the earth beneath, or that is in the water under the earth. You shall not bow down to them or worship them; for I the Lord your God am a jealous God. (Exodus 20:4)

First, the technical stuff. What God forbids here is not two-dimensional pictures, but rather three-dimensional sculptures. Hence, while ancient Israel had beautiful mosaics and paintings, unlike Greece and Rome, there was no sculpture. (The way that a modern-day religious Jewish sculptor gets around this is by making an imperfect sculpture, usually leaving it incomplete or with something broken off, thereby rendering it unfit for worship.) The reason is that the ancients worshiped gods hewn of stone. Idol worship was based around totem poles and perfect sculptures of the gods. Later, people even came to worship God's handicrafts like the sun and the moon.

And this is what God was saying. Symbols are very important. They represent very special things. But the moment they cease representing them and begin *replacing* them, the moment they supplant the objects they represent, then they are not symbols but false gods. A symbol is meant to be like a glass window. You're supposed to see right through it to the object it symbolizes. But the moment it becomes an entity in its own right, then its whole purpose is defeated. The moment the symbol becomes more important than the object it represents, it becomes a foreign god.

The great Jewish philosopher Maimonides explains how people came to worship the sun and the moon. At first, people would look at the sun and instantly think of the greatness of God. After all, if this incredible fireball in the sky is merely one of God's creations, can you imagine how great God Himself must be? The sun was thereafter employed by the ancients as a symbol of God's might. The Bible itself contains many references to God and the sun. Witness, "For the Lord God is a sun and shield; he bestows favor and honor. No good thing does the Lord withhold from those who walk uprightly" (Psalms 84:11). The problem began when people forgot that the sun was merely a symbol and manifestation of God's glory, and instead started worshipping the sun as a god unto itself. This is what God is outlawing in the second commandment, Uri. What the

Bible really outlawed was not symbols or images which are representations of higher truths, but images which came to supplant and replace higher truths.

For example, the holiest object in the Jewish faith is a Torah scroll and great care is taken to safeguard its holiness. A whole plethora of laws, including the prohibition of having sex in a home in which a Torah scroll is not properly stored, serve to maintain our respect for this quintessential object of Jewish sanctity. But this is not because the Torah scroll is itself holy. Rather, it contains within it the word of God which is holy. The moment people begin to ascribe holiness to the Torah scroll itself, then it too has become a foreign god, an object which masks God rather than leading us to Him.

And herein lies one of the great problems of modern life, Uri. Today, we read ancient history books and tour places such as the great Greek and Roman temples and we wonder how these highly intelligent people could have been so silly. How could they really have believed that the sun and the moon were gods? How could they have bowed down to marble and gold? How could they have taken inanimate objects and ascribed such great powers to them?

But in asking that question we overlook all the other "molten images" and "golden calves" which are today worshiped in society. Do you remember when in 1993 the Uffizi gallery in Florence was bombed? Although people died in the blast, the main thing that was reported was that some artistic treasures housed in the museum had been irreparably damaged. The purpose of art is to enhance and beautify life, and never to replace it. The moment artistic treasures become more important than life itself, we have lost our values and worship the symbols more than the substance.

Ironically, Uri, some of the people who are most guilty of worshipping symbols rather than the objects of their representation are religious people themselves. As the new Christian millennium approaches, we have to ask ourselves why so few people today are religious. Religion has so much richness, everyone agrees. Then why are so many people so passionately secular? The principal reason is that we religious people can often be bad representatives of our faith. We do not inspire our secular counterparts to embrace our lifestyle. A religious Jewish man would never ever contemplate taking off his *yarmulke*. But does that mean that he will always be honest in business? Will he similarly vow never to remove his ethics? The crusaders would never have contemplated taking an axe to a crucifix or an image of Christ. But that did not stop them from taking an axe to every symbol which Christ was meant to represent, like love, joy, acceptance, and piety.

It's time we all came to the vast recognition, Uri, that perhaps the greatest idol of all for the past two thousand years has been religion itself. That's why so many today are discarding the traditional western religions—Judaism and Christianity in favor of spiritualism and New Age sentimentalism. They accuse religion of having become a vast empty shell, filled with symbols of little substance. So, they are discarding what they perceive to be the empty forms of religion in favor of mysticism and spiritualism which still inspires the spirit.

With every passing day, I see religion becoming more extreme. In Israel, religious Jews are becoming more judgmental of those who adhere to lesser standards of observance. I am sure that I am not the only one who is alarmed at reading increasingly frequent newspaper accounts of incidents betraying intolerant groups within Judaism which is estranging more and more Jews from their faith. Similarly, if you watch evangelical Christian television, the preachers sometimes seem far more interested in condemning sinners than welcoming penitence.

We hear of far too few religious representatives who protest against extremist elements. But what is at risk here is something far more serious than human discord and intolerance. Rather religion risks overstepping into idolatry as it replaces the worship of God with the worship of individual religious tenets and the deification of faith.

In Oxford, I lectured my students on the importance of never desecrating the Sabbath, of marrying within the faith, and celebrating the festivals, because it was incumbent upon them to be good Jews. I spoke of the beauty of Jewish life and Jewish tradition and how we could not allow ourselves to be the generation which severed the link with the faith of our ancestors.

I still of course believe all of those things to be true. But there was something else I had to question. What about God? How often did I talk about God? I was beginning to speak of Judaism as if it were some end in itself; as if the preservation of its traditions and an adherence to its laws was the ultimate purpose of the Jew, and not that religion was the means by which man achieved a proximity to, and created a relationship with, God. What was I promoting? Judaism and religion as an end in itself, or as the road by which man brings God into his life? And was there any point in enforcing a Godless Judaism? To most of us it is inconceivable that religion and God can be at odds. But this is precisely what happens when we make religion the goal instead of the means, the destination rather than the road. When we promote religious tenets to the exclusion of God then we are guilty of deifying symbols which are designed to bring us closer to the ultimate truths which they represent.

I am sure you would agree with me, Uri, that the binding of Isaac presents one of the most problematic stories of the Bible, especially for a man with a very strong orientation towards peace like yourself. What was God's intention in commanding Abraham to sacrifice his own son? My great teacher and spiritual mentor, the Lubavitcher Rebbe, Rabbi Menachem Schneerson, explains that the only way the story makes sense is if we understand that Isaac was more than just a person. He represented Judaism. Ishmael had already gone off the path. He had abandoned Abraham's monotheistic ways. If Isaac died,

Judaism would die with him. God was commanding Abraham to close up shop and murder the religion which he had fathered, to kill the one man through whom the tradition would live. In essence, the test which God presented to Abraham was to choose between his God and his religion. God gives you a command which pits His Will against the essential tenets of your faith. Which would Abraham put first: his relationship with God, or his new-found faith? Would Abraham tell God, "Sorry, but I can't murder my son. I can't murder my successor. The continuity of my faith is too important to me. Isaac will be the first Jewish missionary. If he dies, Judaism dies with him. I will not discard my beliefs, even if You tell me to, because my religion is more important to me than you, God. I will have to ignore Your express commandment. I would rather keep my traditions than follow Your will." What made Abraham great was that he never made the mistake of replacing God with his faith. He loved his religion only insofar as it brought him closer to God, which was the real object of his love. Hence, Abraham merited to be referred to by the Almighty as "Abraham my beloved."

The current overall direction of religion raises the same question which God asked of Abraham. In Judaism, the word *halakha*, which connotes the whole body of Jewish religious law, means path, and is indicative of the fact that *halakha*, as the supreme embodiment of the divine Will, is the only means by which to please God and draw near to Him.

If we want to merely be religious and spiritual, then we can do anything that makes us feel holy and elevated. For some, it might be smoking cannabis; for others, it might be having a ritual orgy. Still others might find looking at a beautiful sunset and writing poetry about it the most meaningful spiritual experience. There is one problem with all of these things. While they may indeed make you feel spiritual, they will not draw you any closer to God. In order to do that, you must undertake not that which makes you feel spiritual, but rather that which God says will please Him. The emphasis must be on His will rather than on individual human emotion.

Once in a low moment in rabbinical seminary, when I was feeling mystified by the myriad details of my faith, I asked the head of my academy to sum up Jewish belief. He said, "The essence of Judaism is that one should take God very seriously, and never take oneself seriously." I felt uplifted by such profundity. But many within the religious officialdom are today guilty of precisely this: they *become* religious, and they begin to take themselves far too seriously. They become self-proclaimed guardians of the faith and take offense at everything they perceive to be heretical. Jews cannot study the Torah because they want to be great scholars or be respected for their learning. It cannot be about our own individual journey. Rather, they must do so because they want to know what pleases their Master. Christians cannot read the New Testament because they want to be inspired by Jesus' teachings. Rather they must do so because they want all their actions to conform to God's wishes. Jews marrying outside the Jewish community is wrong not because it endangers the continuity of our small people, but rather because it distances the individual from God who wished for the Jews to serve as a light unto the nations. They must therefore be a strong and spiritual nation and cannot weaken their ranks.

But we speak today of religion as if it were a deity, an end in itself. Worse, we are even seeing how religion is often used to prevent individuals of lesser faith from coming closer to their Father in heaven. If we always followed the criterion that the purpose of religion is to establish a bond between God and man, then we would not make tragic mistakes that allow for religious imperatives to serve as a fence which isolates mankind from the Creator. To be sure, homosexuality is prohibited by the Bible. But that is no excuse for religious attacks against homosexuals or for religious homophobia. We can assert our right to promote religious values without making people feel like freaks as a result. As a Rabbi in Oxford for eleven years, I have heard the pain of so many gay Jewish men and women who are prepared to accept that this aspect of their lives is lived outside of religious law. But they still want to know that God loves them. And He does. So why do we ostracize homosexuals from our communities and from their God? In the same vein, why are Jews who have married outside our faith still not encouraged to participate in other areas of Jewish life to the best of their ability, in light of their circumstances?

My friends tell me that I can be too hard on religion. But this is simply because I am passionately religious. New age religion may be all right for some. But for me, I want to feel that I am not merely *feeling* spiritual. I want to know that I am connecting with God. And this means turning to God's revealed teachings via His authentic prophets as contained in the Bible. My Judaism is my very life. There are many things that I wish for my children, among which are health, success, and happiness. But there is nothing that I wish for them more than to be good Jews and human beings, and to live up to the great legacy of being compassionate like Abraham, their ancestor. For me, touchy-feely religion, the kind that makes you all warm inside, is nice, but ephemeral. While it may cater to the human need to feel inspired, it does not raise us to a true cosmic consciousness. For me, there is only one Judaism: that which was given to Moses at Sinai. I am not a great or very spiritual man, but I know enough to comprehend that we must all focus on rehabilitating a stagnating religious culture rather than continuing to passively witness wondrous world religions going off the deep end and alienating good men and women who may be fallible but who are all still God's children. This is why we must terminate the *idolization* of symbols, while not terminating the symbols themselves.

We must continue to embrace and restore religious symbols, but we must also never worship them. We rather must worship the loving God who is behind them. Witness our love for money. Really, money should be treated as nothing more than a means to an end. Money is a facilitator that enables us to purchase things which enrich the quality of our lives. But what happens when the symbol of success—money—ceases to be a symbol and replaces life itself? What happens when people begin to devote all their lives to the acquisition of money? What happens when the symbol replaces the object it is meant to bring about?

Two years ago, I was strongly guilty of this myself. Debbie and I always wanted to have a large family. We both saw children as the ultimate blessing. Moreover, the only thing that got me through my parents' divorce was the love of my siblings. We were all very close in age and therefore best friends. And we nurtured each other through all the pain that a divorce causes. Therefore, I wanted my children to be close in age as well. We already had five young children, thank God, and Debbie and I decided on having a sixth. Three summers ago, I took Debbie to Spain alone for a week, and she told me very excitedly that she was pregnant. But rather than be excited, I was miserable. I cannot adequately communicate to you just how depressed I was at the news. I was a young rabbi on a rabbi's salary. Reality set in. How was I going to support yet another child? My mood soured our holiday and my wife had to bear the ignominy of telling her husband that she was expecting another child and being treated as if she had done something criminal.

I called a good friend in New York and told him of my depression. He scolded me harshly. "What the hell is wrong with you?" he asked. "God gives you blessings and you spit in His face. What would you prefer? Another car or another kid? But besides losing your values, you've also lost your faith. Don't you believe that if you work hard, God will provide?" He was absolutely right. I went to my wife and apologized. Instead of moping, I decided to try and do the things that would earn us more money to sustain all the blessings that God in His kindness had given us. God kept his side of the bargain. I sat down to write another book, and tentatively titled it *Kosher Sex: A Recipe for Passion and Intimacy*. I never thought it would have any market outside the small Jewish community. Why would anyone want to hear about sex from an unshaven thirty-year-old father of six, who was a Hassidic rabbi to boot? At first, I couldn't even get a publisher. It was rejected by six. But the seventh decided to gamble on it. And lo and behold, it became an international bestseller and kept our family going for an entire year. And I am convinced that the success of that book was in the merit of that child.

Nowadays, I look at our beautiful baby, whom we affectionately call Baba, who has become one of the most beautiful things in my life, bringing me boundless joy, and wonder how indeed I could have been so stupid? How could I have worshiped the symbol rather than the representation? How can I have put money before all the rich blessings that money is meant to buy?

I too hope that the woman who approached you found her wedding ring. But even more, I hope that finding it ensured that she found a newer and deeper love for her marriage and her spouse. And I hope that every time her husband looks at *his* wedding ring, he is reminded of the greatest blessing he has in life, a devoted and loving wife.

With the gift of this letter as the symbol of our friendship and devotion,

Yours,

Dear Shmuley,

A good friend dropped by today, a professional magician. A conjurer. A sleight-of-hand wizard. You may have seen him on TV—you'll know him if you took the kids to see *Star Wars*,

Episode One: The Phantom Menace, because his act featured in a car ad before the movie screened. You remember—he's the wise-cracking, super-confident guy who walks up to groups of girls in the street and shows them magic. He hurls a pack of cards at a car, and one of the pack sticks to the window, inside the glass. His name is David Blaine.

David phoned me from New York one morning, introduced himself, and said I had been a hero of his since he was a child. I said, "Drop over some time"—he said, "Really? You really mean that?" and took the next flight from JFK. He ate dinner that night with my family. "Show me," he said, "show me that thing with the spoon." I showed him. "OK, I want to see it again," he insisted, shaking his head in disbelief. I explained I couldn't just keep bending spoons, especially when I was with only one person. I need to draw energy from my audience—a group of excited children are great, they buzz around me like little battery charges, and a two-hundred-strong crowd at a book signing or a business conference can keep me energized for half an hour or more. But bending a spoon for one hyper-skeptical conjurer, who is more interested in seeing "the trick" than witnessing a phenomenon, is draining.

"How do you do it?" David begged me. "C'mon, how? How?"

"With my mind."

"Your mind never touched this spoon." He held the warped metal up to the bridge of his nose and closed one eye, and swore fluently and softly. "What touched this spoon was your fingers."

"I don't do magic, not sleight-of-hand. I do MindPower."

He let out a long sigh. "I don't know how you did that. Man, you're good. But I'm going to find out."

He keeps on flying over and eating with us. I keep on bending spoons and telling him how it's done. He's a convinced believer in the paranormal now.

I've been trying to think how I can prove to David that the mind can work any magic. I could read passages from classics in my library, like Nandor Fodor's *Encyclopedia of Psychic Science* and Father Herbert Thurston's *Physical Phenomena of Mysticism*. I could show him a biography, edited by Sir Arthur Conan Doyle, of the Victorian super-psychic Daniel Dunglas Home, who levitated through open windows. David would nod and tell me, "That's a great trick." David is famous for his levitation act—no one has ever proved it isn't a psychic feat, because he rises four or five inches off the ground when you're close enough to reach out and touch him. I could show him film clips of Nina Kulagina, the Russian woman who could make objects slide on a table by staring at them. Her concentration was phenomenal, and before the energy burst out of her body, her heart-rate could top two hundred beats per minute. At the moment of psychokinesis, Soviet researchers noted Nina appeared to have a massive physical orgasm. I can relate to that—serious PK can be as immense as sex. I think David would understand the sex part, but he would never believe Kulagina was more than just a clever conjurer—or that the KGB had not faked the film.

David is very different to how I was at his age, enjoying fame in my mid-twenties. I believed everything, and I believed everyone. I thought all the people I met were sent to help my career and that every piece of flattery was truly meant. I believed the claims, I trusted the motives, and I accepted the promises. I must have been one easy guy to lie to. When the CIA were checking me out, lying all the way because lying was an instinct to them, I thought I was being taken into their fullest confidence. When I look back, I can see I was just being taken in.

People think that because I can read images from their minds, I must always know what everyone is thinking. That's not so. Suspicion kills MindPower. Skepticism drains me. If I want to keep my inexplicable energies, I have to carry on being open-minded. To believe in myself, I have to carry on believing in everyone.

I have made a conscious decision about this. Of course, I have been let down by people I believed in, people I loved and trusted—it happens to everyone. I resolved a long time ago, when I was barely out of my teens, that no matter how much I saw of the bad side of human beings, I would always turn my gaze back to the good side. In America, decades ago, I overheard someone use the phrase "positive thinking" and I thought "Yes! That's it. I'm a positive thinker."

Throughout my career, and especially since my children began to grow, I have given the same advice to anyone who has asked me for help: "Think positive. Smile often, because smiling releases the tension in your face, and makes other people happy. Smiling even encourages your brain to generate more happy hormones. Start smiling and you have to feel better, you can't help it. And keep your thoughts focused on the plus-side to everything, the Yes-words, the upbeat. All your thoughts are prayers—whatever your mind rests upon, that's your prayer. When you daydream of a holiday in the sun and a big lottery win, that's a kind of prayer. Keep all your thoughts positive and, when your prayers are answered, good things are bound to happen to you."

I believe that totally. I know without doubt that positive thoughts bring positive results. The mind that dwells on good things begins to expect good things, and the mind that expects good things starts to look out for them. We can will good luck to come to us, just by concentrating clearly on positive images. When people are really keen to learn strong MindPower techniques, I teach them to visualize—to daydream deliberately. "Focus your mind on what you want," I urge them. "First you must know what it is. Make your mind up—what do you want? How can you pray for something unless you have defined the question you're asking God?" Often that's enough to bring a result. Many people know they're looking for something but haven't decided what they need. When I nudge them to make up their minds, the whole answer, including the path they must take, presents itself immediately.

When they know exactly what they want—a baby, for instance—I say: "Imagine you have your heart's desire. That baby is yours. You're holding her. You can feel her warm fingers on your face, smell her skin and her fluttering breaths as you clutch her close to you. I want you to fill in all the details in your mind—picture the bedroom you're in, how the pillows are arranged behind you, how the light falls through the window. Fix it fully in your mind. I want this image to be utterly real to you. Every moment that you are able, return to this vision. Dream it and live it. Believe in it."

A vision this intense can change a person's whole body. Instead of anxious thoughts about miscarriages and blocked tubes and low sperm counts, the mind turns to positive images. Instead of expecting disaster, the mind becomes impatient for hope.

Positive thinking can change lives—in the most wonderful images, like these daydreams of a newly given baby, it can create life.

If the mind can turn a life around, small wonder it can bend a piece of metal.

Positively your great friend,

[signature]

Dear Uri,

I much appreciated your last letter about positive thinking. The most important things in life are usually the most difficult to achieve. There are three deep human desires that form the very stuff of our humanity. The first is the will to meaning. The second is the will to goodness. And the third is the will to happiness. In the end, they are all really one. Because they are special, they require hard work. And no goal is more difficult to achieve than happiness and positive thinking. The disparity between how strongly we wish to be happy and how seldom we achieve this goal is staggering.

We are the most prosperous generation of all time. We live longer, have more money, travel further, and have more entertainment than any generation the world has ever known. And yet, in the wealthiest country of all—the United States—one out of every three Americans has either been treated for clinical depression or is currently on an antidepressant like Prozac or Zoloft. (The other two are on Viagra.)

This is an important subject to me, Uri, because I am not always positive. I witness many of my colleagues and friends who are always jovial and naturally see the cup as being half full. You are one of them. You're always jolly and patient. Although you accomplish so much, you never seem rushed or harried. For our friendship, you seem to have all the time in the world. But I have the "half empty" syndrome. I get frustrated quickly. Unfortunately, there seem to be far more people like me than like you. Many people today seem unhappy. They feel that they are not maximizing their potential, that their lives are not what they quite want them to be. Even those who are not clinically depressed are still consuming endless amounts of television and movies or reading frivolous magazines about the rich and famous. If we are so happy with our lives, then why are we always trying to escape? If we are satisfied with who we are, then why are we always gossiping about someone else? And why has modern life been reduced today to the endless pursuit of meaningless distractions?

We seem to be chasing elusive goals that are always just outside our reach, causing gloom and despair. No matter how much we achieve, we rarely attain a sense of satisfaction. Like my father, I live daily with a sense of insatiability. Things will, thank God, go well one day. But in the end, who cares, because tomorrow you have to start all over again. I take little joy in the things I achieve. The sense of fulfillment is fleeting. The feeling of inadequacy long-lasting. The tremendous opportunity that has opened up to all segments of society in this entrepreneurial age has caused us all to compare ourselves to others, making us feel unworthy. Hyper-competition undermines the innate value of human self-worth. Many of the people I know have ceased to judge themselves on the content of their character, but do so instead on the content of their bank account. But this criterion is bound to push people over the precipice. We can never find satisfaction or satiation because we always watch yet another of our colleagues overtaking us in the pursuit of personal fortune or fame, creating bitterness, jealousy, and resentment.

These feelings of inadequacy, as well as many other factors, are what leads us into depression. Other causes I have witnessed as a rabbi that can lead to serious depression and unhappiness are broken relationships, financial difficulties, or serious illness. I have also seen many people who just seem to get depressed for what is seemingly no reason at all. They just get down.

So, one of the things I appreciate most about our friendship, Uri, is your joy. You're always up and you're always trying to bring me up. Truth be told, I can't remember ever seeing you down. You have a natural propensity for joy (and maybe this explains your extraordinary power). In Jewish thought, joy is the very stuff of holiness and spirituality. God is infinite. He has no limitations. The holy man is he who transcends his human limitations. The spiritual woman is she who can soar. The very essence of joy is to experience a loss of boundaries and limitations. To be joyous is to feel that we are more than mere mortals. Joy is an enlargement of the self. Scripture even says that "good news makes the bones enlarge."

The Talmud tells a story of how, when Vespasian, who had laid siege to the city of Jerusalem, heard from Rome that he had become Emperor, he became so happy that he could not take off his shoes. The essence of happiness is to experience an inflation of life, an enlargement of the self. When we are happy, we are filled with exuberance and energy. Like Superman, we are able to overcome large hurdles in a single bound. We can even overcome heavy emotional obstacles. The Talmud says that when a man dances at the wedding of his son or daughter, he is even prepared to dance with his worst enemy. All the negative emotional baggage associated with an old adversary immediately vanishes and the full joy of the human heart is manifest. There is a common misconception that the religious man or woman is meant to look pious and be serious. Nothing could be further from the truth. God commands us to worship Him with exultation and joy.

One of my favorite verses, recited by religious Jews every morning as part of their daily prayers is this: "Worship the Lord with gladness; come into his presence with singing" (Psalms 100:2).

You speak eloquently, Uri, of the warmth and beauty of the human smile. Smiling at people brings out their humanity. Whatever warmth or hope is trapped within them can be released with a smile. Once when I was gloomy over things not going according to plan, problems that I felt could not be solved, I came home about ten o'clock, and my four-year-old daughter, Shaina, was still awake. Rather than scolding her for having gotten out of bed, I let her climb all over me as I sat to sulk on the couch. She ran and got her tzedakah box—her charity box—and insisted that I put some coins in. I put one in, and she insisted on more. Two, and she still wanted more. Three, and she said, "Tatti, I want all your coins." So she cleaned me out, and when she didn't believe that I had any more coins to give, she stuck her tiny little hands in my pocket, and low and behold she found another five pence. Upon discovering the treasure, she looked up at me with the most devious little smile. And that smile shot a wave of joy through my heart. I knew that my children were, thank God, still smiling—they were healthy and alive—so things couldn't be that bad. In fact, they were wonderful. In that instant, I was enveloped by the light. Or rather, I saw the light that had always been there.

Do you know why God wants us to be happy, Uri? It's because He wants to know that we know how to appreciate, how to say "thank you." He wants to know that we are cognizant of all the blessings He showers upon us. To be depressed is to be an ingrate. It is saying to God, "Sure you've given me so much. But how about all the things you haven't given to me?"

As you know Uri, when I was twenty-one years old, I arrived in Oxford to serve as Rabbi to the students. I quickly set up the L'Chaim Society to cater to the students' needs. We started to get some big speakers and the society was taking off. It was then that I read former President Ronald Reagan's autobiography, *An American Life*. In the book, he writes that he had attended a simple university called Eureka College. He goes on to say that later, as president, although he had visited all the great universities of the world, he would never have traded in Eureka because of how warm and earthy it was. So I wrote him a letter and I told him that it would be wonderful if he brought some of that humor, warmth, and charm to a place that can be as cold and stuffy as Oxford. Amazingly, he wrote back and said that he would be happy to deliver a lecture to our society. We were ecstatic. Two years into our organization's existence, we had secured a former American president to speak at our Society, and President Reagan was kind enough to waive any expenses or fees.

We worked our guts out organizing the event. The costs were still astronomical—publicity, banquet dinner, three full-time staff organizing it, etc. In addition, we were opening a new student center in Oxford, smack in the city center. It was beautiful, but equally expensive. I was despairing of being able to afford it. We asked President Reagan to open the center, and he agreed. I approached the publisher Robert Maxwell, who was an Oxford resident, and asked him to cover the expenses of the center for the first year. Because he wanted to help, and with the prestige of someone like President Reagan opening it, Maxwell agreed. We agreed to name the center after his relatives who were murdered in the Holocaust. It was all happening.

I had to go to New York just a week before President Reagan arrived. I was sitting in a kosher restaurant watching CNN when a newsflash suddenly came up on the screen: "Publishing magnate Robert Maxwell missing at sea." First, of course, I was saddened at the news. It was shocking to hear that Mr. Maxwell might have met with a terrible tragedy. I was saddened for his family and especially for his wife, Elizabeth, who had attended some of our events. And, for us, this tragedy also spelled the ruin of our plans.

I departed to London that night. The next day, I arrived at Heathrow airport and saw the headlines. Maxwell's body had been found, drowned. I sympathized with the grief his poor family must have been experiencing and tried to put a call into his wife, Elizabeth. I also understood that President Reagan's visit was now in jeopardy. What will we do now? A few days later, much controversy over pension funds started appearing in the press, another unexpected turn of events. I could see the event unraveling. Sure enough, during the *Sukkot* celebration, Judaism's most joyous holiday, the phone rang, and it was President Reagan's office. "Due to an unforeseen scheduling conflict, the President will not be able to deliver the lecture." It didn't make a difference to us what the cause of his inability to appear was, my heart sank. So much for a joyous festival!

First we had to clear up the mess of the cancellation. We were tens of thousands of pounds out of pocket, and also we were humiliated. Everyone thought, "There must be something wrong with the organization if Reagan cancelled." Far worse, we didn't have the money to pay for the fitting out of the new center, let alone the rent. I had never been so depressed. The organization that I had so painstakingly built was about to go belly up.

At this point, it was too late to cancel the workmen. I would come into the office every day, and my heart would sink. I have always prided myself on being very active. But I could not deal with this situation. It simply sank me. I would literally put my head on my desk and keep it there for an hour, too listless to do anything to get myself out of my problems.

Many friends came to talk to me, "It's gonna be all right. Don't worry. It'll work out." I felt they were just being naïve. "My career is over, and nothing can help me. Our debts are out of control. Soon people will be pressing to be paid, and there is no money." These were my only thoughts.

One day, my friend Sandy called me from New York. "You jerk. Something this small has broken you? Stop feeling sorry for yourself. Get up and fight back." Those simple words, "Get up and fight back," did it for me. Yeah, why wasn't I fighting? I was engaged in a struggle for survival. But God had endowed me, like every other human being, with health and talent. So why did I assume defeat? It was a mental thing. I had presupposed my own doom, had envisioned my own collapse. I was the architect of my own downfall, which needn't have been real. As you have told me so many times on the phone, Uri, I was translating my own negative thoughts from the potential into the actual. I was becoming the conjurer of my own nightmare. With my gloom, I was blocking out the light of the sun.

Depression is based on a false idea that man is meant to have victories, that life is meant to be smooth. Neither fact is true. The essence of life is the struggle. Defeats are not defeats, they are just part of the ongoing battle. The greatest blessing of all is life, and so long as you have breath in your lungs and blood pumping through your veins, you can engage the battle and rise to see another day. As long as you can struggle, even if you sometimes have to writhe and squirm to get back up, it's OK. Because you are still alive. But the moment you can't pick yourself up to fight back, then depression has claimed another victim.

There is a solution to depression, however. Death has to be countered with life. Unhappiness must be battled with joy. And depression must be fought with action. If you make an effort to start doing the things you don't feel like doing, chances are that

your heart will follow suit and kick in feeling where it was previously frozen. One of the great secrets of life, Uri, is that the
hands are the masters of the heart, action the champion of the
emotion. And if you start doing that which you don't feel like
doing, soon enough your heart will respond and create the
emotion which fills the vacuum. The more heat you generate in
the form of action, the more depression will thaw. Since
depression is based on a lie that the battle is lost and the situation unrecoverable, you've got to pick yourself up and just start
doing again. Don't reason with your depression. Don't dignify
it by giving it the pretense of authenticity. Don't afford darkness the credibility of reality. Simply turn on the light, and all
the darkness will go away. You are battling a mythical dragon, a
phantom, a mirage. You'll be lost in the illusion, you will be
defeated by a nonentity. You can't have an antithesis against a
nonexistent thesis. Rather, stop thinking, stop worrying, and
just start doing. Soon, you'll feel the blood pulsating through
your veins again. You'll know you're alive. And you will live to
see the sun break through the clouds.

But I discovered something even more important, Uri,
through that bout of depression. I discovered that the best way
to feel good about myself was to try and do good things for
other people. That big center that we certainly couldn't afford
was soon filled with students. After hearing that President
Reagan had cancelled, Israel's housing minister at the time, the
legendary war hero Ariel Sharon, agreed to come and open it.
Soon, Friday night *Shabbat* dinners were buzzing with excite-
ment as both Jewish and non-Jewish students joined together
to enjoy each other's company. The office's central location
made it much easier for students to stop by during the day to
speak to me about their problems over a falafel or tea. And
slowly, I began to discover my own inner strength to fund the
center and make it work.

We human beings want three things in our lives, Uri: meaning, joy, and goodness. The first two are predicated on the last.

There is no greater fulfillment than to feel that you are having a positive impact on the world and the people around you. And there is no greater joy than to practice goodness. Sometimes, when the flame in our own heart has seemingly burnt out, it needs to be lit by the flame of another soul. In fact, it is impossible to be joyous without being good.

Happiness and joy are predicated on inner harmony. You can't be happy when you feel that your innards are at war. Perhaps the greatest source of despondency is lack of inner peace. When your heart tells you one thing and your mind another, and they cannot be reconciled, that inner tension robs you of happiness. How can one be joyous when there is a millstone grinding away on the inside? So, happiness and joy are predicated on the total integration of our inner and outer selves. Our innermost convictions must match our outermost actions. Only then do we feel whole and therefore happy.

And since goodness is our deepest and most heartfelt desire, and we can't be happy unless there is a total integration of our inner and outer selves, it follows that we can't be happy unless we are good. And that's why smiles are as powerful as you say in your letter, Uri. Because smiling is the quintessential act of goodness. First, a smile is given to a total stranger, even someone who has done nothing to merit our love or indeed may not even be deserving of our love. As such, it represents an act of unconditional love. Second, a smile is given with no hope or expectation of receiving anything in return. While it's a great song, it's simply not true that "when you're smiling, the whole world's smiling with you." Often when you smile at someone, you receive only a cold grimace in return. Finally, the purpose of a smile is to uplift the other person and raise them out of their gloom. A smile picks them up to a higher level of energy and consciousness. As such, it represents not just any gift, but the gift of enlightenment. It is the gift of the eagle, allowing the other person to soar. And it is you who has set them on the launching pad simply by raising your cheeks and curving your lips.

That's why when you do a really good deed, you will notice that a wonderful feeling of pleasure follows. It is so important to experience that feeling of pleasure, of happiness, the joy that follows selflessness. When we feed the hungry, offer someone a loving compliment, give a needy man a good job, or apologize for an outburst of anger, we always feel wonderful after the event. All of these undertakings involve effort and sometimes even unpleasantness before we decide to do them. But they are followed by phenomenal and immense joy as soon as they are over. Because nothing feels better than goodness.

A successful Jewish investor friend of mine named Joseph, who had led a secular life totally outside the Jewish community, just recently started getting more involved with the Jewish community and paid half the cost of a new synagogue. His friend Marty, another secular Jew, called him. "Come on, Joseph," he said, "who are you kidding? You couldn't tell a synagogue from a mosque or an ashram. You're not doing any of this stuff because you're interested. You're doing it only because you feel guilty. You feel bad that you haven't continued the tradition and you're trying to make up for it. Just get over it already."

Joseph called and told me what Marty had said. "Well, what do you think about Marty?" he asked me. "Do you think that maybe he's right?"

"I think that Marty is a thief," I told him. "He has robbed you of the feeling of meaning and goodness that comes from doing the right thing." When a person gives charity, he has every right to feel a deep sense of satisfaction. Robbing people of that satisfaction by questioning their motivation is horrible. There is nothing selfish, either, about feeling really good about the good things we do. We don't do it for that feeling. Rather, the pleasure of goodness is the immediate and automatic outcome of addressing and satisfying our most deep-seated desire to be good and decent people.

Another friend, a chiropractor, told me of how he almost succumbed to temptation. "I was at a national convention, far away from home and my wife, when I struck up a conversation with a woman from Minnesota. One thing led to another, and suddenly I was up in her hotel room having a drink. She started taking off her blouse. But somehow I summoned the strength to thank her for the drink, get my jacket, and get the hell out of there. But it was really hard, Shmuley, giving up all that pleasure and going back downstairs."

"Hard?" I asked him, "You didn't give up that pleasure and simply receive nothing in return. You didn't merely go back to an empty hotel room. Rather, you gave it up for an even greater pleasure. When you walked away from that woman in order to uphold your marital vows, you walked away knowing that you are a man of greatness. You are a man of honor, integrity, loyalty, and commitment. You're one of those great men of history. How good does it feel to be all those things? Whatever enjoyment and gratification you could have had with that woman that night could never have compared with the pleasure of doing the right thing!"

There is an inner voice, Uri, that whispers to us everyday. It is a still, small, voice that not everyone hears. It's the voice of the spirit crying out. It wishes to be set free. It wishes to be liberated from the confines of a life lived in mediocrity, a life devoted to ephemeral pleasures that give no satisfaction and have no permanence. It wishes to attach itself through kindly deeds to another soul and, finally, be permitted to take off and soar with the eagles.

Because the natural gravitation of the human soul is not downward, like the dead. It is upward, with the living.

Giving this one for the Gipper,

Love,

Dear Shmuley,

I have this idea for a TV gameshow. Take three couples, all of them desperate for a child. Fill their homes and their workplaces with spy cameras, so that viewers can tune in and observe them sleeping, eating, talking, showering, arguing, watching TV, working, socializing, twenty-four hours a day. Bring them to a television studio two or three times a week and grill them in front of a baying audience. And at the end of a month, let the viewers—millions of them—vote on which couple wins.

The prize will be a baby.

The TV company will have legal guardianship of a baby, and the winning couple will be given that baby and all the help they need to successfully complete the adoption procedure. There will be a cash award too, to make sure the child has a good start in life financially.

It's not hard to buy a baby these days. There are surrogate mothers, and countries such as Russia where the adoption procedure can be manipulated easily. There are orphanages in Mexico and South America and Eastern Europe that will gladly sell a child. There are websites that will help to organize it. There are millions of mothers in total poverty who would sell their newborn son or daughter to a Westerner from a TV company who promises a future of hope for the infant. There are street children on every city in every country of the developing world and in most of the cities of Europe and America too— who would miss one vanished baby?

A child for a desperate couple, a new life for a child without hope, and stratospheric TV ratings. How can a concept that will give happiness to so many possibly be wrong?

You think I'm joking. I'll remind you that you took part in a TV show to find husbands for Roseanne Barr's three daughters. Those girls, and their suitors, were all consenting adults, and you might argue that a baby cannot give consent—but ask anyone, "If you were about to die, and God gave you the chance to be reincarnated, what would you choose—to be born and live in a Brazilian slum or a Palestinian refugee camp, or to be adopted by loving American parents in a blaze of publicity?"

Ask yourself, Shmuley: Which would you choose?

I'm not joking. I am going to do it.

I can't do it on TV, of course. I don't run a network. But I can do it on the internet. As fiction.

My new novel is called *Nobody's Child*. I will be publishing it week by week, via a website at www.uristory.com where readers can subscribe to have each chapter e-mailed to them. The first ten thousand words will be freely available at the site—anyone can start reading, without having to register. Read the page: if you like the story, you can sign up for the next installment. You'll meet the contestants: Denny and Nat Monroe are black and appear well-off, living in a pleasant L.A. suburb; Andy and Mouse Beck are poor, white Southerners in a trailer park; Terry Impey and Colin Lord are gay—they've got cash to spend and a sumptuous apartment in Atlantic City.

The show's host is a savvy shock-jock named Rob Roy McClean. Right now he's not saying how he found the baby. It's nobody's child...until America awards it to the winners.

Each chapter contains between two and three thousand words and costs just thirty cents. I aim to finish the book in a year's time, but however long it takes to complete, I guarantee that you'll only have to pay for a maximum of fifty installments. That makes the total price $15, considerably less than you'd pay for a new hardback. And you don't get to pay for hardbacks in installments.

I'm doing this to satirize trash TV and its contempt for human values. But I'm also doing it because I believe the Internet can turn conventional publishing inside-out. Everything I hate about publishers is bypassed on this site. Most important of all, I am in direct contact with my readers. I'll be writing each chapter during the few days before it is mass-mailed to subscribers, so it is effectively a live performance. Before every installment, I'll be getting feedback on the story's latest twists.

This has never happened in fiction—previously, I've only been able to gauge public reaction to my books months after the writing is finished. I'm making it as easy as possible for readers to have their say—they can email me directly or post comments on an electronic board. My IT team is also planning to set up a chat room, where web users can discuss the book online. Each week, readers will be able to vote on which characters they want to be killed off or plunged into crisis, on which couple they want to win. I don't have to obey the voting—fiction is not a democratic form. But it will be fantastic to see the reactions. All these features will be free—you only pay for the book itself.

It's more than a century since novels were published in installments—usually monthly ones. But the format is a core element of television programming, with most of the best stories of the past fifty years broadcast as serials. Soap operas and shows such as *The X-Files* and *Twin Peaks* have screened weekly to audiences who remember every detail from the previous episode and who count the minutes to the next one. Written fiction lost its momentum when publishers stopped using installments—I want to restore that energy.

If this experiment works—and it will—I believe it will blow publishing wide open. Anyone will be able to copy the format, and I expect many established writers to try it for themselves. Stephen King is already having a go with his novella *The Plant*, though I think he made two serious mistakes when he set the installments a month apart and when he invited subscriptions without supplying a hint of what the storyline would be. King knew his fans would want to read anything he wrote, even a shopping list. I want to reassure my fans that what they'll read will be a gripping story with an outrageous concept and fascinating characters—and if you don't agree with that assessment after reading the opening chapters for free, you simply don't subscribe for the rest.

I expect to be savaged by the publishing world. They'll criticize the format, the story, even the idea of dispatching the chapters by email instead of posting them on a website for readers to download. What about the pleasures of browsing in a bookshop? they'll say. What about the dangers of copyright piracy? What about our cut?

The publisher's cut has been too deep and too bloody for too long. Most writers have been cut right out of the business by the people responsible for producing and selling books. Some retail chains take 50 percent of the cover price—even the biggest names in fiction cannot command more than 15 percent of the retail price, and for the lesser-known authors, already struggling for income, the royalty is usually around 10 percent. You have to sell a lot of books at 10 percent to make a living (do I have to tell you this, Shmuley?) If writers sell direct to the public, they need to move far few copies to make more money.

I do understand that the book world is filled with enthusiasts—and that many of the most committed, most enthusiastic publishers and booksellers are being hit hard by powerful global brands. No independent publisher can expect to hang on to a successful writer when major agencies and multinational houses are offering megabuck three-book deals. And no corner bookshop can compete squarely against cost-cutting websites operating at a million-dollar-a-week loss.

The future that I predict gives a greater chance to those small players, if they are prepared to adapt. Publishers who help their writers get online and communicate directly with readers will have an edge over the top-heavy corporations who take three weeks to convene a committee meeting. Readers want immediacy, and they want it now. The only people who can deliver that are the enthusiasts.

This is a world where consumers can watch a couple meet and marry (and consummate too, pretty soon!) inside an hour. If the Internet can offer bestsellers on screens within a few moments, why should anyone expect to wait months as the typesetting, printing, promotion, and distribution drags on?

These changes will make life richer for writers, readers, and—if they can adapt—publishers and booksellers. I wish I could be so confident about a richer life for viewers and TV presenters.

I believe that, within five years, a TV show with a concept like *Nobody's Child* will be a reality. Someone will begin life as a game show prize. Maybe it will happen in less than five years—maybe inside the next twelve months. That's another reason I am so excited about publishing this book myself, live online: it's an immediate concept. I don't have to wait eighteen months before my work reaches the public, I don't have to pray that the distributors get their timing right so that my publicity tour coincides with the book's release. I am putting this story online myself, so I know it will be available on time. Last year, I was trapped in a disastrous promotion schedule, going on TV and radio and into bookstores to talk about my biography—while the books remained in warehouse limbo, not even available to newspaper reviewers. I am never going to let that happen again, not to me and not, if I can help it, to any other author.

We have the Internet. It is the most powerful communication tool ever developed. Let's use it.

With deep affection,

Dear Uri,

There is one thing you haven't factored into your publishing plans. How are you going to give me a signed copy of your book? Or anyone else, for that matter? And can publishing really succeed once it loses its personal touch? How about the vanity side of having your name on the cover of a book, one of the principal motivating forces behind authors writing them? And what about using your favorite book barker? But aside from these considerations, I think your idea is great. Will you be my publisher too?

What's really wrong with reality television, Uri, is the reality it betrays, namely, that people are incredibly bored with their lives. This is a generation that is so intent on escaping the everyday reality of their own lives that they will even escape into someone else's reality! That everyday life no longer engages us is the number one cause of the breakdown of marriage and relationships. The leading complaint that I hear from wives about their marriages is that their husbands ignore them. Instead of talking, they watch television or play on their laptops.

Now, some people would say, What's the big deal? This has always been a problem, and there's nothing really new about boredom in everyday life. But something has changed. When life once bored us, we all chose to escape reality by delving into fantasy. And that's why fantasy films and television from *The Wizard of Oz* to *Star Wars* have always been so popular. But the idea of escaping our reality by immersing ourselves into someone else's reality is truly novel. It means that it's not life in general that is boring us, but rather *our* life in particular. So, having a shower ourselves is utterly boring. But watching someone else have a shower, well, what do you know? I'll vegetate in front of the TV and watch that. Sounds great! Could you imagine that someone finds their life so stultifyingly boring that rather than speak to his wife, he would rather watch someone else speak to *his* wife?! Rather than eat dinner themselves, they would rather watch someone else eat dinner. And, most important of all, rather than watch his own wife undress, he would rather watch someone else's girlfriend undress. So we're no longer escaping life into fantasy. We're escaping life into life, but someone else's life.

This is yet another example of what I call "Generation O" (as in "Oh"): the generation with everything on the outside and nothing on the inside. We are so prosperous and lack for nothing. So since we have everything, we search for nothing. Having everything on the outside makes us totally oblivious to what we're missing on the inside. But what we're oblivious to is that when a man or a woman is missing a spiritual center, a convictional core, a purpose-oriented essence, then they quickly burn out on the inside and the outside. Boredom becomes the bane of their life and they begin to tire of their own existence. And as it begins to hurt more and more, and we feel the emptiness of our lives, we continue to reach outward rather than inward to alleviate the problem. We expand horizontally rather than vertically. We swell rather than grow. This is what's currently happening with all those people who would rather be someone else than be themselves. Rather than become interesting themselves, they would much rather simply slip into someone else's skin in order to get more passionate about life. But this is yet another silly escape.

When Adam and Eve were in the Garden of Eden, they were bitten by the wily snake, a metaphor for desire and insatiability. Suddenly, even being in the Garden of Eden wasn't enough. They needed some more stimuli in order to feel complete. God allowed them to partake of every single tree in the Garden. But that wasn't enough. They longed to eat of the forbidden fruit. It's that attitude that says, "If only I just do this, or if only I could just be like so and so, then, finally, I would be happy." All of us who lack a spiritual center are susceptible to the snake. The only way to inoculate ourselves against his poison is to have a life that is gratifying because it is useful to others and meaningful to ourselves and is not just devoted to ambition and acquisition.

And what makes that other person that you're watching on the reality TV program so much more interesting than you, anyway? Are they prettier or smarter with livelier personalities? The answer is no. They are just ordinary people, which is the whole point of reality TV. It is rather the medium in which they are presented that is more interesting than they are. Anything that comes to you through your television set is by definition interesting. Eating meatballs is itself not very interesting. But if it's projected by a diode tube on a TV screen, it's suddenly the equivalent of a lightsaber duel to the death between Obi-Wan Kenobi and Darth Vader.

Television has the power, in our minds at least, to raise the ordinary and make it extraordinary, to take the natural and make it miraculous, and to take the everyday and make it unique. And the reason for this, Uri, is the modern day confusion between celebrity and dignity. We are prepared to watch anything that comes across our TV set because we are consumed with the cult of celebrity. Television is reality. Our everyday life is the fantasy, and a poor fantasy by comparison. We all want to be famous or, as a poor substitute, at least be allowed to watch the famous. I recently saw a late-night celebrity interview with one of America's leading movie actors. For twenty minutes he told the most banal story of how, the week before, he had burnt lasagna in his kitchen and his concerted efforts to remove the black melted cheese from the bottom of the pot. Any wife who would have spent twenty minutes to tell her husband a similar story would have sent him into a deep coma from which he would never awake. But that didn't stop husbands across America from watching that night and feeling entertained while they did! Such is the power of celebrity.

And why are we so consumed by the cult of celebrity? Because we have lost our dignity. A generation that has squandered its natural inner light has become completely dependent on the external spotlight. We no longer feel special and dignified naturally, so we have to achieve it artificially. Because we don't feel inwardly distinguished, we all need the corroboration of an outside audience.

To be sure, Uri, we are not the first generation of individuals who wishes to be famous. Since the beginning of time, men and women have endeavored to escape the horrible facelessness of anonymity by becoming recognizable to their fellow humans through grand gestures. The great men and women of history have always sought to rise from the undistinguished morass of the general populace and be noticed, like a towering wave that swells from the pool of the oceans. Twenty-five hundred years ago, Alexander the Great of Macedonia, the first truly famous man in history, took along on his campaigns chroniclers and historians who would later tell the tale of his wondrous conquests to the generations that followed. Later, Augustus of Rome minted dozens of coins with his likeness. He wanted his vast achievements as the towering administrator of the world's greatest Empire known throughout the world. In an age where the majority of the population were illiterate, the best way of becoming famous was visually rather than verbally. Even in the last century, Charles Lindbergh became the most famous man on earth when he fearlessly conquered the seemingly vast distance of the Atlantic Ocean as a lone flier, and indulged in an orgy of ticker-tape parades and never-ending interviews. So, no, as a generation, we are not distinguished by our lust for celebrity.

What does make us different, Uri, is that we are the first generation ever who is prepared to lose our dignity in the quest for celebrity. We are veritably a generation who is just as willing to be famous for our flaws as for our virtues. Notice that in all the aforementioned scenarios what is common is how the protagonist always wishes to be famous for some great accomplishment. Throughout history celebrity was a means by which an individual magnified his own dignity and respectability by having the masses know of his triumphs. Men pursued celebrity with the express intention of promoting their dignity and uniqueness. To be sure, we can debate today whether Napoleon was a liberator or a tyrant, whether someone who finds glory on the battlefield is a bully or a victor. But be that as it may, in his own age, military conquest was glorious and thus Napoleon wished all the earth to know that the glory was his.

In short, celebrity was the art of exalting human achievement, and people who wanted to be special undertook great enterprises and made sure that their neighbors read of their success. But who has ever heard of wanting to be celebrated for being a jerk? Who has ever heard of desiring to be famous for one's ugliness? Since when is infamy the equal of genuine fame?

Usually people try to hide their mistakes and their character defects. They want to be famous for the good, not the bad things. But today our dark side is one of the prize things we trumpet most on daytime talk shows. Remember the controversial yet highly successful Fox TV show *Who Wants to Marry a Multi-Millionaire?* The show had an audience of more than twenty-six million. Just think about that for a moment. A producer of a show will come to a group of women and tell them, "Who wants to go on a show where you will be making a laughingstock of yourself as a shallow, incredibly vain gold-digger and marry a man you have known for only one hour just because he has a few million dollars?" And so many will run to their own ruin that the producers will have a hard time reducing the number to fifty. Why are so many people prepared to go on a show and tell the rest of the country how silly they are just for the sake of shameless self-promotion? Because we are so desperate for just a little bit of attention these days, we are so thirsty for recognition, that we will chase it even to our own detriment.

Two weeks ago, I watched a TV talk show where a young woman, just sixteen, said she had already slept with fifty men. Then the host asked, "What else do you have to tell us today?" She said, "Well, I'm pregnant, and the father can be any one of six men." But why was she talking about this on national TV? Clearly, there was a connection. She slept with the men in question because it made her feel loved, at least for a little while until the pain came back. And she told it to the camera because that also made her feel loved. Celebrity made her feel important, that is, until she had to live with the consequences of her actions.

Whereas in previous generations, dignity and celebrity were partners, today they are enemies, at odds with each other.

Nearly all of us are prepared to sacrifice our dignity in the pursuit of celebrity. We are prepared to face humiliation and public ridicule just to get our fifteen minutes in front of the camera. Going in front of TV lights today usually involves being stripped of our human dignity. But basking in the warm glow of the TV cameras, we do not even notice that we are naked, that is, until the lights go off. Then you actually have to live with the confessions you made on TV and the ass the producers made of you just to boost ratings.

In the absence of the attention we are meant to feel from our parents and spouses from each other, we search for artificial attention instead. We have become shameless seekers of recognition, even when it is an affront to our dignity.

The only remedy to this downward spiral of shame is for people to start giving each other more attention. Rather than getting into a cab and immediately getting on our cell phones, we should be speaking to the driver. He's not just a means to an end. He wasn't created by God merely to get us from Midtown to Wall Street. Give him attention as if he's a celebrity. Similarly, every child deserves to be a star. When our kids come running to tell us some seemingly insignificant detail of how their pet hamster was eaten by the neighbor's coyote, we have to put down the newspaper and give them our undivided attention. If Chelsea Clinton came to tell us the same thing, we'd probably listen. Because if we don't give our own children our attention, they will turn instead to those people who will listen, like Jerry Springer. And none of us should be surprised when our kids turns up on our television screens one day telling the whole world how they were irreversibly scarred by an indifferent and unconcerned parent.

Still, Uri, I welcome the arrival of reality TV. There is indeed a silver lining behind this very dark cloud, and it is this: the obsession with reality television is indicative of the real desire on the part of society to return to authenticity. For six decades, TV has worked its magic on us. The great artists of Hollywood have manipulated our emotions with unparalleled success. They made us cry with the death of Leonardo de Caprio at the end of *Titanic*, they made our hearts swoon with romance in *Gone with the Wind*, they made us rise with outrage in the miniseries *Roots*, and they made travel to another dimension in the adventure of *E.T.* For what seemed like an eternity, we became used to packaged ideas, robotic messages, and a fantasy world all wrapped up in ribbons. And our susceptibility to this manipulation, indeed our demand for it made TV and film not only the most influential medium of all time, but a veritable addiction for billions of people who can't seem to live without it.

But suddenly, there is a backlash. People want authenticity again. They're tired of fabricated stories. They want both the message and the medium to be real. And who says that authenticity in programming won't be the precursor for a return to greater truth in life?

Truth, Uri, is a human necessity. People can only live a lie for so long. Communism and fascism can survive for one or two generations. But then they will crumble of their own accord. A lie cannot last, and falsehoods cannot flourish.

It's quite fascinating, actually, the human yearning for authenticity. Remember the rage for women to have breast implants and how attractive those that did were to men? Well, today there is a complete backlash. The new trend in adult magazines is to use models who have no plastic and are totally natural. Thousands of women (Pamela Anderson among them) have actually had their implants removed! But why should it matter? As long as they look great, and feel soft, who cares if they're made by fatty tissue or silicone? But the men do care and the women are responding.

And look at the 2000 Olympics, Uri. Relatively few viewers in the United States watched because the action wasn't live. Even if people didn't know the results, they still decided not to watch because the coverage was canned and packaged, making it less authentic and real.

And while the reality still has to come through television, it's the first step toward getting back to the real reality. Maybe, just maybe the next step after reality television will be to turn off the television and enjoy authentic human company again. People can only be pushed so far. They can only live in a plastic bubble for so long. Deprived of authenticity for long enough, people are going to rebel and cry out for oxygen. Not that a little fantasy has to be presented in a way that enhances our daily reality rather than undermining it. The Jewish dream of the Messiah is a case in point as is the Jewish observance of the Sabbath. Both pull us toward a higher reality, a world with no crime, death, or disease. But the purpose of being immersed in these dreams is to influence the believer to return to "reality" and make it into a dream, bring heaven down to earth and turn the world into paradise.

But what we were beginning to witness with television was not the creations of a world of fantastic dreams, but unrealized nightmares. Tawdry sex, horrific violence, and a world of broken relationships became our everyday reality. And people said, "Enough." And they decided to watch a bunch of people brushing their teeth in their underwear instead.

I know we're not there yet, Uri, but a better reality might be just around the corner. I can see it happening. One day we're going to wake up. And the everyday will have become unique, the ordinary will have become extraordinary, and the natural will be miraculous.

Looking forward to seeing you in person before I see you again on TV.

Love, your friend,

Dear Shmuley,

I am going to miss you. You called me this evening from the back of a yellow cab in New York City, and I know you called because you were feeling upset and bewildered over a meeting that fell through—but you know, through all the anguished sighs and the explosions of discontent, you sounded at home. At home in NYC, at home in America. You are packing up your house in England, winding up your work in Oxford, but I think your spirit has already made the move. You have the soul of an American, and your soul sounds glad to be home.

I'm glad you and Debbie have found such a beautiful place in New Jersey. I'm glad your career is surging ahead so fast; I'm glad U.S. TV shows can't get enough of you; I'm glad your burgeoning fame is bringing so much outside energy into L'Chaim. I'm still going to miss you.

We only met a few years ago, but when I run an eye over the letters we have exchanged, I realize how close we have grown, and how quickly. Your compassion has enabled me to face parts of my life that I had masked from my own mind for many years. For the first time in a long time, I no longer feel I am in hiding from myself. You coaxed memories out of me without goading me or ordering me to speak—the words came because I trusted you.

Winning confidences is a natural part of your ministry, but I know many others who have developed the same skill—therapists, lawyers, teachers—and they have not inspired me to open my soul. You are a rabbi, but I know many rabbis. You are a friend, but I have other, older friends, very close to me, who knew nothing of the confessions I have made to you.

The quality in you that most deeply impressed me when we first met was one that I have always known I lack. Perhaps it is usual to be aware of other people's virtues when they remind us of our failings. We know what is missing in our own hearts, and we are sensitive when it radiates from others. In me, this provokes admiration, a feeling of awe that you can do what

I cannot. I have no formal qualifications, so I am conscious when I speak with doctors and graduates that they have spent many years at study, which I did not. I am sometimes a little vain about my appearance, and I can't bring myself to care any less about it—after all, my first job when I left the military was as a model, and I should hate to grow flabby and wrinkled—but I do take notice of people whose minds are clearly more important to them than their appearance. When a scientist has soup on his tie, or a government minister wears no make-up on her warts, I always suspect it is because they are preoccupied with thoughts more profound than mine.

I have known some people who are made angry and envious by other people's virtues. They are sensitive to their own failings, and every reminder is a personal affront, an insult. When a foul-mouthed TV guest is confronted by a well-spoken studio manager at an after-show party, the guest doesn't usually stop swearing. If the manager refuses to get flustered, a taunt is always hurled: "You think you're better than me!" I've heard this after many shows, in many countries, whenever the drinks start to flow. And I've heard it at airports, in banks, at motorway service stations, at school parents' evenings, at shop counters, and in village streets. "You think you're better than me!" It always means, "You have a quality I don't, and I'm scared you might really be better than I am!"

The quality in you that I felt I most painfully lacked was commitment. In the months that followed our first dinner together, I saw this strength of yours more clearly. I am not one of those who grudge other people their virtues. I can't take much credit for this—it's just the way I am, and I have never worked at cultivating it. Probably my native optimism is the cause—I see your strength and I think, "Yeah, I could be like that, if I tried." It's a simple reaction, but I'd recommend it to anyone who is plagued by envy. Instead of torturing yourself with, "I want it and I can't have it," tell yourself: "I could get it, if I showed some determination. I want it, I'll have it." Whether or not you end up getting what you want, the immediate response feels so much better—positive and hopeful and active.

I saw the way you lived with complete commitment to your work and your wife and your children and your faith, and I thought: "I could be that committed, if I really tried." But I had to admit that I have been desperately anxious about any kind of commitment all my life.

Maybe it's because I was kicked around by everyone in kicking distance for my first twenty years—my father, my mother's new husband, my teachers, my instructors. I didn't get any say in my own life—not about which lessons I learned in school, or whether that school was in a town or on a *kibbutz*, not even which country the school was in. And all the time weird things happened around me, voices that whispered other people's thoughts and watches that skipped whole hours and metal that snapped in my hands. I couldn't control any of that either. I certainly grew up a perfectionist, unwilling to let anyone do anything I didn't personally oversee and double check. And I believe I also grew up scared of ceding control to anyone else.

I hate signing contracts. I would rather work with a handshake and a promise, even though I've occasionally been cheated by people who reneged on verbal agreements. I hate setting deadlines—what if something more important crops up in the weeks ahead? And I hate pledging my emotions to other people—if my heart feels a natural commitment, why should I put chains around it?

I don't suffer as a result of this failing of mine. But other people do. I am painfully aware that the person who has suffered most, for many years, is Hanna.

There seemed so many good reasons, when we first knew each other, why it would have been wrong for me to make a frank commitment to Hanna. I loved her, and I knew she loved me, but so much was changing around us. My career was rocketing into an unknown sky, and I was afraid of exploding in showers of glory, and even more afraid of screaming out into deep,

deep space. I was afraid too that money, or fame, or America, would change me. Or change Hanna. Or that I would grow up a different man, convert to Buddhism or Taoism or Communism, or that she would be stolen from me by one of the many glamorous men who cast their eyes over her at parties. Every time I heard the word "marriage," I flinched. Of all the reasons I love Hanna, one of the most profound is that, during these years, that word was never spoken by her. But, of course, our friends were marrying, or celebrating anniversaries, or divorcing, all the time— marriage is a hard thing to avoid. And because I knew I was hurting Hanna by shying away from the issue, I was sensitive to all these marriages. My own relationship with the woman I loved should have been the greatest thing in my life—instead, it was overshadowed by everyone else's relationships.

We started living together around 1975, when I stopped switching between cities so fast. We scarcely discussed the move—it was natural. And we wanted children. Hanna especially wanted children. Daniel was born in 1981, and Natalie arrived in 1982. And we still were not married. I didn't advertise this, of course—when we arrived in England in the mid-Eighties, we were Mr. and Mrs. Geller to the villagers. We had children—of course we were married. We had lain together beside the river under a flickering starscape and pledged our hearts to each other forever. Call it a pagan wedding or a sky marriage, it was enough of a bond for us. I never wanted to wear a wedding band or sign a document or make a promise to a registrar, to show the world I loved Hanna. I hope that everything in my life shows the world I love my wife. And the only promises I owe to anyone are to her.

I should have married Hanna when I first met her. I have always known that. My commitment to her was total, and I should not have been scared to say it aloud. I did not find the courage until 1991, when my mother reminded me she was growing old, and would like to see our wedding day. I didn't marry Hanna to please my mother—but Muti's hint kept scratching in my mind, and I knew I was hurting other people by pleasing myself. I hurt my wife, I hurt my mother, and I risked doing a terrible hurt to my children. We were wed in a wonderful ceremony in Budapest, at a register office in Uri Street, which means the street of light. Afterwards we went for a run beside the Danube, because I secretly felt the river had more power to consecrate our love than the civil service.

It is the same fear of commitment that has kept me from getting too close to any one religion. Hanna is a good and observant Jew—I am…well, I hope I am sometimes a good Jew. I am not very observant of the customs. OK, to be honest, I have always enjoyed flouting customs—anybody's customs. If I had become a Buddhist monk, my robes would have been blue, or green—anything but orange. If I had been a communist, I would have flown a yellow flag, or a purple one—anything but red. And if you ever make an Orthodox Jew of me, I will wear a pink hat, or a white one—anything but black.

As our letters have grown in intensity this past year, I have turned to the Bible more and more. First to find the quotes to answer your quotes, then to find the stories to answer your stories. After a while, I was going to the Bible simply for inspiration. And then for enlightenment, and now for pleasure. I have learned that is what the book is for. I don't have to be committed to the Bible merely to pick it up and read it. The verses are there to be read.

I like that. No commitment—I get what I want, on my own terms. It's not a great quality of mine, but I can live with it. When that attitude starts to hurt others, I want to be able to rise above it. That takes strength, the kind of strength you show daily in your passionate commitments. From your strength I have gained strength, and I am grateful to you. Strength is the greatest blessing that a friendship can bestow.

Your friend,

Dear Uri,

I am going to miss you too. I have been humbled by your friendship, and you inspire me and make me want to be a better person.

You flatter me by speaking of my commitment to my religion and to my family. I wish that this commitment had more to do with altruism than selfishness. People tell me that I am young, Uri, only thirty-two. But I am an old thirty-two. I have had too many experiences—not all of them positive—for a man of my years to have witnessed. And the things that have never abandoned me are my God and my family. Like a man who holds on to a life raft in the midst of a stormy sea, I hold on to my religion and my family because they keep me afloat.

But there is one thing to which I believe that I am selflessly committed. And that is the idea of trying to become a better person. Friedrich Nietzsche made the case that goodness makes you weak. And he is right. Being good means never taking revenge. Being good means never retaliating against those who slander you. And being good means lowering your guard and learning to trust people. By being good we become vulnerable. But without goodness we cannot be happy! We may be successful, but we will never have any of the deep inner satisfaction that only goodness can inspire.

Uri, in spite of some of the small victories that the good Lord has enabled me to obtain, there is something still missing from my life, and missing at its very core. That something is happiness. There has always been something gnawing away at me, something that has told me that whatever I may achieve in life, there is still something higher to which I must aspire. As my life has progressed in this way, I have discovered that happiness was ever elusive. So I adopted a new strategy. I talked myself into thinking that happiness was a foreign god, not worthy of pursuit. What was happiness, anyway, other than a feeling of inner contentment? And was not contentment nothing but the guarantor of mediocrity? When you are content, you cease to reach for all things high. Wasn't inner peace, therefore, a prison that precluded the opportunity for further achievement?

But as I have matured, I have regained my will to be happy. I want to be happy, and I want my family to be happy. And I have now discovered what I believe to be life's greatest secret. You have to be good in order to be happy. Goodness is man's deepest desire, his greatest dream. Amid striving always to be true to my rabbinic calling, I have always struggled with the issue of goodness. Unlike many of the people who surround me, goodness has never come naturally to me. I am not the type of person who naturally thinks of getting up and washing the dishes when I finish eating. Nor am I am the kind of person who naturally gives rich and poor the same amount of time and attention. Even less so am I the kind of person who intuitively gives his children more time than he gives his career. But I have always wanted to be all these things.

My wife, Debbie, has no such problems. Uri, I married someone whose capacity to give is infinitely greater than my own. Through all the controversy that my career has entailed—the inclusion of thousands of non-Jews in our L'Chaim Society, the relationship books, the media appearances my wife Debbie has stood by my side like a rock. She has given me superhuman support without which I could never have continued. All she has asked for in return is my undivided attention and affection. Because she is such a good person, I find myself having to defend her all the time. I make sure that nobody takes advantage of her, because she finds it very difficult to say no to all who ask of her.

When I am with Debbie, I wonder to myself, how can she be so good? And why am I not naturally like that? I have tried to live a good life, true to my religious convictions, available to all those who are in need. But it has often been an uphill struggle. Ironically, I have never found the rituals of the Jewish faith challenging. To be sure, eating kosher food in all places, even when you are travelling in Singapore, is no easy thing. You can go hungry much of the time and must learn to survive on tuna fish and lettuce. Likewise, ensuring that you pray and don your tefillin every morning, even when you awaken to a hundred urgent responsibilities, can be immensely trying. But, you learn to do it. It becomes a part of your day, and soon it is automatic.

Goodness is different, however. No matter how many times you do the right thing, the next time will still be a struggle. You'll somehow rein in your temper on this occasion, only to discover tomorrow that the beast within is just as potent as he was the day before.

Sadly, all too many people respond to the call of goodness by trying to be good in the abstract. They love humanity in general, they believe in goodness in general, and they believe that all poor people should be fed. But the moment you ask them to translate these principles from the abstract and apply them to their own lives, it becomes so much more difficult. Sure, they will condemn the violence in Bosnia. But when you approach them for a donation to aid the relief of refugees, their response is that they gave a donation at the office.

Twenty years ago, I stood in front of hundreds of assembled family members and friends, perspiring and nervous, reading from the Bible in public for the very first time. It was my Bar Mitzvah, the celebration of maturity for a boy of thirteen. Like any young man since the dawn of time, I wished to distinguish myself. I was eager to make my mark, desirous of achieving greatness. I wanted to be one of those special people whom the world remembers. I wanted to be a hero, like the great heroic figures of history, Caesar crossing the Rubicon, Hannibal atop an elephant crossing the Alps, or Alexander the Great on a fiery steed cutting swathes through Darius' hordes.

But when I began to read the Bible, I discovered a totally new kind of hero. I read of Abraham, the great knight of faith, whose heroism lay in having discovered an unseeable God in the starlit heavens of Mesopotamia. Abraham, who, rather than defeating his enemies or rejoicing at their fall, rose to the heights of human greatness, sparring with God when informed that the evil inhabitants of Sodom and Gomorrah were to perish for their iniquity. He had the audacity to enter into a debate with God in order to preserve, rather than take, human life:

> Suppose there are fifty righteous within the city; will you then sweep away the place and not forgive it for the fifty righteous who are in it? Far be it from you to do such a thing, to slay the righteous with the wicked, so that the righteous fare as the wicked! Far be that from you! Shall not the Judge of all the earth do what is just? (Genesis 18:24)

In the Bible, Abraham's heroism is depicted as a man who sits at the crossroads looking to find any wayfarer to whom he could offer food and water. Now I was confused. What kind of heroism was this? It seemed so lackluster when compared to people like Genghis Khan or Attila the Hun. Was this not weakness rather than heroism? The Gentiles had great generals to inspire them. And what did we Jews have? Caterers!

The Bible passage that I read at my Bar Mitzvah was about Jacob, my namesake. And what kind of hero was he, as he flees the wrath of his brother Esau? But the key to understanding his heroism lies in the prayer he offers as he flees his brother's vengeance. He prays neither for wealth nor glory. Rather, he prays that God accompany him, like an intimate friend, throughout the ordeal he is about to encounter. Jacob prayed not for gold or silver, but for righteousness. "If God shall be with me and keep me blameless on the path which I now embark upon." Jacob prayed for blamelessness before God. He prayed for innocence.

Later we find Jacob wrestling with a mysterious, angelic foe. Jacob, the untested novice in warfare, weak and unarmed, somehow defeats his superior antagonist. But his moment of heroism did not involve subduing his enemy. His supreme moment of heroism was when he forgave his opponent and allowed him to go free. What was he doing? Was he crazy? Allowing his opponent to escape opened Jacob up to the possibility of further attack, Jacob decides instead to rise up and become a hero. His heroism is manifest in his ability to overcome his animal instincts to vanquish the enemy and to exercise instead his Godly capacity for mercy. He retreats in forgiveness rather than advancing in triumph.

I read in the Bible also of Jacob and Rachel and how they loved each other. But on the night of their marriage, Jacob is tricked by his father-in-law, Laban, in order to extract another seven years of labor. Under the cover of night, he exchanges Rachel for Leah. Yet Rachel, knowing the entire time of the plan, never discloses it to Jacob. And why? Why give up the possibility of happiness and pleasure with the man who owns your heart? It was to spare her sister embarrassment, public humiliation, and rejection. Rachel's heroism was displayed in her ability to sacrifice her own happiness for that of another.

And finally, I read of Moses the great lawgiver. Moses, a man with no legions. A man armed with the word of God alone who, moved by faith and fired by the passion of fighting injustice, brings Egypt—the world's greatest empire—to its knees. Moses, who proves the power of the word to defeat the sword. Moses, who climbs mountains and speaks to God face to face, who is described by the Bible, in the only epitaph relating directly to his person, as the most humble man that walked the earth.

When God saves the Jews from Egypt and brings them to the foot of Sinai to be His chosen people, they build a Golden Calf. God demands their total annihilation, promising to make Moses into the father of a great nation, like Romulus or George Washington. But Moses will have none of it. Desperate for clemency, he offers the ultimate sacrifice, choosing self-destruction, oblivion, and anonymity to save the Israelite nation. "And now, if you will not forgive their sin, blot me out, I pray You, from the book that You have written." (Exodus 32:32). The meaning, "Purge me from the Bible, remove my name from the history books. Let it never be known that I ever walked the earth. Save my people instead." Here, Moses demonstrates a totally new kind of heroism by offering to withdraw from the spotlight, to do the right thing because it is right, to serve the interests of humanity at great personal sacrifice, even though the sacrifice will never be recorded in the history books and no one will ever know.

What I am trying to say, Uri, is that by reading the Bible, you slowly transform from being a classical hero to being a biblical hero, devoted to sharing your inner light with your fellow beings upon this earth, rather than in hogging the spotlight.

The first commandment that God gives humanity is to rise above the selfishness of human nature and to lead a memorable existence. Religion demands greatness. Religion creates heroes. But, whereas the classical hero advances in battle to defeat his enemy, the biblical hero retreats from conflict with his fellow man. Whereas the classical hero battles monsters and dragons, the biblical hero battles his own inner demons. Whereas the classical hero seeks to become a "god," the biblical hero teaches all men to know the one true God. The knights of the round table are born for adventure. But the biblical knight of faith is born for service. And whereas the classical hero is wrapped in splendor and garbed in glory, the biblical hero is naked and innocent before God.

Long ago, in the dusty marketplaces of the holy land of Israel, elderly, frail, bearded Jews—with names like Jeremiah, Isaiah, Zachariah, and Micah—proclaimed that the great men were those who would one day beat their swords into ploughshares, that a superlative father was one who vowed never again to teach his son the art of war. Sigmund Freud spoke of his humiliation, as a young Jew growing up in Vienna, at watching an anti-Semite knock off his father's hat, and yet his father refused to assault the man in return. "This struck me," Freud wrote, "as unheroic conduct on the part of the big, strong man who was holding the little boy by the hand. I contrasted this situation with another which fitted my feelings better; the scene in which Hannibal's father, Hamilcar Barca, made his boy swear before the household altar to take vengeance on the Romans. Ever since that time Hannibal has had a place in my fantasies." Freud felt ashamed of a biblical hero and wished for his father to return to the age of battles. But the Bible introduced us to heroes who traded in power for influence, competition for conviction, and fury for faith.

The true sound of heroism, Uri, is not the sound of trumpets blowing nor the piercing cry of the throng. As Moses told Joshua, "It is not the sound made by victors, nor the sound made by the vanquished." Nor is heroism the scene of a triumphal victory parade through a Roman arch and the searing display of captured prisoners. Rather, its sound is the soothing sound of comfort, and its image that of the warm arms of embrace. When Elijah goes to find God in the wilderness, God said to him:

> Go out and stand on the mountain before the Lord, for the Lord is about to pass by. Now there was a great wind, so strong that it was splitting mountains and breaking rocks in pieces before the Lord, but the Lord was not in the wind; and after the wind an earthquake, but the Lord was not in the earthquake; and after the earthquake a fire, but the Lord was not in the fire; and after the fire there was a still, small voice. (1 Kings 19:11–12, NRSV)

It was in the soothing comfort of that voice, Uri, that God was to be found.

I'm telling you all this Uri, in my last letter to you before I leave the United Kingdom for a new life in the United States, because I want to share with you my greatest confession of all. I have lived my entire life with the phenomenal fear of mediocrity. I have been afraid of being ordinary. I have sat in front of a keyboard for thousands of hours writing books. I have traveled around the world to meet with world leaders and movie stars in an effort get them to speak at Oxford. I have dropped the names of famous acquaintances in conversations at endless receptions. And I have traversed the globe giving lectures and seminars. And all this has been directed to one purpose: to rise and become a hero. My childhood dream has not changed. I still want to be special. What has changed, however, is that I have now come to understand what a real hero is. I had it all wrong before. Before the Bible and my Judaism reshaped my dreams, I wanted to be the guy who is recognized by strangers when he walks into a restaurant. But now I know that the real hero is he who is recognized by his children when he walks through the door at night because he comes home at a decent hour and reads them bedtime stories, rather than staying out late and trying to win over the rest of the world. I now understand, Uri, that so many people I looked up to as heroes were really weak and ordinary men whose lives were impelled by the desperate need for attention so as to comfort their own macerated egos.

Classical man invented the hero in order to soothe his own conscience with grandeur and glory. Men looked at themselves and experienced their own vulnerability, their mortality, their smallness. They experienced the ephemerality of their existence and arrived at the conclusion that they could not cross the Rubicon separating the finite from the infinite. Out of a sense of desperation and in order to soothe their fragile pride— out of a sense of frustration and disenchantment—they invented the myth of the hero. They were like the generation that built the Tower of Babel, proclaiming, "Come, let us build ourselves a city, and a tower with its top in the heavens, and let us make a name for ourselves" (Genesis 11:4). Uri, the essence of the heroic grandiose gesture was that it would compensate for man's insignificance.

But this sort of heroism could not cope with the demands of the sort of goodness that is a requisite of happiness. Uri, witness the final victory of the biblical over the classical hero. The most respected political figure in the world today is Nelson Mandela, a figure who, like the biblical Joseph, forgives his brothers their attempt at fratricide and embraces his enemies. Not only are Mandela and Gandhi not military figures, they are men who refused to go to war. And the least respected figures are people like Slobodan Milosevic and Saddam Hussein, who in ancient times would have been hailed as great tribal chieftains, conquerors who seek to expand the borders of their empires. Today, they are nothing but common thugs.

This change in outlook resulted from the Bible. Religion replaced honor with humility, hatred with harmony, vanity with values, egotism with egalitarianism, mortal conquest with moral courage, and a passion for publicity with a desire for the divine countenance. In the process, a new definition of heroism was born. Our ancient Rabbis proclaimed, "Who is a hero? He who conquers his own selfish inclination." The men and women who refuse to live by the law of jungle, purging pride from their hearts, eradicating envy from their souls, eliminating deceitfulness from their character, and cleansing corruption from their constitution—these are the real heroes.

And even today it is felt and it is heard, that inner voice, thundering forth from Sinai, piercing our hearts and searing our souls. It is a voice heard only by the most sensitive of spirits, the most introspective of individuals. It is the voice of God crying out, "Who today will rise and be a hero?"

A woman called me crying, "Shmuley, can you bring back my husband to me?" He was a world-famous musician who, after thirty years of marriage, had run off with his young apprentice. "Why should I give her up?" he asked me. "She makes me feel young and alive."

"Why should you give her up! Because you have conquered the entire world. The easy part is over. Now the hard part begins," I told him. "You must now master *yourself*. Go home. Go home and be a hero. Only a small man surrenders to a fleeting passion. A great man honors his commitment to the woman who is his very flesh."

Every day, God's voice thunders forth from Sinai, shattering the cedars of Lebanon, appealing to our sense of majesty: "I created you to be heroes." The woman who restrains her lips from gossip, the teenager who rejects the ecstasy pill rather than try and be "cool," and the son who refuses to lose his temper with his father. These silent, unspectacular, everyday acts of heroism represent true human beings at their greatest.

I don't know if I ever mentioned this to you, Uri, but one of my greatest heroes is Victor Frankl, the founder of Logotherapy. In the gorge of hell that was Auschwitz, Frankl described how the Nazis robbed him of his freedom by incarcerating him. They robbed him of his human dignity by placing a number on his arm. And they robbed him of his happiness by murdering his family. But there was one freedom that even they could never take away: that was his freedom to choose heroism over submission. The savages could not rob of him of the choice to share his few bread crumbs with other emaciated inmates, nor the freedom to comfort his brethren succumbing to disease, nor *his* determination to live and bear witness to their courage.

Yes, courage. We speak of the martyrs of the Holocaust as victims, when in fact they were the greatest heroes. Not even the evil within man could break their attachment to God.

Fifty-five years ago, in a burned-out house in the Warsaw ghetto, which was being shelled every moment by the Nazis, a man named Yossele Rakover pulled out a pen and wrote a letter to God. He had already witnessed the murder of his wife and six children by bullets and starvation. He held in his hand his very last Molotov cocktail to stave off the Nazis, and he knew that within a few moments he would be dead. In his letter, he expressed his anger at God and his sense of having been abandoned. But rather than be defeated, he ended his letter with defiance. "My God and God of my father, You may insult me, You may strike me, You may take away all that I cherish. But I will always believe in You, I will always love You...You have done everything to make me renounce You...but I die exactly as I have lived, an unshakable believer..." Like so many millions, he departed with the ancient words of faith on his lips, "Hear, Oh Israel, the Lord is our God, the Lord is one."

It was heroism, Uri, that gave Noah the nobility to swim against the tide of civilization when "all the earth's inhabitants had corrupted their ways." It was heroism that inspired Abraham to plant the seed of monotheism that would eventually destroy all the false gods of the earth. And it was heroism that led Joseph away from judging his brothers' act of fratricide to forgive them and feed them instead.

My father's family came from Iran to Israel in 1952. Like so many other Israelis, they somewhat discarded their Jewish observance. They no longer completely rested on the Sabbath. One might say that they embraced the great symbol of heroism of a nation fighting for its very existence. Like so many young men and women they became Westerners, they enjoyed their nightlife and sometimes went to the cinema on the Sabbath eve and to the beach on the Sabbath day.

As I grew older, I saw my father becoming more and more observant. He put us into a Jewish day school and we observed the Sabbath. He started reading the Bible with us every Saturday after synagogue. I asked him what had changed in his life. He said he was haunted by a vision of his departed father. You see, every morning this frail old man would rise early and put hundreds of pounds worth of carpets on his shoulder and go to the marketplace so he could feed his thirteen children. But having made enough money to meet their needs for that day, he would return early, spread out a carpet, and read from the holy books. When he reached the passage of the Bible which states that Moses was the most humble man who walked the earth, he would break into tears and was inconsolable. My father told me that after his lifelong dream of making money and owning a big house, he has re-embraced his father's example. After all those years, my father understood. His own father had become to him a hero.

Real heroism consists in not being in the spotlight, but in shining the spotlight on others. It is the heroism of a father, of whom the Talmud says that man is jealous of every other man in the world with the exception of his son and his student. In both cases he takes pride in having facilitated their success and achievement. Influence is the real power in the world, not power itself. It is the starting of events that may take centuries to achieve, but which ultimately secures victory. It is what we call principle-centered leadership—men and women who allow their cause to be in the spotlight while they remain on the side-lines. It is where men and women take greater pride in seeing their legacy than in vainly looking at themselves in the mirror.

My students in Oxford often ask me, "Where have all the heroes gone?" But they are blind, because they are all around us.

I witnessed the heroic backbreaking labor of a single mother working to raise five children. She asked what gift I wanted for my Bar Mitzvah. I said I wanted to grow. "You mean you want to be a Rabbi, grow spiritually?" "No, Mom, grow literally. Haven't you noticed that I am pretty darn short?" So she took me to a hormone specialist, who showed us a tablet the size of a horse pill, told me I'd have to take one of these each day, and that it would cost thousands of dollars. "We can't afford this, Mom," I said. "Don't worry. I can always start working nights again." And never in the history of parental endeavor has so great a sacrifice produced so little for one so small.

Hence the Bible says, "Honor your father and mother." Not *love*, but *honor*. Set them up on a pedestal. Look up to them as heroes. They fed you when you were helpless, now go and feed the stranger. They clothed you when you were cold, now go and dress the naked. They saw your beauty when everyone else saw your ugliness, now go and make all of God's creatures feel special.

I decided to become a Rabbi after someone made me feel special, as I related to you earlier, Uri. It was in a meeting with the great Rebbe of Lubavitch at the time of my Bar Mitzvah. I told him that my parent's divorce had made me a cynic. I believed that every star would one day cease to shine. The world was made of incongruent pieces of a puzzle. Nothing fit. His beautiful blue eyes welled up with a sea of compassion. "You have an obligation to ensure that no child utters such despairing words again. I bless you today to become a light and inspiration to the Jewish people and the world." Here was the leading Rabbi in the world helping a child with a broken heart, at three o'clock in the morning, believe that his life could make a difference. Because the test of true greatness is the ability to inspire greatness in others.

You see my point, Uri. The Bible is not a book of *history*, but a book of *heroes*, both past and present. The past heroes consisted of the great personalities of the biblical age. The present ones consist of the kind of people both you and I can be if we are but inspired by their example.

Hence, the moving biblical narrative closes with a story of the greatest act of heroism of all. "Then Moses, the servant of the Lord, died....And God buried him in the valley....And no one knows his burial place to this day." (Deuteronomy 34:5–6) Moses retreats from the world stage, silently and without fanfare. It was just him and God, intimate and alone. He had done his duty, he had served the people, and then, like footsteps in the night, he was gone. There were no massive hordes of distraught followers, no honor guard, and no twenty-one gun salute. He didn't want nor did he need a great monument built to him in a public square. He didn't care if he was going to be remembered because he never thought of himself. Rather, he served God and man to the best of his ability and then just faded away.

I remember the heroism of my mentor and guide, the Lubavitcher Rebbe. As I wrote you, I was in London in June 1994 when I heard that he had passed away, and quickly rushed to catch an airplane. Only hours later in New York, I stood along in the midst of a throng of fifty thousand people, waiting for the coffin to arrive and the funeral to commence. There stood with me men of distinction, famous rabbis, the governor and mayor of New York. And then, as the wailing and the cries of the women reached a crescendo, the coffin came out. A simple, pine coffin, constructed from the wood of the Rebbe's prayer lectern. They carried the body a few hundred feet, and then it was placed into an ambulance and carried off. But wait? What about the eulogies? This is the most famous rabbi in the entire world. Why not the governor, why not the mayor, why not the Chief Rabbis of Israel? Because the Rebbe was a hero. He ordered no eulogies. He worked forty-five years toward the perfection of the Earth, advancing the welfare of its inhabitants in general, and the Jewish people in particular, and then, in a moment, he was gone. Again, there were no trumpets blasting or cannons firing. It was enough that God knew. He had done his duty, quietly departed the stage, and without fanfare, he was gone. This is a hero.

Now, as the second Christian millennium closes, we, all earth's inhabitants, must make our own peace with God. We must embrace the simple path laid out by the prophet Micah. "He has told you, O mortal, what is good; and what does the Lord require of you but to do justice, and to love kindness, and to walk humbly with your God?" (Micah 6:8 NRSV).

We are all mortal, and one day we too will retreat from the stage, and our life will be remembered by one of the clergy. It will be either an ordinary remembrance, or one of greatness. The ordinary one will say that he was the chairman of a multi-national conglomerate, paparazzi flashed bulbs wherever he went, and that he was the confidante of presidents and prime ministers. Or there will be a eulogy of greatness. He always gave charity and his table was brimming with guests. He forgave slights and only ever had kind words to speak of others. He read his children bedtime stories and made his wife feel cherished at all times. Before God and before all mankind, he was a hero.

And speaking of making your wife feel like a queen, Uri, I have one final offer to make to you, only in partial recognition of all your love and friendship. You know the way you and Hanna got married by a justice of the peace? Well, how about a real Jewish wedding? Replete with a real *chuppa*. Performed by a real rabbi. I would love to do it for you. The offer is there. And I will ask Daniel and Natalie to be best man and bridesmaid.

And oh, I almost forgot. It's all free of charge, and it comes with a great wedding present—a new house built entirely from...you guessed it, unsold copies of *Moses of Oxford*.

Hoping that you will take me up on my offer so that we can describe it in Book Two,

Your loving friend (and small-time hero),

Dear Shmuley,

I am sure you and your family must have watched in horror as the U.S. news networks repeatedly broadcast footage by a French camera crew of a boy's death at Netzarim Junction. Mohammed al-Durah was huddling beside his father as a crowd of Palestinian protesters hurled rocks and the Israeli military returned fire with bullets. Mohammed died, again and again, on screens all over the world. His father tried to protect him with his own body and could not. It is a horrific image, made all the more sickening by the later discovery that this child was not part of the mob—he and his father were simply in the wrong place, on a calamitous day.

This image is a gift to any politician who wants to attack Israel. But that it not why I call it a tragedy.

This image has murdered the seven-year peace process to integrate the Palestinians within Israel. But that is not what makes it so tragic.

This image is being twisted to show Jews as callous killers, and to heat up the bilious hatred of our people that poisoned the twentieth century. And even that is not what makes me call it tragic.

For me, the tragedy is personal. A boy of ten or twelve dies a needless and brutal death. And that is how Gadi died, ten or twelve years ago. He was not even born—seven months old in the womb. And in a hideous accident, he was slaughtered.

Hanna and I were anxious for a third child, after the birth of our daughter. We were settled in England, and you know our home in Sonning is large enough for sixty children. Hanna persuaded me that one more baby would be quite enough.

We waited till Natalie was a toddler, and then conceived again. With the children we were open: a baby brother or sister was growing for them inside their mother's tummy. (I do not think it's right to burden a young child with too much biological detail—they don't really understand, and "tummy" is more meaningful a word to them than "womb" or "uterus.") But I don't believe either that pregnancy should be hidden from children or that we must tell them lies. They knew about the baby, and they were excited.

What we did not tell them was the more worrying medical aspect, that Hanna and I have incompatible blood types. This imbued each of her pregnancies with risk: her immune system might detect the baby as an infection, and try to fight it. The result could be fatal—both for my wife and our unborn child.

The doctors at the hospital carefully explained this problem and told us there was a simple diagnostic procedure called amniocentesis which would determine whether Hanna was in danger. An amnio is also used at an earlier stage to detect whether the fetus has Down's Syndrome, but it was not this disability that concerned us. If the baby had Down's, so be it— it would be born, our child, and we would do all we could to care for it. Hanna was in her thirties, and the risk of Down's increases with the mother's age, but neither of us had any thought of a termination in the event that the test revealed a survivable disability. In any case, an amnio for Down's is done much earlier than at seven months. I explain all this to you, because I want you to understand that our concern was solely about the possible threat to both Hanna's life and the babies.

Amniocentesis involves taking a tissue sample from the fetus, by plunging a needle into the womb. In about 1 percent of cases, we were told, it results in the death of the baby. This chance seemed very small. We were wrong.

It seems to me now that the medical profession's use of statistics is misleading. On a broad scale, this test may kill one unborn child in one hundred, but that does not mean that any individual operation has a 99 percent chance of success. It's the same when a doctor says you have a 70 percent chance of recovery from cancer, or a ten thousand to one chance that your child may be autistic. Those statistics are about the big picture. For you, the individual, the odds are always the same: fifty-fifty. Either you die from cancer or you don't. Either your child is autistic or it isn't.

Either the amnio will kill your baby or it won't.

I blame myself for my complacency as we prepared for the test. I still believed in a 99 percent success rate. I didn't realize that Hanna and our baby needed my prayers more than at any other time. I thought everything would be all right. After all, everything is always all right, isn't it?

We had already decided to call the child Gadi. We'd seen him on a sonar scan—we could even see his tiny face. He was clearly a boy. This scan is our only tangible memory of our son now. No bigger than a Polaroid print, it is framed and hangs in our bedroom.

The amnio needle did untold damage. I have never been able to discover whether that was an unavoidable accident or the result of surgical incompetence. It is hard for me to believe that, when sonar can show us the face of a child in the womb, it can be impossible sometimes to avoid ramming a needle through the umbilical.

He died slowly. We don't know how long Gadi lay dead inside Hanna's womb, but at the next scan, he was no longer alive. The shock of that will haunt me for the rest of my life—and for Hanna, it has been a pain she still suffers every day.

Gadi was delivered by an induced labor. I can imagine no greater torture for a woman than that. We asked the midwife to let our children hold the swaddled body for a few moments. He was their brother.

Now, when I see any child who is about the age Gadi would be today, I cannot help but remember those awful days. When I saw Mohammed al-Durah die needlessly, huddled beside a father who was unable to protect him, I felt an agonizing kinship with them.

There is a spark of comfort for me in the words the father spoke to an American news crew shortly after the tragedy: "I am a man of peace. We two peoples must live together. There is no other possibility."

I am praying for all the people of Israel, Jew, Christian, and Muslim. Most especially I am praying for the children.

Shalom,

Uri

Dear Uri,

It's been a long while since we communicated by formal letter, and as I write this particular one to you, I am reminded of how much I have enjoyed our correspondence over the past two years. To be sure, we've spoken by phone many times, and a mark of the strength of our friendship is how each of us makes the effort to stay in touch amidst being separated by a vast ocean and hectic schedules. While the phone is nice, a disembodied voice is a poor substitute for your warm smile and reassuring voice that I grew so accustomed to when I lived in England. You became like an older brother to me. I used to feel that there was no way that I could ever repay the love and kindness you have always shown me. But I now feel that the love you have for me actually brings out the best in you, a fact attested to by the wisdom and advice you offer me. You have seldom been wrong. And when you offer me advice over the phone, it's almost like you go into a trance—your voice becomes as focused as a laser and sharp as a razor.

But for all the comfort of our phone conversations, there are things that an oral conversation can never capture, beyond its transient nature. The celebrated American columnist William Safire once said that the telephone destroyed the American language. Before its invention, there were only letters—you had to think about what you wanted to say, then organize your thoughts, and finally choose the words and express it in an eloquent way that was worth putting on paper. These exercises built our vocabulary and gave us a command of language. Now we just call each other up and say, "How's it going?" And I've noticed since moving back to the States, Uri, that we Americans love using the word "thing" and use it to connote, well, almost every*thing*.

But more than just our language skills shrinking, when we speak on the phone, our hearts can shrink as well. It's so difficult to speak about really personal issues, like the ones about which we have been communicating. And the truth is that aside from these letters, I have few other outlets to unburden my heart.

You will say that I, thank God, have my wife. And there can be no doubt that Debbie is an immense blessing to me in being able to be intimate about every matter. But there are things that Debbie, due to her own inherent goodness, will never completely understand. She is not the tortured soul you and I sometimes are, and thank heavens for that. But you have wrestled with many of the same conflicts as me. And in your latest letter, you write of the conflict that most grips me, namely, the pain caused us by children. For you it is the tragic loss of an unborn child, and may God always comfort you for that loss and protect all of us from anything like that ever happening again. While for me it is the constant pain—and guilt—of not prioritizing my children sufficiently.

I am an incredibly blessed man, Uri, having never experienced close tragedy like what you describe, may God be blessed. To be sure, Debbie endured two miscarriages in close proximity, and one caused her to be hospitalized, which deeply traumatized both of us. But children followed in quick succession after those episodes, which allowed us to overcome those painful experiences with scant memory of them.

Hence, it was highly ironic that the day that I read your letter to me, the second day of the Jewish festival of *Sukkot*, we narrowly averted just such a tragedy, God forbid. The whole family was walking home from Synagogue and I was pushing the baby in her stroller. The last part of the walk to our home involves a steep hill, and as I pushed hard up the hill, I saw the opportunity to cross the street, and ran across with the stroller. Little did I know that Mendy, my seven-year-old and only son, would follow me without looking at the cars. As I reached the other side, I suddenly heard the screeching of tires and my son scream. A terror gripped me like never before and I turned around while shouting, "Meeennnddddy!!!" The car swerved at the last second and missed my son by perhaps an inch. And it was all my fault. I did not take my son by the hand and lead him across the street. So he followed me into terrible danger.

The shock of what almost happened to my son stunned me for the rest of the day. In the aftermath of that incident, I found myself holding him throughout the day, asking him banal questions just to hear his responses. I was looking upon him as if he were given to me anew. I stared at him, wanting to discover everything about him. The mere thought of losing him, God forbid, now made me appreciate him so much more.

Surely this is one of life's strangest facets, Uri. What is it about the nature of man that he becomes complacent about life's most precious gifts until he is threatened with their loss?

I always wanted to be a good father. I would love to say that I try my best. But I know that I am failing in one very important sphere, namely, putting my children *completely* before my career, making them feel that I am always available to them, come morning, noon, or night. They hate it when I travel. But travel I must if I am to support them, as well as advance my professional profile. When an American TV channel interviewed me and asked what my favorite song was, I chose Harry Chapin's "Cat's in the Cradle," his famous song about a father who never has time for his kid, only to grow old and discover that his son now has no time for him. Even as a child, whenever I heard the song's final lament, I would cry. I was the boy in the song, and, as I grew older, so was my son. The song, as you know, has captured the tragedy of a father who commits the ultimate error of depriving his son of his affection.

There is a terrible cycle, Uri, that has to be broken in families like mine. Because my parents fought much and eventually divorced, they could not, through no fault of their own, give me the unconditional love and support that they wished and which I needed for the formation of a strong and stable character. How could they? They wanted to, but were too busy nursing their own wounds. As a result, I grew up feeling anonymous, that I had to earn a name, become somebody. So now, I work myself very hard in order to become a somebody, a man whose accomplishments and achievements afford him a sense of worth. I want to rescue myself from the abyss of nothingness, drag myself out of the pit of namelessness. But in so doing, I do not always sufficiently give my children the love and attention they need, and the cycle is repeated.

It's ironic that all we modern parents claim to want to give our children "all the things that we didn't have when we grew up." We're lying, and we know it. The one thing we didn't have when we grew up was enough love, and that's what our children want more than anything else.

So I've made a huge effort to change, and I'm getting a lot better. And I'm doing it by totally reversing the dynamic. Parents are today encouraged to spend time with their children for the sake of the children. They are told that their children need them for the formation of their characters and development of their personalities. A child needs to know that he is valuable and loved. And how can he feel valuable if his own parents don't put him first.

The problem with this argument is that it makes it all sound like a sacrifice. There are so many fun things to do out there in the grand old world. But you're gonna have to give them up because your kids need you.

The truth is the reverse. *We* need our kids much more than they need us. God gave us children for *our* sake, to teach us what it's like to be children again. To remind us of joyfulness and playfulness, innocence and blamelessness, imagination and creativity, exuberance and passion, curiosity and adventure.

I have always wondered why you and Hanna, with the enormous strength of your marriage, never had more children, and your latest letter sadly explained it. I have always watched you with *my* kids. You have a special gift for children. My children adore you, and you love them. When we lived in England, having you and Hanna visit for *Shabbat* was the highlight of their week. The patience you would show my children as you told them your fascinating stories—you have a gift for making everything sound fascinating—made their Friday nights come to life.

But is it possible, Uri, that the phenomenal powers that you possess, and which you are at a loss to explain, actually stem from being childlike? Maybe you just don't know what you aren't supposed to be able to do. Children don't know their limitations. The ancient rabbis used to say that now that the Temple is destroyed it is only children who can prophesy. The reason: their minds are totally open. The infinite can commune with them because they have no restraints. And maybe that's why you love children, Uri, because you feel a kinship with them. Maybe you feel that they alone can understand you. They may not speak your language, but they experience your experiences.

I am often asked by women, "What should I most look for in a guy? How do I know that he is husband material?" I tell them to watch his interaction with children. A man who loves a child's innocence is himself innocent. A man who loves a child's playfulness is himself playful. And a man who has patience for children is a patient man.

And yet, Uri, I have never been one of these people. On the contrary, prior to having my own children, I had little patience for children. I was just like one of the many modern people who treated children more as a burden than a blessing. I lacked that innocence. I did not gravitate naturally toward children because I never focused on what I could learn from them.

I still remember how, in my second year as Rabbi at Oxford, a Hassidic couple came to stay with my family for the Jewish festival of *Sukkot*. Following dinner with several students, a young woman looked quizzically at the couple's ten children surrounding their mother. "Are all these yours?" she asked. The mother proudly assured her they were, to which the student responded, "Don't you think that that's a bit much?" The mother's eyes reddened, and she excused herself. I followed her into the kitchen and apologized for my students' remarks. "That's OK," she said, while gently sobbing from the humiliation. "I get it all the time. But the Lubavitcher Rebbe told me never to be embarrassed for having a lot of children."

Just the other night I had a similar experience. A female writer friend of mine, who has written two bestselling books and is a proud "career" girl, had a meeting with me to discuss a possible joint writing venture. When I told her that Debbie and I were, thank God, expecting our seventh child, she honestly looked at me in horror. Her first words were not "Congratulations" or "That's wonderful." Rather, the only thing this articulate woman could muster at the time was, "That's ridiculous." She went on about how big a burden all of those children must be and couldn't I learn to take it easy.

I said to her, "I find your words puzzling. Surely, if I told you that I had just made seven million dollars, you wouldn't have said to me, 'That's awful. What a terrible burden to look after all that money, to have to invest it, protect yourself from losing it, and just generally worry about it.' The same is true if I would have told you that I just purchased my seventh antique sports car, you wouldn't have said, 'What a pain. To have to service them all, oil them, keep the tires pumped. You poor thing.' But when it comes to seven kids, you're offering me your sympathy."

"Well there's a difference," she defended herself. "The money, the cars, they bring pleasure. Kids bring work. And what kind of sex life can you have if you have seven kids?"

I responded, "Well, as far as the sex is concerned, I'm the one who has the kids, while you don't. Which would seem to mean that we know something about my sex life, while we know absolutely nothing about yours. And, by the way, children do wonders for your sex life. Adults who don't have kids have a terrible sex life."

At this she was aghast. "I'm not letting you get away with that, Shmuley. Kids destroy your sex life. They run into the room, sleep in their parent's bed, and leave you way too exhausted to have the energy for sex."

I said, "You discipline kids to respect their parents' privacy, and they do. You teach them that Mommy and Daddy's bedroom is a private place, and they have to knock before entering, and they get it. But the reason that children are so essential to their parents' sex life is that they teach them *playfulness*. As we adults get older, we slowly calcify. We become rigid. We become serious. Just look at the way you react when you get a bad review for one of your books. We lose the ability to laugh at ourselves and simply enjoy life. But then we come home, in our expensive Armani suits and silk ties. And our kids jump all over us, wipe their snot on our clothes, and make us tumble on the ground. And gradually, we lose that seriousness. Isn't that what great sex is? Two adults at play? Teasing each other, rolling around on the floor together, tickling each other and making each other laugh, not being afraid what all that sexual play is going to do to our clothes, to our image? And if you don't know how to let go, how can you make love?"

"I wouldn't know," she replied. "I've never had sex like that. Mine is much more civilized."

The exposure to my children has taught me, Uri, that we should all grow up on the outside, but forever retain the child at our center. As we grow older, the pain of the world around us forces us increasingly to close off our hearts. Were not Adam and Eve, the uncorrupted progenitors of the human race, depicted as children, naked and innocent, in the Garden of Eden? Around children you can feel free of pretension and inhibitions, released from rigidity.

We all come into this world innocent but quickly compromise our incorruptibility. We pride ourselves on our "adult" manners and "mature" values. But often the word "adult" becomes nothing more than a euphemism for "cynical," untrusting, manipulative, and scheming. Niccolò Machiavelli was the quintessential adult who encouraged us all to grow up. The pain of the world around us forces us to close up our hearts, just a bit at first, then some more. And like a tooth that quickly rots when its daily calcifications are not removed, so too our hearts become punctured and our childhood purity seeps from its chambers as the daily disappointments and frustrations accumulate.

There's an ancient Jewish tradition that says that not all people were expelled from the Garden of Eden. There are still those saintly individuals who live at an exalted plane where life is everlasting, beauty is eternal, cynicism is nonexistent, and playfulness is abundant. And who are those people who still inhabit Eden? Why, our children of course. And from their exalted plane in a perfect world, they call out to us, beckoning us to join them, entreating us to follow them. And all it takes is the simple belief that we have something to learn from them. To open our hearts to others without first evaluating their usefulness to us. To quickly forgive after an argument, without bearing a grudge. And not being afraid to love, because we have overcome all hurt.

Not only is your unborn son in the Garden of Eden, Uri, he has taken you there as well. He has called out to you, and you have followed him. Or why else would you love the company of children so much?

I'm working on joining you there by being an ever better and more loving parent and more devoted friend.

And finally, Uri, I read recently that the average child smiles seventy-four times a day, while the average adult smiles only nine times a day. So where do all those smiles go?

And rather than answer that question and try and locate the adult lost smile repository, I suggest we just all start smiling a whole lot more. Because when you're smiling, the whole world smiles with you. So I close this letter by only slightly contradicting how I began. I lamented how the telephone undermined the English language. But one thing it has done is bring people unexpected smiles. Because when I'm walking down Fifth Avenue, or in the back of a New York City cab, and you surprise me with a call on my cell phone, it brings an immediate smile to my face that words are too limited to describe. So I'll just draw a picture instead:

Yours in comfort, yours in loneliness, and yours in joy,

GLOSSARY

Avodah: worshipping the Creator through prayer
Bar Mitzvah: celebration for coming of age for Jewish boy of thirteen
Cabbala: Jewish mysticsm
Cabbalist: Jewish mystic
Chassidic: see *Hassidic*
chuppa: Jewish wedding ceremony and/or canopy
explorology: the study of the unknown
galgalim: mystical celestial spheres
Gemillat Chassadim: acts of loving kindness
Haganah: Jewish defense forces prior to the establishment of the State of Israel
Halakha: the complete body of Jewish law
Hassidic: a Jewish sect, emphasizing mystical study, prayer, piety, and joy
Kaddish: Jewish prayer of mourning
kibbutz: Israeli socialist settlement
kibitz: joke with
kippah: skullcap
kosher: food conforming to Jewish dietary law
L'Chaim: Jewish toast for cheers, means "to life"
Mishnah: oral Rabbinic law
mitzvah: divine commandment
moshav: Israeli communal settlement
Mossad: Israeli Secret Service
neshama: soul
Passover: Jewish festival celebrating Exodus from Egypt
seder: Passover festive meal
Shabbat: the Sabbath
Sukkot: Feast of Tabernacles
Talmud: compendium of the Rabbinic oral tradition on Jewish law, compiled third to fifth century C.E.

tefillin: leather boxes containing scriptures, worn by male Jews for morning prayer

Torah: The Bible, the Talmud, and Rabbinic literature about the creation of the world

tzimtzum: the Cabbalistic mystery and condensation, describing the paradox of God's simultaneous presence and absence

yarmulke: skullcap worn by orthodox male Jews

Yeshiva: higher academy of Jewish study

Yom Kippur: Jewish Day of Atonement

BIBLIOGRAPHY

Books by Rabbi Shmuley Boteach
Dating Secrets of the Ten Commandments: Take the Two Tablets and Find Your Perfect Soulmate, Doubleday, 2000.
Dreams, Bash Publications, 1991.
An Intelligent Person's Guide to Judaism, Duckworth, 1999.
The Jewish Guide to Adultery, Hodder and Stoughton, 1999.
Kosher Emotions, Hodder and Stoughton, 2000.
Kosher Sex: A Recipe for Passion and Intimacy, Doubleday, 2000.
Moses of Oxford: A Jewish Version of Oxford and its Life, Volumes I and II, Andre Deutsch, 1994.
Wisdom, Understanding and Knowledge, Jason Aronson, 1996.
The Wolf Shall Lie with the Lamb, Jason Aronson, 1993.
Wrestling with the Divine. A Jewish Response to Suffering, Jason Aronson, 1995.

Books by Uri Geller
Change Your Life in One Day, Marshall Cavendish.
Dead Cold, Headline Feature, 1999.
Ella, Headline Feature, 1998.
The Geller Effect, Henry Holt/Jonathon Cape/Grafton, 1988.
Mind Medicine, Element, 1999.
My Story, Praeger/Robson, 1975.
Nobody's Child, an Internet publication at: www.uristory.com.
Shawn, Goodyer Associates, 1990.
Uri Geller's Fortune Secrets, Sphere, 1987.
Uri Geller's Little Book of Mind Power, Robson, 1998.
Uri Geller's Mind-Power Kit, Penguin/Virgin, 1996.
Uri Geller's ParaScience Pack, van der Meer, 2000.

Books about Uri Geller
The Amazing Uri Geller, (Martin Ebon), New American Library.

The Geller Papers, (Charles Panati), Houghton Mifflin.
The Geller Phenomenon, (Colin Wislon), Aldus Books.
In Search of Superman, (John Wilhelm), Pocket Books.
The Metal Benders, (John Hasted), Routledge and Kegan Paul.
Mysterious Powers, Orbis Books.
The Strange Story of Uri Geller, (Jim Colin), *Raintree*
    (for children).
Superminds, (John G. Taylor), Picador.
Uri, (Andrija Puharich), Doubleday.
Uri Geller, Magician or Mystic?, (Jonathan Margolis), Orion.

Most of Uri Geller's books, mind games, and lots of other fascinating information and pictures, relating to him and his work, including his biography, are available on his website: **www.urigeller.com**.

You can email Uri Geller at: **urigeller@compuserve.com**. Uri's latest book, an online novel, *Nobody's Child*, is available at: **www.uristory.com**.

You can email Rabbi Boteach at: **shmuley@hotmail.com**, or **shmuley@htwf.com**. You can find out more about Rabbi Shmuley Boteach at any one of his three websites:

To find out about L'Chaim Society, go to: **www.lchaim.org**

To join Rabbi Boteach's online matchmaking service or to get guidance or advice about relationships, go to **www.love prophet.com**

To find out about the Heal the World Foundation, go to: **www.healtheworld.com**.

INDEX

ABOUT URI GELLER

Uri Geller is the world's most investigated and celebrated explorologist. Famous around the globe for his mind-bending powers, he has led a unique life shrouded in mystery and debate. He is also related to Sigmund Freud.

He was studied by scientists who worked with Albert Einstein, and the world's most prestigious scientific magazine, *Nature*, published a paper on Uri's work at the Stanford Research Institute—a unique endorsement, and an irrefutable proof that his powers are genuine. His work with the FBI and the CIA has ranged from using MindPower to wipe out KGB computer files and tracking serial killers, to attending nuclear disarmament negotiations to bombard and influence delegates with positive thought waves. For decades, this aspect of his work was too confidential and controversial to discuss.

A vegetarian and fervent promoter of peace, he has used his gifts to detect oil and precious metals, which has provided him the freedom to help others. He is the MindPower coach to Premier League footballers, industrialists, Formula One drivers, and racing cyclists, and cycles twenty seven miles daily on his exercise bike. As a columnist, he is syndicated in newspapers and magazines around the globe. The honorary vice president of the Royal Hospital for Children in Bristol and of the Royal Berkshire Hospital, close to his Thames-side mansion, he is the father of two teenagers, the owner of five dogs, and the author of ten bestsellers, including the novels *Ella* and *Dead Cold*, which was listed in the UK by *The Times* as a contender for the Golden Dagger award.

ABOUT RABBI SHMULEY BOTEACH

Rabbi Shmuley Boteach served for eleven years as Rabbi at Oxford University and is Founder and Director of L'Chaim Society, a high-profile education organization, with branches in Oxford, Cambridge, London, and New York which hosts world leaders lecturing on values-based leadership. He is the author of eleven popular books including the bestsellers *The Jewish Guide to Adultery, Dating Secrets of the Ten Commandments,* and *Kosher Sex,* the international blockbuster which was translated into eleven languages. Rabbi Boteach has quickly established himself as one of the world's leading relationship experts, appearing frequently on television and radio on all continents. He has also been profiled in all the major newspapers of the Western world. His weekly essays on the Internet are read by a vast following and are syndicated in major U.S. and UK publications In 1999, he was voted *The Times* Preacher of the Year, receiving more points than anyone in the competition's history. In 2000, he established the global "Heal the Kids" initiative, together with his close friend, the singer Michael Jackson, who also appointed Rabbi Boteach as president of his "Heal the World" Foundation. Born in Los Angeles, Rabbi Boteach lives in New York with his Australian wife Debbie and their six children.